Cognitive Dissonance

Cognitive Dissonance
Fifty Years of a Classic Theory

Joel Cooper

SAGE Publications
Los Angeles ▪ London ▪ New Delhi ▪ Singapore

First published 2007

Apart from any fair dealing for the purposes of research or
private study, or criticism or review, as permitted under the
Copyright, Designs and Patents Act, 1988, this publication
may be reproduced, stored or transmitted in any form, or
by any means, only with the prior permission in writing of
the publishers, or in the case of reprographic reproduction, in
accordance with the terms of licences issued by the Copyright
Licensing Agency. Enquiries concerning reproduction outside
those terms should be sent to the publishers.

SAGE Publications Ltd
1 Oliver's Yard
55 City Road
London EC1Y 1SP

SAGE Publications Inc
2455 Teller Road
Thousand Oaks, California 91320

SAGE Publications India Pvt Ltd
B 1/I 1 Mohan Cooperative Industrial Area
Mathura Road, New Delhi 110 044
India

SAGE Publications Asia-Pacific Pte Ltd
33 Pekin Street #02-01
Far East Square
Singapore 048763

British Library Cataloguing in Publication data
A catalogue record for this book is available
from the British Library

ISBN 978-1-4129-2972-1
ISBN 978-1-4129-2973-8

Library of Congress Control Number 2006935541

Typeset by C&M Digitals (P) Ltd., Chennai, India
Printed and bound in Great Britain by Athenaeum Press, Gateshead
Printed on paper from sustainable resources

CONTENTS

LIST OF FIGURES

ACKNOWLEDGEMENTS

Writing a manuscript for a solo authored book is not an individual venture. I want to acknowledge all of the people who helped turn my thoughts into manuscript pages and then into a book. Because this book is the culmination of research that transpired for a long time, my debts to my teachers and advisors run deep. The late Edward E. Jones inspired me to be an experimental social psychologist and taught me how to ask the questions that were worth pursuing. With almost equal gratitude, I thank Darwyn E. Linder and Jack W. Brehm for their patience, guidance and good will. All of my colleagues during the course of my career shaped my perspective on cognitive dissonance, but I would be remiss if I did not single out John M. Darley, Mark P. Zanna and George R. Goethals as being just a little special. I also want to acknowledge my former graduate student, Russell Fazio, and my former postdoctoral fellow, Jeff Stone, for being constant sources of ideas and for the collaborations that fill many of the pages of this book.

I also thank my family whose support and encouragement are the bedrock of my life. My wife Barbara stands at the top of the list, but so too do my children Jason, Aaron and Grant and my daughters-in-law, Sharon and Ana. My grandchildren, Reuven and Judah cannot read this book yet, but just gazing at them is the source of so much inspiration.

I also gratefully acknowledge the many people who read chapters and offered their assistance at many points along the way. Matthew Kugler, Amir Goren, Jessica Salvatore, Jeff Stone, Russell Fazio, Grant Cooper, Aaron Cooper, Dink Asano and Ana, Dragomir and Ljubica Bracilovic are among those people. I am also grateful to Vera Sohl for doing all of the hard administrative work to move the project through to fruition. Finally, I wish to thank my friend and series editor, Michael Hogg, and my editor at Sage, Michael Carmichael, for believing in this project.

For Barbara

FORWARD
Or, Why I Wrote This Book

Cognitive dissonance is a theory that has had an amazing fifty-year run. It began as a gadfly, an iconoclast exception to the way social psychologists typically thought about social processes. It generated excitement and anger – two elements that frequently lead to controversy, new data, and eventually to a synthesis. That certainly has been true of dissonance. The theory continues to generate exciting new data in our journals and conference presentations, and animates our classroom lectures. It has become a commonly used phrase in the popular press, frequently making its way into the pages of the *New York Times*. This book is about dissonance. And this book, like dissonance itself, is about many things.

It is a book that pays homage to Leon Festinger, the social scientist who started the research tradition that for fifty years has been a dynamic and innovative theory. It paints a historical portrait of dissonance that sets the twenty-first century issues in the context of the excitement of its early years.

But this is not a book about history. It is about an exciting evolution that has seen the theory change many times. What began as a simply stated theory about inconsistency is no longer about inconsistency. Or is it? That, too, is the subject of controversy. And one thing that can be said confidently about research in dissonance theory over the decades is that its controversies have not been mellow; they have usually been provocative and productive.

Readers who are new to the field will quickly learn the basics (Chapter 1) and then begin the journey to the current issues facing the theory. Readers who are well versed in dissonance theory, who have taught it to their classes or who have conducted research using its principles, will be challenged to consider the implications of the new issues and controversies facing the field. Along the way, we will weave together such disparate concepts as autonomic somatic arousal, individual conceptions of the self, as well as cultural perspectives in modern-day dissonance theory.

This book also has a personal agenda. All research compendia are necessarily selective. They have to be viewed through the author's lens. In the current volume I have selected what I believe to be a fair representation of the thousands of publications that bear the stamp of cognitive dissonance. But the lens is my own. I will necessarily disappoint some scholars and excite others. Readers should be aware that different experts, just as knowledgeable about dissonance as I, might have written a different book, highlighting different ideas and data. This book is my best judgment of where dissonance theory began and where it is going, and I hope the reader will catch the excitement that I still feel after contributing my own work on dissonance for forty years.

What does dissonance look like as it reaches 50? Well, answering that now would prematurely give away the end of the story. It is safe to say that dissonance at 50 looks a little like self-discrepancy and a little like motivated cognition, a little like judgment and decision making and a little like self-esteem. And although it has been informed by these concepts and contributed to the development of concepts outside the framework of dissonance, the theory has maintained its own framework which continues to make it exciting to study.

1

COGNITIVE DISSONANCE

In the Beginning

There are times in modern history that are relatively peaceful and quiescent, a taking stock of where we are and where we've been. The middle of the 1950s was such a period. The United Nations police action known as the Korean War had ended and Nikita Khrushchev, the Premier of the USSR had not yet threatened the Western hemisphere with nuclear missiles. It was a time for *I Love Lucy* and *Milton Berle* on the relatively new electronic gadget called television, Fred Astaire and Ginger Rodgers at the cinema, and the love affair with the Brooklyn Dodgers in baseball.

In the academic arena of psychology, the discipline of social psychology was blossoming. The geographic locus of theory and research was the United States, with much of the energy and enthusiasm coming from scholars who had emigrated from Europe during the build-up to Nazism, fascism, and the Second World War. During the war, much of the effort of psychologists was directed at issues that were important to the war effort. For example, in Kurt Lewin's laboratory at MIT, central questions involving the efficacy of democracy vs. autocracy were examined, as were more practical issues such as persuasion techniques that could encourage American families to eat formerly shunned cuts of meat – an important issue for a country trying to feed itself in times of war. Similarly, at Yale University under the guidance of Carl Hovland, a stellar team of psychologists had been examining techniques of persuasion that could convince American citizens to make the sacrifices necessary to allow the US and its allies to pursue the Second World War to its conclusion in Japan after the surrender of the Axis powers in Europe.

During the quiescent 1950s, the emphasis of social psychology was examining the way people functioned in groups and the influence that groups – or simply other individuals – had on an individual citizen. Only a few general theories had captured the imagination of social psychologists. Harold Kelley and John Thibaut created a framework for understanding social interaction (Thibaut and Kelley, 1959), Leon Festinger created social comparison theory to understand group influence on the individual (Festinger, 1954) and Hovland and his colleagues produced volumes applying a learning theory perspective to the analysis of persuasion (e.g., Hovland, Janis, and Kelley, 1953).

And then came cognitive dissonance.

Getting started with dissonance

Leon Festinger, whose work on social comparison theory had already made him an influential figure in social psychology, made a very basic observation about the social lives of human beings: we do not like inconsistency. It upsets us and it drives us to action to reduce our inconsistency. The greater the inconsistency we face, the more agitated we will be and the more motivated we will be to reduce it.

Before formalizing the definition of dissonance, let us imagine some inconsistencies that can happen in social life. Imagine that you prepared at great length for a dinner party at your home. You constructed the guest list, sent out the invitations, and prepared the menu. Nothing was too much effort for your party: you went to the store, prepared the ingredients, and cooked for hours, all in anticipation of how pleasant the conversation and the people would be. Except it wasn't. The guests arrived late, the conversations were forced, and the food was slightly overcooked by the time all of the guests arrived. The anticipation and expectation of the great time you were going to have are discordant with your observation of the evening. The pieces do not fit. You're upset, partly because the evening did not go well, but also because of the inconsistency between your expectation and your experience. You are suffering from the uncomfortable, unpleasant state of cognitive dissonance.

Imagine a second scenario. You are an avid baseball fan living in the United States. You believe that the World Series, played each year in a US city, truly selects the best team in baseball. Yes, you know this sport is played in Australia, Brazil, Panama, the Dominican Republic, Canada, Japan, and a host of other countries, but it rarely enters your consciousness. Baseball is American and the best players live there. But then a tournament is organized featuring most of the nations of the world that play the game. The United States is eventually eliminated and Japan wins. Once again, the pieces do not fit. You feel perplexed, agitated, and uncomfortable. In addition to being disappointed by the outcome, your suffering is compounded by the experience of cognitive dissonance.

Festinger was adamant about one point. People do not just *prefer* consistency over inconsistency. It is not that the baseball fan would have preferred his country's team to have won; it is that he must deal with the inconsistency that losing has created. The party host does not just wish the party had gone better; he must deal with the inconsistency between the hopes, aspirations, and effort that he put in prior to the party and the observation that the party did not go well. How can that be done? Surely, if the host changes his opinion about how well the party went, then there is no longer an inconsistency. Perhaps the guests loved a slightly blackened lamb and their quietness at the table reflected their enjoyment of the meal. The baseball fan can deal with his inconsistency by believing that the International World Tournament was not a true reflection of baseball ability. After all, many US players did not play; some played for teams representing countries their parents were born in rather than playing for the United States and, mostly, the US players were more involved in spring training for their upcoming season than taking this tournament very seriously.

Festinger's insistence that cognitive dissonance was like a drive that needed to be reduced implied that people were going to have to find some way of resolving their inconsistencies. People do not just *prefer* eating over starving; we are *driven* to eat. Similarly, people who are in the throes of inconsistency in their social life are *driven* to resolve that inconsistency. How we go about dealing with our inconsistency can be rather ingenious. But, in Festinger's view, there is little question that it *will* be done.

Preparing for the end of the world

A article that appeared in a Minneapolis newspaper gave Festinger and his students an ideal opportunity to study inconsistency in a real-world setting. The article reported on a group of west coast residents who were united in a belief about a significant event: the belief that the Earth was going to be annihilated by a cataclysmic flood on December 21, 1955. All of the people would perish in the cataclysm except for those who believed in the prophecies emanating from the planet Clarion; they alone would be saved from the flood.

Festinger reasoned that if Earth survived December 21, then the people in the little group, dubbed The Seekers by Festinger, Riecken and Schachter (1956), would face a considerable amount of inconsistency on the next morning. While the rest of the world awoke to just another day, The Seekers would face a calamitous amount of inconsistency. The world's very existence would be inconsistent with their belief that the world as we know it was to have ended on the previous evening.

The Seekers was a serious group: this was not a collection of individuals who had a mild premonition of the world's demise. Their beliefs were specific and strong. As the December day approached, Seekers members sold their possessions and quit their jobs. Some, whose spouses did not share their beliefs, divorced. The Seekers members were united in their support

3

of their leader, Mrs Marion Keech, who believed she was the medium through whom the unearthly beings on the planet Clarion communicated their wishes. She received her messages through automatic writing – a paranormal belief that a person's hand is seized by the spirits in another world and is used to communicate messages from the Great Beyond.

Clarion was specific. The group was to gather at Mrs Keech's home on the evening of December 20. They were to await the arrival of a spaceship that would come to Earth and whisk the group away from danger.

The Seekers were not publicity hounds. They sought no attention for their beliefs or their prophecy. When the reporter whose story appeared in the Minneapolis newspaper attempted to interview them, they grudgingly gave only the briefest interview. Publicity was not their goal; protecting themselves from the cataclysmic end of the Earth was.

As a social psychologist, Festinger saw the immediate relevance to the theory he was generating. If people are driven to deal with inconsistency, how would Marion Keech and her followers react to the morning of December 21 when the sun rose, the sky brightened, and the spaceship from Clarion failed to appear? The clear and specific anticipation of the world's demise, the elaborate preparations for the group to be saved, the broken marriages and other personal sacrifices, all would stand in stark contrast to the world's having made just another turn around its axis. Festinger and his colleagues predicted that the dramatic inconsistency would create the state of cognitive dissonance and the group would be driven to find some way to reduce it. They would need to find some way of restoring consistency to their mental maps of the cosmic events.

One of the researchers, Stanley Schachter, infiltrated the group. He carefully observed the group's preparations and specifically observed the events as they unfolded just after midnight on December 20. The group gathered near midnight, waiting for the arrival of the spacecraft. Tension and excitement were high. They had followed the Clarions' instructions meticulously. Mrs Keech's grandfather clock ticked the final seconds to midnight. No spacecraft. Someone in the group checked his watch and saw that his watch still read only 11:55. All watches were reset. At 12:05, even by the ticking of the newly set watches, there was still no spacecraft. Another member of the group suddenly realized that he had not fulfilled all of the instructions given by the Clarions. They had insisted that all metal objects be removed from the human space travelers. Thus, they came with no zippers, belt buckles, or bra straps. But now a Seeker realized that he had a metal filling in a tooth. He removed it. Still, no spacecraft.

There followed a terrible few hours following the midnight disconfirmation of the prophecy. People sobbed and wept. Had they been abandoned by the Clarions? Had they been wrong all along, just like their more cynical spouses and former friends had told them? Shortly past 4:00 am, Mrs Keech received her final message from Clarion. The message provided the answer to their questions, and also provided the opportunity to restore consistency between their doomsday beliefs and their observation that the spaceship had not come and there had been no Earth-destroying cataclysm.

A message shows the path … to restore consistency. The Clarions' final message was brilliant. Through Mrs Keech's trembling hand, it said:

> 'This little group, sitting all night long, has spread so much goodness and light that the God of the Universe spared the Earth from destruction.'

So that was it. The beliefs had not been wrong after all. God had been planning to destroy the Earth. All of the preparations for the cataclysm had not been in vain. In fact, it was precisely and only because of the preparations, sacrifices, and faith of the group that the Earth still existed on the morning of December 21. The sun still shone because of them; people went to work because of them; people still had homes to return to and families to love them … all because of the determination of the small group of Seekers.

Before December 21, Festinger et al. (1956) had made a prediction. They hypothesized that The Seekers, who shunned publicity and notoriety, would take their cause to the public following the disconfirmation. And The Seekers did that with gusto. As soon as their new belief was in place – as soon as they had generated the story that their actions had saved the world – they took their case to the public. They looked for social support for their story. They desperately wanted others to see that their actions had not been in vain, that their prophecy had not been disconfirmed, that there was no inconsistency between their belief in the cataclysm and the bright sunny day that had dawned on December 21.

The premise of dissonance theory is that people do not tolerate inconsistency very well. The Seekers had found a way, post hoc, to make their actions feel consistent to themselves and they now sought validation in having the world believe them. They printed flyers, called newspapers and magazines, offered to talk on radio programs, all in an effort to bolster their new found consistency.

There are probably many factors that influenced the group of Seekers in their actions. Who can guess what had initially influenced these individuals to believe in the prophecy and the automatic writing? Who can guess what motives each individual may have had in the wake of the disconfirmed prophecy? But one thing seems certain. Caught in a major inconsistency among their beliefs, behaviors, and observations of reality, The Seekers did just what Festinger and his colleagues predicted they would do: they were driven to find a way to restore their consistency – driven to find a new belief that would make sense of what they had done and driven to convince a sceptical world of the truth of their new position.

The theory of cognitive dissonance: the original

A year after Festinger et al. (1956) reported their observations of the dooms-day cult, Festinger (1957) published *A Theory of Cognitive Dissonance*. It was a relatively uncomplicated theory with a small number of basic proposi-tions. Although it seemed, on the surface, to be similar to other theoretical notions, which held that people prefer consistency to inconsistency, disso-nance theory would soon stir up a proverbial hornets' nest of controversy and propel it to become one of the best-known and prolifically documented theories in social psychology.

One of the brilliant innovations of cognitive dissonance theory was its use of a relatively new concept called 'cognition.' A cognition is any 'piece of knowledge' a person may have. It can be knowledge of a behavior, knowl-edge of one's attitude, or knowledge about the state of the world. Anything that can be thought about is grist for the dissonance mill. Using 'cognition,' dissonance theory could refer to many different types of psychological con-cepts. An action is different from an attitude which, in turn, is different from an observation of reality. However, each of these has a psychological representation – and that is what is meant by cognition.

The state of cognitive dissonance occurs when people believe that two of their psychological representations are inconsistent with each other. More formally, a pair of cognitions is inconsistent if one cognition follows from the obverse (opposite) of the other. An example will help: A person believes that he should give money to the poor but he passes by an indigent person on the street without contributing money to the man's cup. These two cog-nitions are dissonant because not giving money follows from the obverse of his belief. Not giving money follows logically from a belief that one should *not* contribute to the poor. But, in our example, the person held a belief that did not coincide with his behavior. We can say that the two cognitions were inconsistent or dissonant with each other.

> If a person holds cognitions A and B such that A follows from the opposite of B, then A and B are dissonant.

We have millions of cognitions; some are currently in awareness but most are not. I may know that I am watching television and I may know that I am hungry. I can also become quickly aware of the day of the week, the distance between Los Angeles and San Francisco, or who won last year's Super Bowl. Most cognitions coexist peacefully in our minds, shar-ing nothing in common (e.g., my knowledge of my hunger and my knowl-edge of last year's Super Bowl winner.) Festinger divided cognitions between those that are irrelevant to each other and those that are relevant. It is in the latter category that cognitions can be consistent or inconsistent.

We are comfortable with our consistent cognitions (e.g., I believe in giving to the poor and I donated coins to a poor person today; I was hungry so I ordered a meal in the restaurant.) Inconsistent cognitions, on the other hand, require some work in order to reduce the inconsistency. Why? In Festinger's terms:

> The holding of two or more inconsistent cognitions arouses the state of cognitive dissonance, which is experienced as uncomfortable tension. This tension has drive-like properties and must be reduced.

Dissonance has a magnitude

One of the features of the concept of cognitive dissonance that makes it different from other theories of inconsistency is that dissonance has a magnitude. The more discrepant two cognitions are, the greater the magnitude of dissonance. Imagine that I am a person who believes that the poor deserve my charity and that I should donate to them whenever I have a chance. One day, a volunteer knocks on my door and asks me for a donation to a local soup kitchen. If I give nothing, my decision will be markedly discrepant from my attitude and I should experience a large amount of the uncomfortable tension known as dissonance. If I write a generous check, I should experience no dissonance because I have acted in accord with my attitude. It is also possible for me to reach into my pocket, find a fistful of change, and then donate 10 cents to the volunteer. That should generate a lot of dissonance, because a 10 cent contribution does not make much of a dent in the budget of the soup kitchen. Nonetheless, it is less discrepant with my attitude than no contribution at all. So, the magnitude of cognitive dissonance will depend on the degree of discrepancy between the two cognitions. The greater the discrepancy, the greater the discomfort, and the more motivated I will be to reduce it.

The many ways to reduce cognitive dissonance

Once dissonance is aroused, it needs to be reduced. The more of the tension state I have, the more I will need to do to reduce it. By analogy, a person who is very thirsty is more likely to find a way to get a drink and is likely to drink more than a person who is only slightly thirsty. So, too, with dissonance.

The many ways to reduce dissonance coincide with a more comprehensive view of the factors that affect its magnitude. Reducing the discrepancy is the most straightforward way to reduce dissonance. If my knowledge of my behavior and my knowledge of my attitudes do not match, I can change one or both. If I think contributing to the poor is a good idea, I can resolve to give considerable money the next time I see a beggar or write a larger check to the soup kitchen.

However, in my example, I have a dilemma. I have already refused to give any money to a beggar and I gave only a few coins to the soup kitchen. That's the reality, and the reality has limited my choices about how to resolve the discrepancy. It is difficult to distort the reality of my behavior. My cognition about my attitude, on the other hand, is more fluid and flexible. If I come to believe that I don't really support giving money to the poor, then my opinion will have been consistent with my behavior. The cognitive dissonance that was aroused because of the discrepancy between my attitude and my behavior would no longer exist.

In general, it is difficult to change a cognition about one's behavior. Therefore, when behavior is discrepant from attitudes, the dissonance caused thereby is usually reduced by changing one's attitude. The resistance to change of the behavioral cognition is what makes dissonance theory seem to be a theory of attitude change. Although all cognitions are important for cognitive dissonance theory, the relative ease of changing one's attitudes rather than one's behavior has made dissonance more relevant to attitudes than to any other concept.

Dissonance is impacted not only by the existence and the degree of discrepancy between cognitions but also by other factors. In my soup kitchen example, it may well be that there were good reasons to give only a small amount of money to the kitchen. Perhaps there was no money in my checking account and a few cents were all that I had. Perhaps I did not trust the beggar's authenticity, or perhaps I had contributed a large amount of money to a different social service organization that benefited the poor. All of these might be considered cognitions that are *consonant* with my small contribution.

In general, cognitions that are consonant with one of the discrepant cognitions can serve to reduce the total magnitude of dissonance.

Just as the magnitude of the discrepancy between two cognitions increases the tension state of cognitive dissonance, so the magnitude of consonant cognitions lowers the tension state. In the need to reduce dissonance, a person can work to lower the discrepancy between cognitions, or can work to add cognitions that are consonant with one of the cognitions. Another significant factor in determining the magnitude of dissonance is an assessment of the importance of the cognitions. Not all cognitions have equal importance.

The more important the discrepant cognitions, the more cognitive dissonance I will experience. The more important the consonant cognitions, the less will be my cognitive dissonance.

That provides another avenue for reducing dissonance. If I am suffering unpleasant tension because of my behavior toward the poor, then I can reduce the importance I place on my attitudes toward the poor. I can decide that my attitudes toward the poor are not very important to me compared to other major issues and values or that my behavior toward them was trivial and inconsequential (Blanton, Pelham, DeHart and Carvala 2001; Simon, Greenberg and Brehm, 1995). I can also work on bolstering the importance of any cognition that supported my behavior toward the poor (Sherman and Gorkin, 1980). In my example of contributing toward the soup kitchen, I may decide that the horror I would experience from writing a bad check was so important that it justified my only reaching into my pocket to see what coins I had.

Before leaving the overall picture that Festinger painted in his original theory, it may be useful to summarize it with the following formula for the magnitude of cognitive dissonance:

$$\text{DISSONANCE MAGNITUDE} = \frac{\text{SUM (all discrepant cognitions} \times \text{importance)}}{\text{SUM (all consonant cognitions} \times \text{importance)}}$$

That is, the total magnitude of the tension state of cognitive dissonance is proportional to the discrepant cognitions a person has (the elements above the line in the formula) and inversely proportional to the number of cognitions that are consonant (below the line), each weighted by its importance.

As we shall see in this book, the research paradigms that have been used to test predictions from dissonance theory have relied upon attitude change as the predominant method to reduce dissonance. By focusing on the discrepancy between behavior and attitude, the direct reduction of dissonance by attitude change is the most likely and predictable means. But it is important to keep in mind that attitude change is not the *only* means of dealing with cognitive dissonance. Research has shown that, consistent with the general formula above, changes in importance of cognitions are an effective means of dissonance reduction (Simon et al., 1995). Similarly, research has shown that bolstering the supportive cognitions – those 'below the line' in the above formula – (Sherman and Gorkin, 1980), seeking new, supportive cognitions that support the discrepant action (Frey, 1981; Mills, 1965) also serves to reduce dissonance.

In fact, the doomsday cult studied by Festinger et al. reduced their dissonance by adding cognitions consonant with their behavior. Through the last-minute intervention of the Clarions, The Seekers had invented a cognition consonant with their prophecies, predictions, and sacrifices. It was only *because* of their prophecy and sacrifice that the world was saved. And to magnify the importance of that cognition, they celebrated that idea with news releases and interviews. Gaining public support for that belief made it seem all the more important. While The Seekers' thoughts and actions were undoubtedly determined by many factors, their post-disconfirmation scramble to find credible supporting cognitions seems to have been at the service of reducing their state of dissonance.

Liking what you choose: the first experimental verification of the theory of cognitive dissonance

Jack W. Brehm was a PhD student of Leon Festinger's during the time that dissonance theory was being conceived. His doctoral dissertation provided the first experimental test of hypotheses derived from the theory. As a thought experiment to help bring Brehm's story to life, imagine that you are in the market to purchase a new car. Imagine, too, that you have done considerable research on various cars, consulted with your friends, and thought hard about how various cars make you feel. With this careful research, you have now narrowed your choices to two: a previously loved (i.e., used) Honda Civic and a new BMW sports car. Each has advantages and disadvantages. One is expensive, the other is cheap; one is attractive, the other is not; one is sexy, the other is not. You have made a list of advantages and disadvantages that looks something like this:

If I choose …			
Civic		**BMW**	
Advantages	**Disadvantages**	**Advantages**	**Disadvantages**
Inexpensive	Ugly	Attractive	Expensive
Fuel costs	Not sexy	Fast	No room for
		Sexy	groceries
		Hi tech features	

You want to make the correct choice. You dispassionately examine your list make the most rational, unbiased decision you can make: you choose to purchase the BMW. You sign the paper, pay your deposit, and are ready to receive your car. However, something may feel just a little wrong. Do you notice the twinge of regret? Do you notice that you are a bit uncomfortable? Dissonance theory explains why. Even though you have made a rational choice – the best you could have made in the circumstance – you nonetheless experience the unpleasant emotional state of cognitive dissonance.

Here is why: you have a cognition about your decision – i.e., you are going to own the BMW. But, remember that you thought the BMW had disadvantages. It is small, providing little room for groceries, and it is very expensive. These cognitions are discrepant with your decision to buy the BMW. Think, too, about the good features of the Civic: It has low fuel costs and is inexpensive. You could have bought two Civics for the price of the BMW. How do you reconcile those cognitions with your decision to buy the BMW? These discrepancies create cognitive dissonance. These discrepancies lead to an unpleasant emotional state and, akin to the experience of aversive drives, you need to reduce it. And you will!

Your choices for reducing dissonance are several. Remembering the dissonance formula, your dissonance is high because you have discrepancies between several pairs of cognitive elements. You bought the BMW, which is discrepant from the cognition about its price tag. You rejected the Honda, which is discrepant from your cognition about its fuel economy. You can reduce dissonance by reducing the discrepancy. The easiest solution (one that does not involve changing your decision) is to change your attitude about some of the features of each car that are discrepant with your decision. For example, you can decide that it is wise to make a major financial investment in something as important as a car. And who needs good fuel economy anyway? By changing your opinion about these features, the discrepancy between the features and your decision is minimized and dissonance is reduced.

In addition to these strategies, you can recruit more ideas that are consistent with your decision to purchase the BMW. Suddenly, the thought of how many people will become friendly with you in your shiny new car strikes you as something you had never thought of before. And don't forget that the Civic only comes in colors you do not like and it is probably difficult to add air conditioning to the base car. Now, you have added consonant cognitions (below the line in the earlier formula) and successfully reduced dissonance.

You can reduce even more dissonance if you work on the importance of the various cognitions. If all of the cognitions that are consonant with your purchasing decision are very important and the cognitions that are discrepant with it are trivial, then dissonance is reduced still further. If it seems more important than ever before to have a car that is sexy and even more trivial that its repairs are expensive, then the magnitude of dissonance declines. With the change of importance, you do not need to switch the valence of a cognition – i.e., convince yourself that a feature you used to think was good is actually bad. You just need to change how much to value that particular cognitive element in the total array of consistent and inconsistent cognitions.

There is a beneficial and measurable consequence to the various machinations that help you reduce dissonance. Not only is the tension state of dissonance reduced, but your overall liking of the BMW will also be raised;

similarly, the degree that you like the rejected Civic will be reduced. All of the changes of cognitions about the BMW (e.g., how much you like paying for it; how sexy it is; how important it is to attract more friends) and all of the changes in your thoughts about the Civic (e.g., how important it is not to be stuck with an unattractive car; how bad the air conditioner is likely to be) make you like the Civic less. If we measured your feeling about the BMW after you have reduced your dissonance, it should be more positive than it was before your decision. Similarly, the rejected Civic should be liked less after the dissonance reduction than before. Note that before your decision, you were logical and thoughtful. You had considered all of the features of the cars dispassionately and without distortion. You concluded that you liked the BMW more than the Civic; that's why you bought it. But after the decision, logic and dispassionate thoughtfulness were not the guiding principles. Rather, the guiding principles were at the service of distorting and modifying cognitions to help reduce cognitive dissonance.

Brehm's (1956) dissertation at the University of Minnesota was designed to measure the changes in attractiveness of decision alternatives in the laboratory. Women from the Minneapolis area were invited to come to the laboratory to offer their opinions about a number of household gadgets. They were shown an array of kitchen items such as a blender, a mixer, and a toaster. The participants rank ordered the items in terms of preference for owning one. They were also asked to rate the items on a scale of 1–100, representing the degree to which they liked each item. Then Brehm offered the women an opportunity to have one of the items. He told them that the research firm that was sponsoring the research had authorized him to allow the participants to have one of the items, and he then presented each woman with a choice. At this point, Brehm introduced an experimental manipulation. For some of the women the choice was between two items that they had ranked very highly – specifically, whichever item they had ranked second and third on the list of seven items. Other women were given a choice between their second and seventh ranked items.

Let us consider what the women may have been thinking. A decision selecting one of two household items, like a decision between the two cars in our thought experiment, should be made logically and dispassionately. Considering all of the good and bad features of both items, it would make sense that the participants would choose the higher ranked item, and they did so.

But wait! The choice of the higher ranked item brings with it any of the bad features of that item. A blender, beloved as it might be, is also noisy. And the rejected toaster is both quiet and reliable. These cognitive elements that were inconsistent with the choice of the blender create dissonance and, as with our automobile example, require work to reduce it. By the time the dissonance is reduced, we can predict that the degree of liking for the chosen alternative will be higher than it was before the choice and the degree of liking for the

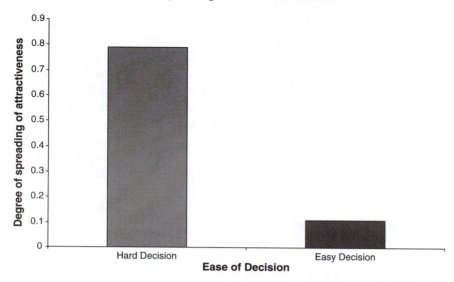

Spreading of Choice Alternatives

Figure 1.1   Attractiveness of the chosen and rejected alternatives following a decision
Source: Adapted from Brehm (1956)

rejected alternative will be less than it was before the choice. Brehm asked the participants to rate the alternatives a second time in order to see if this is what occurred.

There is also a more nuanced prediction that was important in this research. When both items were liked very much, the choice was relatively difficult to make. The lower ranked item, although liked less than the chosen item, was still pretty nice. It clearly had features that the housewives valued, for the item was ranked almost as highly as the item that was eventually chosen. The magnitude of dissonance resulting from this choice must have been quite high, which in turn made the discomfort high and motivated considerable work to reduce it. By contrast, choosing between the second and seventh ranked items was an easier one. True, there must have been some reasons to like item 7 and some reasons to be wary of item 2, but the magnitude of the dissonance should have been much lower. Following the decision, the participants should have been experiencing considerably less discomfort and have less of a need to distort their opinions of the two items.

Brehm's prediction was that women in the difficult decision condition would raise their evaluation of the chosen item and lower their evaluation of the rejected item – and would do this significantly more than they would in the easy decision condition. Figure 1.1 shows what happened.

The results show that the prediction was supported by the data. The participants in the difficult decision condition showed a spreading of the alternatives such that they liked the chosen item considerably more, and the rejected item significantly less, than they had rated the same items prior to the choice. One other finding is noteworthy. Some participants had been run in a control condition. In this case, Brehm gave each participant her second-ranked item as a gift. There was no decision that needed to be made. Brehm reasoned that the control condition would not arouse cognitive dissonance. After all, the participant had not made a decision that resulted in giving up some good feature of a rejected alternative or accepting an unwanted feature of the chosen item. She was simply presented with the item. Her feelings about what the good and bad aspects of that kitchen item would remain the same. Her rating would remain the same. Indeed, the participants in this condition showed no change whatsoever in their rating of the item they received as a gift.

A summary of dissonance following free choice

In the language of dissonance theory research, Jack Brehm's experiment established a paradigm known as the free choice paradigm. His landmark study left us with several lessons:

1 Cognitive dissonance occurs following decisions.
2 It is reduced by attitude change that spreads the attractiveness of the choice alternatives. The chosen alternative becomes more attractive; the unchosen alternative becomes less attractive.
3 The more difficult the decision, the greater the dissonance.
4 Cognitive dissonance is a ubiquitous phenomenon. We make choices all of the time. Choosing among consumer items was merely a way to assess dissonance in the laboratory. However, in the real world, we make many decisions everyday. At universities, we choose courses to take, courses to teach, books to buy. At home, we choose television programs to watch, vacations to take, and even automobiles to purchase. Each time we make one of those decisions, we are subjected to the experience of cognitive dissonance and we are likely to take action to reduce it.

Saying what you do not believe: dissonance arising from induced compliance

As the 1950s drew to a close, dissonance theory emerged as a major player in understanding people's desire for consistency and, when consistency is disturbed, provided a theoretical framework for viewing the distortions people undertake in order to restore it. Festinger, Riecken and Schachter's (1956) study was as dramatic as Brehm's (1956) laboratory study was compelling. But the major controversy was yet to come. It is perhaps a stretch to say that the Soviet Union's launching of the Sputnik satellite shook up world politics and stimulated American technology in much the same way as the publication of Festinger and Carlsmith's induced compliance study in 1959 shook up experimental social psychology. Nonetheless, in a small way, the analogy holds.

Festinger and Carlsmith (1959) posed a relatively straightforward question which they answered with an ingenious experiment. They asked what the consequence would be if someone were induced to act in a way that was contrary to his or her attitudes? In a more modern frame of reference, we could ask the following question: what would be the consequence for a person's emotional state if she argued publicly for the value of bringing democracy to Iraq via the 2003 military invasion when, privately, she was against the war? The inconsistency between attitude and belief would bring about the unpleasant state of cognitive dissonance. Needing to reduce that dissonance, the speaker would need to reduce the discrepancy between what she said and what she believed. Because it is nearly impossible to change what she said or to deny that she said it, the most straightforward way to resolve the dissonance would be to change her attitude in the direction of the speech. Therefore, dissonance theory predicts that being induced to make a counterattitudinal statement would lead to attitude change in the direction of the speech. The speaker giving a speech in favor of the Iraq War would likely be motivated to change her private attitude to become more favorable to the war in Iraq. Once again, dissonance theory comes into focus as a theory of attitude change because, in the battle between changing one's attitude and changing one's behaviour, attitudes are the easiest to change.

In a laboratory at Stanford University, Festinger and Carlsmith staged an experiment that was creative in its manipulations and startling in its results. Let's set the stage as a participant in the experiment may have viewed it. You arrive at the research building at the appointed time, you take a seat in the waiting room, and after a short period of time the researcher's door swings open and you are invited inside. He tells you that he is researching various 'measures of performance' and he would like you to perform a straightforward task. You are shown a peg board on which there are several dozen rectangular pegs. Your job is to turn each of the pegs a quarter turn with your left hand and then turn them back again. You will repeat this task with your right hand. When that is over, you will do it again. Then, you will move to a board on which there are several dozen spools of thread. You will take each spool off with your left hand, replace them, and repeat the process with your right hand.

Is the experimenter fooling? Apparently not, because he has a stopwatch and clipboard in his hand and he instructs you to begin. After several minutes of following these instructions, you are bored nearly to tears by the monotonous drudgery that constitutes the tasks of this experiment. Finally, you are done. The experimenter thanks you and is ready to send you to the department secretary who will give you the experimental credit that you were to receive for participating. Of course, he will first 'debrief' you by telling you a little bit more about the experiment. The experimenter now begins a complicated story designed to convince you to comply with a request to make a speech in which you will take a position that is at variance with your attitude.

He tells you that you were actually in a control condition of a more complicated experiment. If you had been randomly assigned to the experimental condition, he continues, you would not have been sitting in the waiting room alone while you waited for him to open the door. Instead, a confederate of the experimenter would have entered the room, told you that he had just completed the experiment, and that you would be happy to know that it was one of the most fun and enjoyable experiences he'd ever had in a research study. The confederate would have said this because (the experimenter tells you) the true purpose of the study is to compare the performance on these peg-turning tasks of people like yourself who had no particular expectation of how good and fun it would be with people who were expecting it to be fun. In fact, he says, the next student who is in the waiting area is in that experimental condition and will soon be greeted by that paid confederate and told how much fun the task will be.

But where is that confederate? The researcher, talking partly to himself and partly to you, mentions that the confederate should have been here already. 'Where is that confederate?' he muses. He missed a session yesterday, too. And then, the researcher is struck with an inspired thought: 'Hey, I have an idea! Why don't you serve as the confederate? I can hire you to be a confederate, and you can be "on-call" whenever my regular confederate can't make it. Would you like to do that? It would certainly help me out. You can start today … right now. All you have to do is to go out to the waiting room, pick up your books, and casually tell that student sitting there how much fun this study was, how exciting it was to be in it, and how much you enjoyed it. Would you do this for me?'

If you were the research participant, what do you think you would do? Almost all of the students agreed to help the researcher. They entered the anteroom, found the student waiting there, and told him how much fun they should expect the study to be. When finished with the little play-acting, the students went to the departmental secretary, received credit for their participation, and filled out a general department survey in which they rated how much fun they actually thought the experimental task had been.

Almost all of what the students had been told was a ruse designed to get them to say something they did not believe. There was no measure of performance study and there was no 'waiting subject' sitting in the anteroom.

The 'waiting subject' was really a confederate; the real subject was not. By having the real participants engage in a task so overwhelmingly tedious, Festinger and Carlsmith could be certain that they would have formed negative attitudes about the task. Indeed, a control group of participants who only performed the peg-turning and spool-sorting tasks rated it as boring and unpleasant. Experimental participants had made a forceful statement about how interesting the task was but, in truth, their private opinion of the task was that it was boring. Clearly, the situation was set up so that cognitive dissonance would be aroused. The way to reduce it was to reduce the discrepancy between attitude and behavior, which could be accomplished by changing their attitude toward the task. That is precisely what the participants did.

Festinger and Carlsmith's study may seem like an elaborate ruse just to convince someone to say something that was at variance with their attitudes. However, we now need to introduce another independent variable in this study. What I have not told you yet was that all of the students, except those in the control condition, had been offered a financial inducement in order to comply with the request. When the experimenter thought of his ingenious plan to sign the student up as a substitute confederate, he offered a financial incentive. For half of the students, he offered the sum of $20; for the other half, he offered $1. There was no difference in the compliance rates. Students were willing to tell the waiting subject that the task was terrific whether they had been offered the small or the large sum.

Did the magnitude of incentive make a difference in students' final attitudes? Would people be more likely to believe what they said if they agreed to say it for a small or a large amount of money? Here, Festinger and Carlsmith (1959) made a prediction that seemed less than obvious in terms of everyday wisdom but which followed logically from the theory of cognitive dissonance. They predicted that the speech given for a small amount of money would produce more favorable attitudes toward the task than the speech given for a large amount of money. Remember our dissonance formula above. The discrepancy between believing the task was boring but saying it was exciting created cognitive dissonance. But dissonance is not just about discrepancy. It is also about cognitions consistent with the behavior. The cognition about the inducement was such a cognition. It goes below the line in the formula and serves to reduce the total magnitude of dissonance. A large incentive ($20) was much more important and influential than a small incentive ($1) and therefore served better to reduce the total magnitude of dissonance.

Because people experienced more of the unpleasant tension of dissonance in the $1 condition than in the $20 condition, Festinger and Carlsmith predicted that participants offered $1 would come to like the task more than participants who had been offered $20. The results shown in Figure 1.2

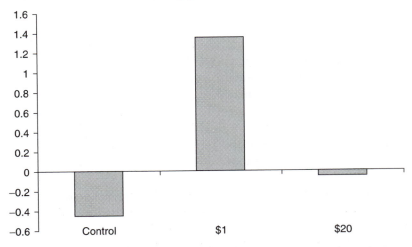

How enjoyable were the tasks?

Figure 1.2   Evalutation of boring tasks: degree of positive feelings toward a task
Source: Adapted from Festinger and Carlsmith (1959)

support this prediction. When asked how much they enjoyed the task, participants who had been offered only $1 to make the counterattitudinal statement to the confederate rated the task as significantly more enjoyable than students who had either been paid the larger sum of $20 or in the control condition.

Political attitudes and induced compliance

One of the methodological considerations that went into the study by Festinger and Carlsmith was to try to create an attitude in the laboratory that was novel. The peg-turning and spool-sorting tasks were novel; people had no pre-existing attitudes, and the boredom of the tasks made virtually everyone believe that the tasks were uninteresting. A very positive feature of this procedure was the control over the initial attitudes that people had before they reduced their dissonance. Republicans, Democrats, Libertarians, and Greens would have no reason to differ on their attitude toward the task. The less positive feature is that the attitude issue seems contrived and less relevant to real-world issues.

The first study to use the induced compliance procedure on real-world attitudes was conducted by Bob Cohen and reported in Brehm and Cohen's (1962) influential book, *Explorations in Cognitive Dissonance*. In the early 1960s, students at Yale University were embroiled in a controversy with the

New Haven, CT, police department and generally felt negatively toward the police. They specifically were angry at the severity of the actions that the police had taken against the students. Participants were contacted in their dormitories and were asked if they would write 'a strong and forceful essay' taking the position that the extreme actions of the New Haven police were justified.

Participants complied and wrote the essay favoring the New Haven police. As an inducement, they were offered either a very small incentive (50 cents), a large incentive ($10), or a variety of incentives in between $1 and $5). When their attitudes toward the police were assessed after the writing of the essay, Cohen found an inverse linear relationship between incentive magnitude and attitude change. Consistent with Festinger and Carlsmith's findings, the lower the incentive, the greater the attitude change. The higher the incentive, the smaller the attitude change.

Although Festinger and Carlsmith's landmark study is probably the best remembered of the induced compliance research, it was Cohen's methodology that established the research paradigm for the hundreds of studies to come. Asking people to write essays or make speeches on topics with which they did not agree became the essential method for creating the discrepancy that aroused cognitive dissonance. Looking for the inverse relationship between the magnitude of incentive and the degree of attitude change became the signature of cognitive dissonance following induced compliance.

Induced compliance: why the controversy?

Festinger and Carlsmith's (1959) experiment set off a flurry of controversy. There was a boldness and a swagger to the early dissonance experiments. Festinger and his students were confident of their ability to bring interesting and important issues into the laboratory and make them real for experimental subjects. There was a flair and a stagecraft not only to Festinger and Carlsmith's experiment but to so many that followed shortly thereafter. Festinger and his students, including Elliot Aronson, J. Merrill Carlsmith, Judson Mills, and Jack Brehm invented elaborate scenarios to study the effects of such issues as threat, effort, and expectancies on the arousal of dissonance. There was no issue too abstract or too difficult to put into the laboratory and no manipulation that they could not carry off in a believable way to research participants. Creating involved participation in elaborate scenarios became a hallmark of the dissonance research.

But more important than the style of the research was its substance. Here was a theoretical stance whose basic assumptions seemed straightforward enough, but whose predictions and derivations flew in the face of the prevailing zeitgeist of the time: learning theory. In the 1940s and 1950s, B.F. Skinner, Clark Hull, and a number of influential psychologists were in the midst of arguments about how to conceptualize the role of reinforcement in shaping learning. The emphasis of learning theory was the study of non-human animals, but one implication for human behavior was clear and common to all learning theories: Organisms learn by reward and punishment. The greater the reward, the greater the learning.

Although learning theory had not been applied with great precision to the human condition (although see Skinner, 1953), its general principles were assumed. In the study of attitudes, for example, Carl Hovland and his colleagues at the Yale Communication and Attitude Change program had published volumes on how persuasion works, and all of it was guided by general notions of reinforcement. We change our attitudes when we are rewarded to do so. We like objects we are rewarded for interacting with. We want to believe what experts believe because having similar attitudes as experts is rewarding (Hovland, Janis, and Kelley, 1953).

Money is an obvious example of a reward. Suppose you find a sum of money on the street. There is a good chance that you will come to have positive affect about that street and perhaps visit that street more often in the future. If you make a statement that someone pays you money for, there is a good chance that you will like what you said and be willing to say it again. The higher the reward, the more this should be true.

The results of Festinger and Carlsmith's study contradicted this framework. The participants liked what they had said the *less* they were paid for it. The smaller the reward for saying that the boring task was interesting, the more the participants believed what they had said. The higher the reward, the less they believed it. Learning theory had been the underlying principle of work in psychology, particularly in the United States. Now the theory of cognitive dissonance was threatening to question the dominance of reinforcement and learning. At the very least, it had made clearly derived predictions about the relationship of rewards to attitude change and supported those predictions. This was not going to be left unchallenged. There will be more to say about the controversy after we look at another of the iconoclast predictions made by dissonance theory.

Liking what you suffer for

What does a punishment feel like? It makes us feel bad, it discourages us from performing the behavior for which we were just punished, and it serves as a reminder to avoid the stimulus or situation that provoked the punishment. Punishments come in many varieties from severe corporal punishment to the more mundane negative reactions we may suffer from friends, teachers, or relatives who disapprove of something we do. Overall, it is safe to say that, at a minimum, we do not like being punished and that punishments typically produce negative affective states. Words like dislike, harm, aversion, and suffering seem to fit within the general rubric of being punished.

Imagine a situation we might be in that brings us pain and suffering. We are in a group that decides to learn to rock climb. We find an instructor in the Yellow Pages who, it seems, has a somewhat sadistic sense of what it takes to learn to climb a wall. He puts us through a tortuous training program designed to make us confront our fear, toughen our skin, strengthen our legs, all for the purpose of climbing a rather ordinary 20-foot wall. Did the suffering the instructor put us through make us thoroughly dislike the wall-climbing experience? Were we sufficiently punished to refrain from wall climbing in the future, to have a negative reaction to the thought of wall climbing, to hate the instructor and his 20-foot wall?

Although there is logic to predicting that the punishment, suffering, and effort that went into the wall-climbing experience would produce negative reactions, Elliot Aronson and Jud Mills (1959) used the theory of cognitive dissonance to predict otherwise. They reasoned that the suffering that goes into a given activity is inconsistent with people's desire not to suffer. In the case of the wall-climbing example, the ordeal that we allowed ourselves to undergo with the instructor is inconsistent with our typical preference not to suffer. These two cognitions are inconsistent and therefore should lead to the experience of cognitive dissonance. In addition, the wall we climbed was a rather ordinary challenge that, to a dispassionate observer, should not have required the suffering the instructor put us through. How can we reduce the dissonance? One effective way would be to raise, rather than lower, our evaluation of the wall climbing. If we thought the wall was an amazing challenge and that wall climbing was an exhiloratingly positive experience, those cognitions would support (i.e., be consistent with) the suffering we endured. Putting it all together, Aronson and Mills (1959) suggested that from the perspective of cognitive dissonance theory, enduring punishing activities such as those our instructor heaped upon us, should increase the positivity of our attitudes toward the activity for which we suffered.

They designed an experiment to test this prediction. Female students from the University of Minnesota were asked if they would like to join a new club being formed on campus – a sexual discussion group. When they arrived for the first meeting of the group, a researcher told them that it was not a good idea for just anyone to join a group on such a sensitive topic as sex. Therefore, they would first need to pass a screening test in order to gain entry. What happened next depended on the experimental condition to which the students had been randomly assigned. Some students were in a high embarrassment condition. They were asked to read aloud some explicit four-letter words and then to read an explicit sexual passage drawn from a lurid novel. Other students were assigned to a low embarrassment condition. Their screening test consisted of a much milder initiation in which they read words like 'love' and 'petting,' but did not have any explicit sexual material to read aloud. When the students finished their screening test, they were admitted to the sexual discussion group.

What Aronson and Mills wanted to accomplish next was to have all of the participants exposed to the same group members who were having the same conversation. That way, the only difference between the two groups would be the amount of embarrassment the students had suffered during the screening test. The experimenters explained that the group session had begun a few minutes before, and there had been some reading that the students had done prior to the discussion, so that it would be best for the new members to listen to today's ongoing conversation via earphones. They would be able to join the group in person at the next meeting. With this cover story, and without telling the participants, the experimenters were able to turn on a tape recording of a staged conversation. All of the participants heard precisely the same voices having precisely the same conversation.

And what a conversation it was! Rather than a conversation designed to be exciting, this one was staged to be boring and monotonous. It stumbled and bumbled its way through several minutes of dry conversation on the secondary sexual characteristics of lower mammals. As Aronson and Mills described it, the participants 'contradicted themselves, mumbled several non sequiturs, stated sentences that they never finished … and in general conducted one of the most worthless and uninteresting discussions imaginable' (1959: 179).

The cognition that the students had suffered through an embarrassing procedure for entry into this sexual discussion was dissonant with the cognitions that (a) the students would prefer not to be embarrassed and (b) the conversation was dreadful. One way of reducing cognitive dissonance was to find something wonderful about the experience that would be consistent with, or justify, the suffering. Despite what the participant heard on the tape, she could decide that the conversation was lively and stimulating; she could decide that the group members seemed lively and interesting people. Those students whose screening test was easy and not embarrassing would have less motivation to distort their evaluation of the group and its members.

Before leaving the session, the students were asked to rate the discussion they had heard and were also asked to rate their impressions of the members. As Aronson and Mills had predicted, women in the high embarrassment group who had a lot of dissonance to reduce, rated the discussion and the group members more highly than did the women in the low embarrassment group. The results are shown in Figure 1.3.

The figure also shows the results of ratings made by students who had been assigned to a control condition. These students also volunteered to be in the sexual discussion group, heard the same conversation as the women in the high and low embarrassment group, but did not have any screening test to undergo. As you can see, the control group subjects thought the group and its

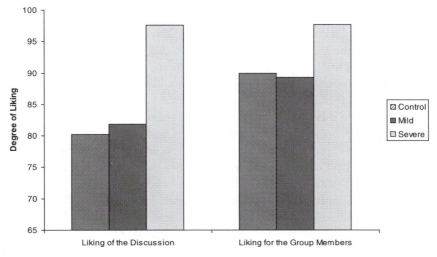

Figure 1.3 Evaluation of interest of discussion by participants
Source: Adapted from Aronson and Mills (1959)

members were dull. So, too, did the students in the low embarrassment group. But the students in the high embarrassment group, who had heard precisely the same tape recording as all of the other students, felt that the conversation and the members were significantly more interesting.

Like many studies that use novel procedures, it is possible to think of alternative explanations. In the case of Aronson and Mills's study, you might have several questions about how well the manipulation of embarrassment really fits the theory. Was reading the lurid passage and four-letter words really embarrassing? If it was embarrassing, is that the same as the kind of physical effort and suffering portrayed in the rock-climbing example? Several studies have replicated Aronson and Mills's basic finding, but the study that probably used the most unassailable manipulation of suffering was conducted by Gerard and Matthewson (1966). For their suffering manipulation, the investigators had participants agree to undergo electric shock in order to join a group discussion. They found that the higher the level of shock, the more the participants enjoyed the group and the discussion.

Threats and expectancies: rounding out the early history

The excitement of the first studies in cognitive dissonance did not stop at induced compliance, free choice, and effort justification. Applying the insights of cognitive dissonance to make novel predictions took several additional forms. Aronson and Carlsmith (1962) posed an interesting dilemma. Suppose you had a child who had a penchant for eating candy. You wanted him to reduce his sweets consumption. It occurs to you that you can use an admonition to stay away from the candy jar, particularly when you are not present to monitor his behavior. So you prepare to tell him that he should keep away from the sweets while you are out of the house. To reinforce what you say, you plan to tell him what you will do if he fails to listen to your directive. You will …

What should come next? Something firm and harsh or something soft and mild? As before, a broad view of reinforcement and learning theory would suggest that a high threat will serve as a deterrent and lead to a negative evaluation of the stimulus – that is, the candy. Dissonance theory predicts something quite different. The deterrence for eating candy should be as mild as possible. It should be just sufficient to convince the child to refrain from eating, but no more threatening than that.

To show that this is true, Aronson and Carlsmith (1963) had children play with some attractive toys. Then an adult experimenter pointed to the most attractive toy in the room, a robot, and told the children, 'I have to leave the room for a moment. While I am gone, I do not want you to play with this toy.' He pointed to the robot and placed it on a table within reach of the children. For the children who had been randomly assigned to the high-threat condition, the experimenter continued his warning by saying, 'If you play with the robot while I am gone, I will be very angry with you. I will have to pick up my toys and go home.' In the low-threat condition, the adult merely told the children that if they played with the robot he would be 'mildly annoyed.'

All children refrained from playing with the toy as the adult had asked them. However, not playing with the toy was discrepant from the children's cognition that they wanted to play with this attractive toy. How could the children reduce dissonance? Aronson and Carlsmith predicted that the children would come to change their attitude about the toy. By devaluing it, they would restore consistency. Not playing with a robot creates no dissonance if you do not like the robot. Children in the high-threat condition had an additional reason to support their behavior of not playing with the robot. The adult would be very angry and take all of the toys away.

This cognition would be sufficient to reduce the children's dissonance. They did not need to devalue the toy because they had a very good reason to support their behavior. When Aronson and Carlsmith asked the children to rate how much they liked the robot, children in the mild-threat condition rated it significantly lower than did children in the high-threat condition. Mild threat led to internal attitude change; severe threat did not. The moral of the story is that if you want to have your child keep his hands out of the candy jar, use a mild admonition and he may well change his mind about how much he likes your candy.

Everyone likes to be successful. Everyone likes to improve his or her skills. Is there a golfer amongst us who would not like a lower score, a skier who would not like to conquer a higher mountain, a chess player who would not like to achieve a higher ranking? Thinking through the implications of cognitive dissonance, Aronson and Carlsmith (1962) suggested that there may be at least one such time: people who think poorly of their ability, who think they are unsuccessful, are people who are likely to expect not to succeed. The expectation for failure is a cognition and any evidence discrepant with that cognition should cause cognitive dissonance. People who think highly of themselves and expect to succeed would suffer dissonance by failing, but people who think poorly of their ability might experience dissonance from success.

Aronson and Carlsmith (1962) tested this notion by giving people a novel task to perform. They were given pairs of pictures and asked to choose which of the pair was actually a picture of a schizophrenic. (In truth, there were no right answers to the task; all pictures were of students enrolled at Harvard University.) Some of the participants went through round after round of the task and were given false feedback that they were almost always wrong. They were very poor at the discrimination of who was schizophrenic. Other students received the opposite (false) feedback and learned that they were very good. On the very last round, participants indicated what their answers were and received feedback. Half of the participants found that they were successful; half found they had given the wrong answers. Feedback on the final round was orthogonal to what students had learned about their ability from the prior rounds. Therefore, the design of the study had four conditions. Some students expected to be successful and found that on the last round they performed either consistently with that expectation or inconsistently with it. The other students expected to be unsuccessful, and found that the last round confirmed or contradicted that expectation.

A mysterious 'accident' then occurred. Through a technological glitch, the experimenters lost the data from the last round. The participants were asked to choose between the pairs of pictures again. They were told they could change their answers or stay with the same answers; they just needed to do the round over. It was a relatively easy matter for the participants to remember what they had chosen before the data were lost. So, they could choose to stay with their original answers, or change them to the other picture in the pair. People who were unsuccessful in the last round could easily become successful by changing their choice.

For participants who had expected to be successful because they had been successful on the first several rounds but who had failed on the last round, choices were changed. That is, knowing that they had made the wrong choice on the last round, they changed their choices to achieve success. Not so for those who expected to fail because they had failed on the first several rounds. They stuck with their original choices and failed again. Even more interesting were those who had expected to fail and found that they had done very well on the last round. All they needed to do was to choose the same pictures on the last round as they had chosen previously. But they didn't. Apparently, the dissonance created by the discrepancy between their negative expectation and their positive performance motivated them to change their answers. It seemed more comfortable to perform as they had expected rather than to suffer the state of cognitive dissonance that would arise from the discrepancy.

Lessons from the early days

The elegance of early cognitive dissonance theory was that it was basic and uncomplicated, yet it made predictions that were novel and non-obvious. It drew on a few basic principles whose a priori basis was appealing: that people are driven to achieve consistency and are motivated to make changes in the wake of inconsistency.

There were several features of cognitive dissonance theory that transcended the basic concept of consistency. The first was Festinger's reliance on the concept of cognition. By focusing on 'pieces of knowledge,' as he phrased it, dissonance theory could consider relationships between concepts that, until then, had been treated separately. Attitudes, beliefs, perceptions of the environment, values, and behaviors all fell under a single rubric and all were grist for the mill to determine the level of consistency or inconsistency.

The second major contribution of cognitive dissonance theory is its prediction of a *magnitude* of dissonance. Festinger was not the first to theorize about the consequences of inconsistency. One of the earliest contributions to the literature in social psychology was Fritz Heider's (1946) exposition of psychological balance. Like Festinger, Heider believed that people intrinsically dislike inconsistent states. It makes us more comfortable if, for example, we like a particular movie and a friend of ours likes the same movie than if we disagreed with our friend. We are pleased by harmonious balance, which is a concept similar to consistency. But Festinger and Heider came from vastly different traditions when thinking about people's mental states in a social environment. Heider came from a Gestalt tradition in which certain relationships among objects in the physical world were simply preferred to other relationships. Heider's genius for social psychology was that he saw that similar principles applied to the social world. Just as we prefer to see such principles as continuity and closure in the perceptual world, so too do we prefer to see consistency in our social world.

By contrast, Festinger came from an intellectual tradition fostered by Kurt Lewin. In that tradition, people navigated a world in which there were motivational pushes and pulls; there were underlying psychological forces that drove our behavior. So, it was more natural for Festinger to expound a theory of cognitive consistency based on forces and drives rather than perceptual preferences. And once the concepts of drive and arousal were introduced, it was not a major leap to theorize about magnitude. There can be more drive or less drive, depending on the amount of dissonance that is aroused in a given situation. It was the ability to predict the *situations* in which there would be more or less dissonance that gave the theory its very special properties. Few would have argued that making a speech contrary to one's attitudes is inconsistent and should lead to change. However, the hypothesis that there is more arousal when the magnitude of incentive is low rather than high is what made the dissonance theory predictions special.

And controversial – which brings us to the next phase of the work in dissonance theory.

2

CRITICISM PROPELS
THE THEORY FORWARD

There is a maxim in research that controversy breeds knowledge. When consumers of a research study find it difficult to believe a result, and the result proves replicable, they need to formulate ideas that can account for it. So it was with dissonance theory. More than a few social psychologists took up the challenge to see if there were reasons other than the ones proposed by Festinger and his colleagues that could account for the data they produced. In the wake of an honest controversy, such as the one that swelled around dissonance theory, the ideas, findings, and results that come from attempts to disprove, reinvent and reestablish create a dialectic that culminates in a deeper understanding of the phenomenon. That is what happened in the case of cognitive dissonance.

I shall relate a story of what I believe to be the first major empirical challenge to dissonance theory and the way it was resolved. I should make clear that my perspective may not be completely dispassionate because this is where I entered the field. However, I think the research controversy I shall describe is a prototype of the early critical analyses of dissonance and the kinds of studies that eventually sharpened the dissonance perspective.

Several laboratories took up the challenge of finding an explanation for the results that was more in accord with the general principles of learning theory than Festinger's dissonance perspective. For example, Irving Janis (see Elms and Janis, 1965), who had been one of the co-investigators on the learning theory-based Yale Communication and Attitude Change program, criticized dissonance theory's conclusions by suggesting that a process known as 'biased scanning' was responsible for the data. Another co-author of the Yale attitude research, Milton Rosenberg (1965), suggested a different approach. Rosenberg suggested that the interpersonal dynamic between the experimenter and the participant might have produced the effect, without any need to invoke the theory of dissonance. Summarizing a plethora of alternative explanations for the dissonance findings I presented in Chapter 1, Alfonse and Natalie Chapanis pronounced with great enthusiasm (and in capital letters) that, five years after the publication of Festinger and Carlsmith's research, the verdict on dissonance theory was 'NOT YET PROVEN!' (Chapanis and Chapanis, 1964).

There is more than a little irony to the reaction of the learning theoretical approach to dissonance theory. Neither Festinger's original writing nor any of the early research reported in Chapter 1 ever mentioned learning theory, still less argued against it. Yet many psychologists believed that it contradicted this basic tenet of human psychology and, therefore, concluded that the results must be due to something else. That belief was the catalyst to many of the research articles that took issue with dissonance theory. And those articles led to further research that helped support, refine, and strengthen the theory. Through the five decades of research in dissonance, there have been and continue to be many controversies about the way in which the process unfolds, and about its antecedents and consequences. But with well over a thousand research articles now in the journals, cognitive dissonance is well established as a reliable phenomenon. The irony is that without the attention paid to it by its critics, the long tradition of dissonance research might never have occurred.

A productive criticism: evaluation apprehension

The first wave of critical reaction to dissonance theory was that there must be some other explanation for the data – some artifact that explained why, when rewards and incentives for a behavior are high, attitudes change less to support that behavior. Rosenberg's was perhaps the most intriguing explanation and he supported it with data. He took as his major theoretical premise that rewards affect behavior in the way one would expect from what we know about learning theory. If people are asked to give a speech about an object, an issue, or an idea, they will come to like it better – i.e., have more positive attitudes about it – the more they are rewarded for it. In Rosenberg's view, it does not matter if the behavior is an essay or speech, whether it is pro-attitudinal or counterattitudinal: the more the inducement or reward, the more one should like and approve the topic of the speech. In Festinger and Carlsmith's (1959) experiment, there should have been a direct relationship between reward and attitude change.

This left Rosenberg to explain why participants in Festinger and Carlsmith's study did not show more attitude change in the $20 condition than in the $1 condition. Here is where *evaluation apprehension* enters the picture. Rosenberg cautioned us to take a long look at the interpersonal dynamic that was occurring in the study. A student enters a laboratory in a psychology department. This is already a social situation imbued with meaning. What do psychologists do? One possibility that may be at the back (or perhaps front) of students' minds is that psychologists always try to evaluate people's personalities.

As the procedure of Festinger and Carlsmith's or Cohen's study unfolded, a psychologist was asking people to perform a fairly simple behavior: for Festinger and Carlsmith, it was to say to a student already in the next room that the peg task was fun; for Cohen, it was to write an essay about the New Haven police. A small incentive may have seemed reasonable and that small incentive, through learning theory principles, might have resulted in positive attitudes toward the peg task or the police issue at Yale. In principle, a large incentive normally would have produced more positive attitudes, but the magnitude of the incentive was overshadowed by the interpersonal meaning of the inducement.

Simply put, $20 (whose value in today's dollars would be greater than $200) was out of line with the task. So, too, was $10 to write a one-page essay. What were the participants thinking about this financial offer? Rosenberg's answer was that the large amount of money must have been seen as a *bribe*. And the bribe clicked with students' notion that they were being evaluated by the psychologist. 'Oh, I get it,' they may have reasoned, 'This psychologist wants to see how I react to a bribe.' Soon, the psychologist asked for the participants' attitude toward the task or issue. This confirms the students' concern that they are being evaluated. 'I'll show that I cannot be bought; I'm not that kind of person.' Concerned with not wanting to appear to be bought, the participants intentionally and purposefully kept their attitudes at the pre-essay or pre-task level.

Rosenberg needed to show that if evaluation apprehension were eliminated as a concern, then participants would have been free to change their opinions, and they would have done so as a direct function of incentive magnitude: i.e., the more the inducement to say something contrary to their attitudes, the more their attitudes would change in the direction of their essay. Rosenberg eliminated evaluation apprehension by running an induced compliance study that was essentially similar to Cohen's study of attitudes about the New Haven police. He had students write an essay that they did not believe for a small or large inducement. However, he had the attitudes collected by a completely different experimenter who was in a different room doing a different study. In this way, subjects would not feel that they were having their honesty and integrity assessed by the experimenter and would not hold back their true opinion. Rosenberg predicted they would show more favorable attitudes with higher rather than smaller incentives.

In order to test this notion, Rosenberg created a clever procedure at Ohio State University in which he convinced students that there were two separate experiments being run. When students arrived for the study they had volunteered for (an attitude assessment study), they found that the experimenter was 'running late.' He apologized to the student and then said that

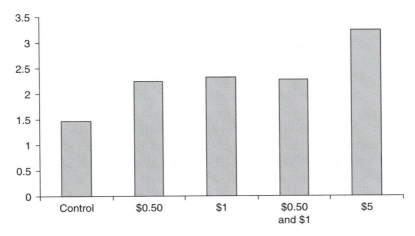

Figure 2.1   Degree of agreement after writing essay
Source: Adapted from Rosenberg (1965)

since they had signed up for an hour's experiment and the assessment really would not take that long, they were to go to another experiment that was being run by another investigator in order to fill the time. Then they could return to the attitude assessment study.

The second study that the student was sent to was research on students' opinions about a controversial issue that had affected the Ohio State campus. There had been a proposal to ban the OSU football team from competing in the Rose Bowl that year. Students were very much against the proposal, so Rosenberg seized the opportunity to run an experiment very much like the basic procedure of Cohen's (1962) study. He asked students to write strong and forceful essays favoring the ban against the football team. They were offered either a small or a large incentive for writing the essay. When they were finished, they returned to the office of the first experimenter who was now ready to receive them.

The first experimenter had a questionnaire that he wanted the students to fill out for his study of campus issues. There were numerous items on the questionnaire, covering a broad range of topics. One of the topics was the students' opinion about the ban on Rose Bowl participation. Rosenberg predicted that, without evaluation apprehension raising its specter as the students were filling out the questionnaire, they would show that their attitudes were more in favor of the Rose Bowl ban as a direct function of incentive magnitude: the higher the reward, the more favorable the attitude.

This is what Rosenberg found. In the absence of concerns about integrity and honesty, without worrying about whether they were being bribed and evaluated, the participants showed the direct effect that Rosenberg had predicted.

A demise or an invitation?

Rosenberg (1965) was not the only scholar to pick up on the interpersonal dilemma that participants were facing when given a reward that seemed too large. Tedeschi, Schlenker and Bonoma (1971) made a compelling case for what they called *impression management* and Schlenker (1980) coined the term *identity negotiation* to describe the way in which the interpersonal dynamics of the experimental situation may have led directly to the result that Festinger and Carlsmith had obtained. But Rosenberg's study was the first and it was instantly influential. Not only did it suggest that the induced compliance results were an artifact of participants' concern with evaluation, but it also produced results that warmed the hearts of the learning theorists. In a counterattitudinal essay-writing paradigm, dissonance seemed to fail where reinforcement theory succeeded.

However, good controversy also leads to further analysis that can offer ideas of why the critics were mistaken. In the best of all worlds, the criticisms of the criticisms are not just endless arguments whose winner is the side that persists the longest. In the best of all worlds, the analysis of the criticisms leads not only to understanding where the critics may have inadvertently created an artifact, but also helps to clarify and extend the original theory. This was the happy outcome of the evaluation apprehension story.

Three of us at Duke University were drawn into the controversy. Darwin E. Linder was an assistant professor who had been a student of the dissonance pioneer, Elliot Aronson; Edward E. Jones was a senior professor who had made enormous contributions to the study of interpersonal perception; and I was a wet-behind-the ears graduate student. We thought that, as good as Rosenberg's work was, it would have been more compelling if he had done a *balanced replication* of previous dissonance work. That is, if Rosenberg were correct about evaluation apprehension being responsible for the results of induced compliance experiments, then it would have been most convincing if he had been able to produce reinforcement results in the absence of evaluation apprehension and, using the very same issue and subject population, produce results that looked like dissonance theory data with evaluation apprehension left in. Because he hadn't done that, we were not sure it was time to give up on cognitive dissonance.

It's all about freedom

We had a different idea about why Rosenberg had produced different data from Festinger and Carlsmith, Cohen, and several others who had used the induced compliance paradigm. We suggested that there was an important difference between the induced compliance procedure as used by Festinger and Carlsmith (1959) and the one used by Rosenberg (1965). When Festinger and

Carlsmith asked the participant if he or she was willing to serve as a confederate and say the task was interesting, the choice to say yes or no was completely open. The participant could have walked away, said he was too busy, or indicated that she could not tell a lie, even for science. Indeed, some participants did refuse, but most accepted. The choice was theirs.

In the evaluation apprehension study, Rosenberg's procedure required that the participant leave the first experimenter, proceed to the office of the second experimenter, and do whatever it was that the second experimenter had in store for the participant. The second experimenter provided no additional choice about writing the essay favoring the Rose Bowl ban. We thought that choice might be an important variable.

Let's consider why. From the perspective of the participant, the cognition that I oppose the ban on going to the Rose Bowl is discrepant from the behavior that I wrote an essay supporting the ban. However, there is also a cognition about my freedom to decline and this cognition must be put into the dissonance formula. It is a large, important cognition in the context of the interpersonal situation of the participant. If I were *required* to write the essay, then that requirement serves as an important cognition consonant with my behavior. Why did I write the essay? Because the experimenter required me to. That cognition might have been powerful enough to eliminate all dissonance.

We designed a balanced replication to assess this possibility (Linder, Cooper, and Jones, 1967). Although the political issue was different, students participated in a study that was very much like Rosenberg's. Like that earlier study, our procedure used the ruse of having two experimenters, the first of whom was running late. Half of the subjects were told that they were to go to the office of the second experiment and participate in whatever research the other experimenter had for them. The other half were also told to go to the second experimenter but were further advised, 'I don't know exactly what that researcher is doing. It will be completely up to you if you want to participate.' Thus, half of the students went to the second experiment feeling committed to whatever the experimenter wanted them to do (low-choice condition) and half knew that the choice to participate was completely their own (high-choice condition).

The second experimenter explained that he was conducting research on a controversial issue affecting the Duke University campus that year. We told the students that the administration was considering banning certain political figures from speaking on campus, a proposal that had been in the newspaper and to which students were strongly opposed. We offered participants either a very small (50 cents) or larger ($2.50) incentive for writing the essay. Most agreed to do so, and then returned to the office of the first experimenter, where they filled out their attitudes on a variety of local and national issues, including the ban on political speakers.

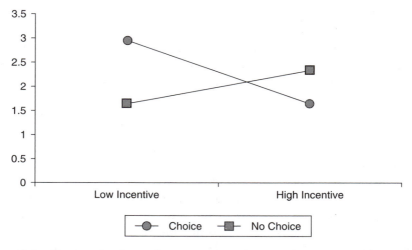

Figure 2.2   Changes of attitudes toward speaker ban as a function of choice and incentive
Source: Adapted from Linder, Cooper, and Jones (1967)

We predicted that dissonance would occur only when the participants believed they had freely chosen to write the counterattitudinal essay. Only then would they experience the arousal of cognitive dissonance and only then would the incentive magnitude play a determining role in the reduction of dissonance. In the low-choice conditions, we expected the lack of decision freedom to extinguish dissonance before it began. Knowing they had no choice but to behave as they did perfectly explained why they wrote an essay contrary to their attitudes. Dissonance would not be aroused and would not need to be reduced.

The results of our study are shown in Figure 2.2. As we predicted, only the students who were in the high-choice condition showed the familiar signature of induced compliance (i.e., the inverse relationship between incentive magnitude and attitude change). The higher the incentive for writing the essay, the smaller was the attitude change. In the no-choice condition, something very different happened. In the absence of choice, with no dissonance to cope with, incentive magnitude played a role, as learning theorists would predict: higher incentives led to more attitude change.

The Linder et al. (1967) study was but a piece of a puzzle in which a landmark study such as Festinger and Carlsmith's was criticized ingeniously by another social psychologist (Rosenberg, 1965). His work, when analyzed through a slightly different lens, showed that the evidence he had obtained for a direct (reinforcement theory) relationship between incentive magnitude and attitude change occurred only because his inadvertent use of coercion eliminated cognitive dissonance. By not allowing participants to exercise a free decision about whether to write or decline to write the attitude-discrepant essay, he had inadvertently eliminated dissonance. The balanced replication of Linder et al. (1967) showed that both direct (reinforcement) and indirect (dissonance) relationships between incentive magnitude and attitudes are possible. Dissonance, however, is the trump card. When dissonance is present because the cognition about decision freedom exists in the minds of the actors, then incentives serve to reduce the dissonance. The higher the incentive, the lower the dissonance.

The beginning of the search for modifiers

The evaluation apprehension studies, far from being a debilitating blow to dissonance theory, began an entirely new phase in its history. Cognitive dissonance had survived its encounter with evaluation apprehension. However, it also began a search for moderators. Under some conditions, dissonance is aroused through behavior that is discrepant from attitudes. But what are the conditions? The Linder et al. (1967) work showed one of those modifiers. Behavior that is at variance with attitudes causes dissonance, but only under conditions of high-decision freedom. In the absence of freedom, there is no dissonance.

The second wave: the data are right but the theory is wrong

The theory of self-perception

A second wave of criticisms took a different tack. Rather than arguing that there was something wrong with the procedure in dissonance experiments, the next round of criticism focused on the theory itself. In a brilliant theoretical analysis, Daryl Bem (1967, 1972) took issue with the entire foundation of dissonance theory. He argued that the very same data predicted by dissonance theory could be predicted more parsimoniously by what he first called 'radical behaviorism' (Bem, 1965) and later referred to as *self-perception theory* (Bem, 1972). Bem had no quarrel with the data from any of the induced compliance, free-choice, or effort justification studies that had focused attention on dissonance theory. He merely asked whether a simpler explanation wasn't readily available that did not involve the drive state of dissonance.

Bem based his theory on the work of Fritz Heider, Edward E. Jones, and Harold Kelley, each of whom had worked out the principles of attribution in interpersonal perception. The key tenet of attribution theory is that people need to decipher the meaning of other people's behavior. We have no immediate insight into what others feel or think. We have no immediate insight into their personalities. All we can observe is other people's verbal or physical behavior. Although the various attribution theories differ in the way they believe people process information about others' behavior, there are two elements they all have in common. In order to know what people are really like, we look at their behavior and the stimulus conditions that provoked that behavior.

Imagine that we want to know how someone feels about immigration policy. We cannot have immediate access to her thoughts, but we can hear what she says. If she says she is for a more liberal immigration policy that legitimizes guest workers, we have good reason to believe that the behavior represents her true feelings. Her behavior is the most critical determinant in our knowing what she believes. The second important factor is our analysis of the environmental conditions that may have led her to say she is for a liberal immigration policy. If she is a lobbyist in Washington DC, employed by the United Farm Workers (UFW) and paid to take her position, we may discount what she said and not assume that her statement reflects her true, personal attitudes. After all, her lobbyist salary may perfectly well have produced the statement. We typically consider people's behaviors to be descriptive of the way they see the world (i.e., accurate reflections of their internal state) unless we deduce that the behavior was under the control of some stimulus in the environment. At that point, we may not know what to believe about the speaker's true attitude. The professional lobbyist who is paid by the UFW may or may not really, truly support immigration rights. If we had to guess her true opinion, we probably would not know what to say. We might choose the normative opinion on the issue (i.e., what most people think) but hold it with little confidence.

Self-perception theory then took an unusual twist. Bem argued that, despite how comforting it may seem to think we have direct knowledge of our own attitudes and beliefs, it is not always true. We do not always have insights into our own attitudes and beliefs, especially when they are not very strong or salient. Bem provided an example. Consider someone who is asked at dinner whether he likes brown bread. He thinks, 'I must like brown bread because I ordered some with dinner the other night.' He infers what his attitudes are by examining his behavior. If he ate brown bread, he must like brown bread. And that would allow him to answer the inquiry into his attitude about brown bread. This inference process works, provided we have no reason to doubt it. We doubt it when we suspect that the behavior was under the control of an environmental stimulus. Thinking back to my eating brown bread, I may not only recall that I ate the bread but I now also recall that I was hungry and the brown bread was the only bread available. That I ate it tells me very little about my attitude toward the bread. Now that I am asked what my attitude is, the best I can do is infer a prototypical attitude toward the bread. Most people think it's pretty good and that will have to describe my attitude as well.

Bem was aware that all of us have some attitudes about which we are very clear and certain. We do not need to use our behavior to infer our attitudes. Ask me if I love my wife, and I do not need to use an inference process. I know I do; I do not have to scan my behavior to make my best guess about my feelings. However, Bem suggested that most of our attitudes are not of that type. When asked about our opinion toward most political issues or attitude objects, we engage the very same process to infer our attitudes as we use to infer the attitudes of others. We look at our behavior, analyze the environmental stimuli, and make a logical inference about our attitudes. If asked whether I like a particular acquaintance that I don't see very often, I might scan my past behaviors and recall that I did not attend a party he threw, have never gone to lunch with him, and have rarely agreed with his position at meetings. I conclude that I'm not that fond of him. Asked if I agree that global warming is an issue that we must be concerned about right now, I scan my behavior, recalling that I signed a petition to my local Congressman to that effect, responded to surveys by taking that position, and even donated money to a candidate for my local city council whose platform contained a strong commitment to lower greenhouse gases. I conclude that, yes, global warming is an issue I'm concerned about. Note that in both cases, I did not have immediate access to my attitudes. I quickly scanned past behavior and made the best answer I could. The answers were the result of inference processes.

Self-perception meets induced compliance

The next step in Bem's approach follows directly from his theory of self-perception. In the induced compliance experiments I have already described, subjects were asked about their reactions to issues that, while moderately important, did not rise to the status of whether the students loved their mothers. That is, they were not asked about issues or people about which they felt very strongly and had 'direct access' to their attitudes. Instead – and as is typically the case with most attitudes – they were asked about attitudes that required an inference process; the very same inference process we have discussed. At Stanford, students were asked if they liked to turn pegs; at Yale, they were asked how much they liked the New Haven police; at Ohio State, they were asked how much they wanted to go to the Rose Bowl; and, at Duke, they were asked how much they agreed with a ban on controversial speakers. How were they to answer these questions?

The Stanford students who answered Festinger and Carlsmith's (1959) questions about their attitude toward spool turning could look at an action that was relevant to their liking of the spool-turning task: i.e., they could remember that they had just told another student that it was fun and interesting. That information contained in their behavior should go a long way toward answering what their attitude was. They could recall going on at some length about how much fun it was. On the other hand, the significance of the behavior for the inference process is mitigated to the extent that it might have been emitted under the control of an environmental stimulus. The experimenter requested the behavior, but he did not demand it. That is, as a participant, I could have said 'No,' but I didn't. 'OK,' the student can reason, 'the behavior is still potentially descriptive of my attitude.' He continues, 'But how about the money?' The experimenter paid me to say that the task was interesting.' As in Festinger and Carlsmith's reasoning about dissonance theory, the difference between the high incentive and the low incentive is important. Behaving positively toward the task (i.e., saying it was interesting) is highly under the control of the environmental stimulus as you now think about it. The inference process continues by the student's thinking, 'I said it was interesting but the $20 payment fully explains why I did it. My behavior is not relevant to my attitude.' The inference process ends with the student having no basis for assessing his attitude. He ultimately reverts to an assessment of how he thinks most people would have felt about a task in which you endlessly turn pegs and sort spools.

A different inference awaits the student who said the task was interesting for only a minimal incentive. For this student, the behavior seems less under the control of the environmental stimulus – i.e., the money – and therefore the conclusion of the inference process is that I must have liked exercising my fingers and turning those spools and pegs. This student infers he had a positive attitude toward the task.

The ingenuity of Bem's explanation is its parsimony. It accepts the predictions and the results of the dissonance theory research. It concurs with the notion that people will come to like what they espoused as an inverse function of the magnitude of incentive. It also concurs with Linder et al.'s (1967) notion that feeling choice is critical for the effect to occur. After all, how much more clearly can we see a behavior as being under the control of an environmental stimulus than if it is demanded by a person with high power, such as the experimenter in a research study? The self-perception explanation accepted all of the findings from induced compliance without searching for artifacts or mistakes in the procedures. It also accommodated the results of other research approaches that we have talked about. If I picked a blender over a toaster in Jack Brehm's study, I must infer I liked it. If I chose to undergo an embarrassing screening test as a student in Aronson and Mills's (1959) experiment, it must be that I really liked discussing the secondary sexual characteristic of lower animals.

Why was it parsimonious? Self-perception did not require that internal states be involved in the process. It did not involve raising and lowering people's level of arousal nor did it need to postulate the drive to reduce that arousal. It simply needed to invoke an inference process – the very same inference process that people use to infer the attitudes and characteristics of others. Its list of advantages included:

1 no need to invoke internal arousal
2 no need to worry about what factors raise and lower the levels of arousal
3 no need to invoke the drive-like quality that leads to dissonance reduction
4 it claimed to accommodate all dissonance findings, including research based on the expenditure of effort and making choices
5 inconsistent behavior was no different from consistent behavior; both were useful pieces of information in the inference process
6 it relied on the same process of attribution that had been studied in person perception since the work of Heider in the 1940s.

These were important considerations, but was self-perception theory correct?

Research support: the interpersonal simulation

The problem with a theory that agrees with all of the research findings of a competing theory is that it is hard to discriminate between the two. Bem had an interesting addendum to his argument that, while not a definitive test of the two theories, was consistent with self-perception theory. Since Bem was arguing that people make inferences about themselves in much the same way that they would make those inferences if they were making judgments of other people, he reasoned that if he told a new group of participants precisely what Yale students were asked to do in Cohen's experiment, or Duke students were asked to do in the Linder et al. (1967) study, they should infer those students' final attitudes and reach the same conclusion that the Yale and Duke students actually reached for themselves. In short, the involved participation of the real subjects, he argued, was unnecessary. Just describe the procedure to people, tell them what behaviors the target people performed and the stimulus conditions that provoked it, and observers will attribute the very same differences in attitudes that dissonance researchers found in their actual experiments.

Bem reported the results of several studies in which he showed this to be true. A research participant in one of Bem's studies was shown a written description of what Cohen's subjects had been asked to do through a verbatim account of that procedure. They were told that the Yale student agreed to write the essay and had been promised $1 for writing it. Other participants were given the same instructions but were told about the original participant having been promised 50 cents. Bem's results so faithfully replicated the original results that Cohen had obtained that the graphs of the data of the two studies could be overlaid on each other with no apparent differences whatsoever. In Figure 2.3, the results of Cohen's study can be seen in the top half of the graph and Bem's results are shown at the bottom.

CRITICISM PROPELS THE THEORY FORWARD

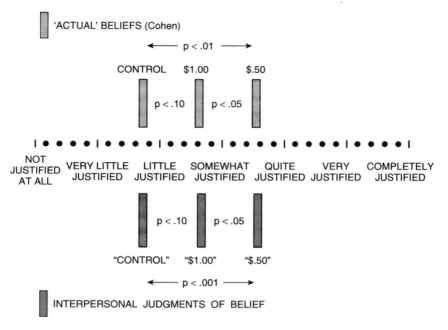

Figure 2.3   A comparision of 'actual' beliefs and interpersonal judgements of beliefs
Source: Bem (1965)

Not everyone accepted the meaningfulness of Bem's interpersonal simulation. Two groups of investigators believed that the meaning of Bem's results rested in part on the assumptions he had made when setting up the interpersonal simulation. A group at Duke University and a group at Yale University independently realized that Bem had based his work on the assumption that students who participate as involved participants do not have a cognition about their initial attitudes. Combining their efforts, Jones, Linder, Keisler, Zanna and Brehm(1968) pointed out that to accept the validity of the interpersonal simulation in the way that Bem reported it was also to accept the premise that the subjects had no insight into their own attitudes. In the interpersonal replication, Bem (1965) had said nothing about initial attitudes, so the only information the interpersonal replicators had to rely on was the essay-writing behavior and the amount of inducement the writers were offered to write the essay. To the contrary, argued Jones et al., the real participants knew what their attitudes toward the New Haven police were. They could use them or ignore them, but they surely had a cognition about their own attitudes. When Jones et al. repeated Bem's experiment and provided the new subjects with the pre-experimental attitudes of the Yale students toward the New Haven police, the results did not replicate those of the original experiment.

Even if the interpersonal simulation is problematic as a research tool, Bem's self-perception theory still posed an immense challenge for dissonance theory. How can the theoretical debate be disentangled? At the very least, the supposition that people sometimes make inferences about themselves is appealing. If that is what participants were doing in the studies whose data had been seen as supporting cognitive dissonance theory, then the theoretical underpinnings of the phenomenon were anyone's guess.

The debate about theoretical mechanisms could not be solved by posing different predictions about changes in attitudes. In almost all cases, both theories made the same predictions. Instead, the debate had to turn on finding a way to collect data on the *process* that occurs following counterattitudinal behavior. Do people change their attitudes to reduce unpleasant tension or are they simply making inferences from their behavior? The search for the internal process and the general resolution to the debate will be the topics of the next chapter.

3

THE MOTIVATIONAL
PROPERTY OF DISSONANCE

Cognitive dissonance was based on an idea of what occurs inside people's heads. Inconsistent cognitions caused tension, the tension is arousing and experienced as an unpleasant state, and people are driven to reduce it. The predictions became particularly interesting when the magnitude of the tension was considered, allowing for the fascinating and non-obvious predictions that we discussed in previous chapters. However, all of this was based on a notion of processes unfolding where we could not observe them. We could estimate how much dissonance we thought would be aroused by particular events in particular social situations and, given what we thought we knew about the arousal and reduction processes, we could predict when there would be more or less change of particular cognitions (usually, attitudes).

Self-perception theory (and, to some extent, the attribution theory of Harold Kelley, 1972), challenged all of that. Did we need the concepts of arousal, tension, unpleasantness, and drive reduction? Did we need to think about inconsistency at all? What is the status of the motivational mechanism that Festinger thought lay behind the dissonance process?

Dissonance: reality or metaphor?

Festinger wrote during a time in which speculation about internal processes was common (although controversial) in all of psychology. In the field of animal learning, for example, Clark Hull (1952) had pioneered a view of learning that was based on internal drive states. Drive states, he argued, provided the motivation to learn; the successful reduction of those drives determined what was learned. But drives were not measured, they were inferred. The length of time the animal went without food, for example, was an indicant of the strength of the animal's drive state. This is not to imply that the research wasn't rigorous and scientific. The dependent variables were carefully measured, as were the antecedent conditions for learning.

On the clinical side of the psychological spectrum, the major prevailing theory was that of Sigmund Freud (1933). Freud's psychoanalytic theory was similarly built on the concept of drive states. Freudian psychology was based on the build-up and reduction of the sexual drive state. In Freud's view, all of human behavior could be understood with reference to a broadly construed view of the human drive for sex. With some assumptions about the need to repress various sexually cathartic experiences, Freud could speculate about the build-up of sexual tension which, in turn, predicted patterns of counterproductive behaviour patterns like phobias, obsessions, and hysteria. Psychologists could measure and assess the neurotic behavior patterns, but not the internal drive state that propelled them.

Did Freud mean his set of internal processes to be a metaphor or did he believe the super ego and id fought battles that resulted in neuroses? Did Hull believe that the arousal of a drive state was real or was it a hidden process whose reality was less important than its ability to predict learning patterns? The unobserved nature of these internal processes prompted critics and alternative views. The famous behaviorist psychologist B.F. Skinner (1953) objected to classical learning theory fundamentally because it relied upon unmeasurable internal states. Although, like Hull, Skinner promoted the importance of reinforcement in learning, he did it in a way that did not rely on any hidden, unmeasurable internal states like drives. In clinical psychology, Joseph Wolpe (1958) and his colleagues brought behavioral therapy to bear on clinical problems whose major idea was to avoid any assumptions about unseen internal processes that had characterized Freudian and neo-Freudian theory.

Leon Festinger had entered this conceptual dialogue on the side of those who found it useful to talk about potentially unseen and perhaps unmeasurable internal states. However, new criticisms arose and his critics, such as Daryl Bem, objected to the use of the internal states in much the same way that Skinner's psychology criticized Hullian learning and Wolpe's behaviorism criticized Freud's psychoanalytic assumptions. For the first decade of research in the theory of cognitive dissonance, there was not much need to worry about whether the proposed state of internal tension was real, or whether it was just a concept whose identifiable tenets created the non-obvious interesting predictions that data ultimately confirmed. With the advent of self-perception theory, it suddenly mattered.

Dissonance as drive: early evidence

Even prior to the challenge by Bem and his colleagues, a few investigators had looked for ways to find evidence that cognitive dissonance functioned as a drive. Without technological tools for measuring a drive, Waterman and

Katkin (1967) devised a clever, indirect method to find evidence for a dissonance drive. They reasoned that one robust finding from the literature on drive states, for humans and non-human animals, is that high states of drive have an effect on how learning takes place. Highly arousing drives facilitate simple learning but interfere with complex learning. Anyone who has ever been anxious before an exam understands this. If you are highly aroused by some form of tension state, it is very difficult to concentrate on new and complex material. The tension and arousal seem to get in the way. On the other hand, if you are asked to answer questions on material that is well learned and easily at your command, then you can quickly and accurately recall the answers.

Waterman and Katkin argued that if cognitive dissonance causes tension and arousal, it should have a similar impact on learning. People who are in the throes of cognitive dissonance should do very well on simple learning tasks but have difficulty on complex tasks. In their experiment, Waterman and Katkin had participants engage in an induced compliance task. The students were asked to write counterattitudinal essays on a topic of interest. Before they could reduce their dissonance through changes of attitudes, Waterman and Katkin presented them with some complex or simple material to learn. The results of the study were supportive but not completely clear. Facilitation of simple learning did occur for participants who were in a high-dissonance condition, but interference with complex learning did not occur. The contribution that this study made to the literature was that it showed a way of studying the question of whether dissonance had arousing properties. The basic tack was an indirect one: if dissonance is arousing, it should work like other arousing drive states. The idea was a good one, but proving it was another matter.

Pallack and Pittman (1972) were the next to take up the question. They also conducted an experiment in which they created high and low dissonance by having participants write counterattitudinal essays under high- and low-choice conditions. In a carefully constructed experiment, they presented simple and complex learning tasks to their participants and found that high dissonance interfered with complex learning but failed to support the prediction that dissonance facilitated simple learning. Again, it was 'half a loaf.' That is, the experiment showed that dissonance does have an effect on learning. However, in principle, it should have two effects. The idea seemed to have truth to it, but confirming it was elusive.

The misattribution studies

The next set of studies in the literature helped to solidify the idea that, just as Festinger had guessed, dissonance is *experienced*, not inferred. Moreover, the research strongly suggests that the experience is an unpleasant state of arousal and *it is to reduce this arousal that people are motivated to restore consistency.*

In order to set the stage for these studies, we should revisit a classic study conducted by Schachter and Singer (1962), as they sought evidence for their two-factor theory of emotion. Schachter and Singer had suggested that the experience of an emotion is based on two factors: one is arousal and the other is the attaching of a cognitive label onto that arousal. Then, and only then, do we experience an emotion. Imagine that you are in a deserted section of your local park and a large dog comes running your way. Your autonomic nervous system automatically is set in motion by the surprise appearance of the dog, its big teeth, and its loud barking. Although it happens quickly, Schachter and Singer argued that people first experience the autonomic arousal and then attach a cognitive label – i.e., an informational explanation for what is happening. So, confronted with the animal in the park, you feel the arousal and then may decide that large + barking + big teeth = fear. This is a dog to be afraid of. When you put the label and the arousal together, you actually experience the emotion known as fear.

The experiment that Schachter and Singer devised provided a methodology which will help solve the question of whether dissonance has arousing properties and is experienced as an emotion. Schachter and Singer knew that the only way they could find convincing evidence for their two-factor model was to be able to separate the stimulus that caused the arousal from the stimulus that provided the cognitive label. If they could activate arousal and then show that the emotion people experience is determined by the cognitive label that is provided for them, that would be convincing. Similarly, if they could show that the label, in the absence of the arousal, did not produce an experienced emotion, then they would have support for their theory.

All of the participants in Schachter and Singer's experiment came to the laboratory as recruits in a study on the effect of a vitamin supplement, known as Suproxin, on people's vision. They were asked to take an injection of Suproxin. In reality, there is no vitamin supplement called Suproxin. What Schachter and Singer administered to most participants was an injection of norepinepherine, a synthetic adrenalin. It produces a general state of arousal in which one's palms may sweat, heart may beat a bit faster, and breathing rate may increase. Schachter and Singer predicted that participants whose autonomic nervous system was aroused would experience an emotion – and the emotion would depend on what cognitive label is provided.

The label was provided in a social context by the behavior of an experimental confederate hired by the experimenters to play a particular role. The confederate was always introduced as another participant waiting for the same experiment. For some of the participants, the confederate acted in a goofy, happy manner, making paper airplanes in the lab room, playing basketball with scrap paper, and generally having a good time. Schachter and Singer expected that the combination of arousal due to the norepinepherine combined with the happy antics of the confederate would make the subject believe that he was happy. On the other hand, the same antics by the confederate were not expected to produce the feeling of happiness in the participant if the participant had not been aroused with the norepinepherine. The results supported the hypotheses: subjects reported that they felt happy, but only when there was a joint occurrence of arousal and a label.

Would any label do? Schachter and Singer thought so and they ran another set of conditions in which participants who were injected with norepinepherine waited with an angry confederate. He regaled against the experiment, expressed his annoyance at the questionnaires and procedures, and made abundantly clear his overall anger at being in the research. Again, subjects who were aroused with norepinepherine reported that they experienced the emotion of anger; they felt angry.

There was an important proviso in Schachter and Singer's theory and results. The coalescing of arousal and a label to form an emotion only occurs when participants have no easily available explanation for their arousal. If participants realized that their arousal was due to the drug they had taken, then they did not seek a label and did not feel an emotion. If they were told that it was the so-called Suproxin that caused the rapid heart beat and breathing, they did not need to use the antics of the confederate to tell them what their emotion was. Indeed, the results showed that participants who were told about the effects of the drug did not experience anger or happiness. They merely understood the reason for their arousal. The happy or angry behavior of the confederate did not affect the participants' emotional experience.

The lesson from Schachter and Singer's study is that the experience of an emotion can be labile. It depends on the presence of arousal, but how it is experienced is deeply affected by the label that is provided for the arousal.

Suppose that cognitive dissonance is experienced as an emotion. It is put in motion by the perception of inconsistency among cognitions. This perception sets in motion a general, amorphous feeling of arousal. Searching for a cognitive label to explain the arousal, people notice that they behaved inconsistently and are thus prepared to come to the conclusion that they are experiencing cognitive dissonance. They know how to reduce dissonance: change a cognition, restore consistency, and feel better.

Now, let's take one more interesting step in the scenario. Suppose that a person who has engaged in an attitude-inconsistent act believes that he or she has a good, adequate explanation for the arousal. Let us say the person ingests a drug prior to engaging in the inconsistent act. The drug actually does nothing. It is purely a placebo with no arousing properties whatsoever. But the person believes that the drug is arousing. He believes that the drug produces agitation and tension. The person's attitude-inconsistent behavior causes arousal but the immediate label is that, 'I'm aroused because of the drug.' With this cognitive label, the arousal that would have been interpreted as part of the feeling state of cognitive dissonance is attributed to the drug instead.

This is a significant attribution. Deciding that the arousal is due to the effects of a drug makes it unnecessary to do the work required to change a cognition and reduce inconsistency. If the unpleasant feeling the participant is experiencing is thought to be a simple side-effect of a drug, then no cognitive changes should ensue.

From two-factor theory to dissonance

Mark Zanna and I decided to use Schachter and Singer's (1962) two-factor theory to test the dissonance theory prediction (Zanna and Cooper, 1974). Our goal was to establish conditions in which the tension state of dissonance – aroused by attitude-inconsistent behavior – was either correctly attributed to the inconsistent behavior or incorrectly misattributed to an external stimulus such as a pill. Consistent with the ideas we had borrowed from Schachter and Singer, we expected to find that the availability of an external attribution for the state of arousal actually caused by inconsistent behavior would eliminate people's need to restore consistency.

Our participants were Princeton University students who had volunteered for a study on the effects of particular drugs on memory. After assuring them that the drug we were about to give them was safe, we told participants that we were examining the impact of drug MC5771 on people's memory. Because it would take a few minutes for the drug, once ingested, to be effective, we had another task for them to do while they were waiting. Some of the students were told that there were side-effects to the drug: they might feel aroused, tense, or excited. These were the subjects who we thought would use that explanation for any arousal they were about to experience from performing an attitude-discrepant act. These were the subjects who we expected would not need to reduce dissonance following the counterattitudinal behavior.

Other subjects were told that MC5771 had no side-effects. It would take a few minutes for it to be effective, but they would not notice any consequences from taking the drug. We expected these students to try to reduce their dissonance following a counterattitudinal act.

The next step in the study was to offer an induced compliance procedure to our subjects. While they were allegedly waiting for the memory drug to be effective, we told them that we had another experiment that we would like them to participate in. The subjects' task was to write an essay favoring a position with which we knew they disagreed – raising tuition fees for Princeton students. Some of the participants were asked if they would be willing to write the essay advocating higher fees. This was a condition of maximal dissonance because the participants received no additional payment or reward and were given the option to decline to participate. Other participants were in a low-dissonance condition as they were told that they were required to write the essay in favor of higher tuition. After writing their essays, participants were given a questionnaire to fill out that included an item that assessed their attitude toward higher tuition rates.

To be clear about our reasoning, we predicted that *if dissonance is an unpleasant state of arousal*, as Festinger had guessed it is, then people would act to reduce their arousal as they normally do when they had no external stimulus to which to attribute it, but they would not act to reduce their dissonance if they thought their arousal was due to the side effects of the pill. It is as though people who wrote an attitude-discrepant essay under high-choice conditions reasoned as follows: 'I feel an unpleasant state of tension. What is it due to?' In misattribution condition, they reasoned, 'Oh, yes, I remember. I took the pill that is supposed to make me feel this way.' For these subjects, that was the end of the story. There would be no need to change their attitude toward tuition increase. For people who did not have a misattribution opportunity, they answered the question of why they felt an unpleasant tension by surmising (with awareness or outside of awareness) that it must have been because of the discrepancy between their essay and their attitude. To reduce their dissonance, these participants would change their opinions.

The results supported this prediction. Figure 3.1 shows the results. As expected, there was no attitude change for anyone in the no-choice conditions. The lack of choice prevented any significant dissonance arousal and the attitude-discrepant essay led to no attitude change. In the high-choice conditions, however, there is attitude change, but only in the condition in which there was no opportunity to misattribute the arousal. When participants could answer the question of why they were aroused by remembering the side effects of MC5771, there was no need for attitude change – and none was found.

Another condition of the Zanna and Cooper (1974) study is worth noting. I did not mention it before, but let's add it now. One third of the participants were given a different explanation of the side effects of the memory drug. They were told that the side effect of the pill would make them feel calm or sedated. They should expect to feel relaxed. Zanna and I thought it would be interesting to see how these participants would deal with the information that they were supposed to feel relaxed but, in the

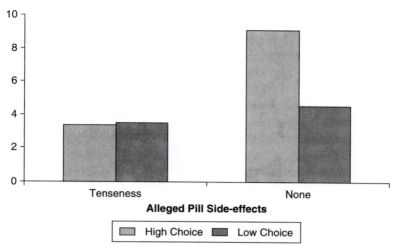

Figure 3.1   Attitude change toward position advocated (1)
Source: Adapted from Zanna and Cooper (1974)

high-choice condition of the essay-writing task, they felt aroused. The pill, we recall, was really a placebo so any arousal they felt from writing a counterattitudinal essay would remain intact. It's an attributional dilemma for people given the information about relaxation. We predicted that subjects in the high-choice Relax condition would reason, 'I feel aroused and tense, despite having a pill that should have relaxed me. That's a lot of arousal. What is it due to? The essay. I must really, really be upset by having written about raising tuition rates.' And the consequence of attributing that high degree of arousal was even greater attitude change.

The full design of the study is shown in Figure 3.2. The left-hand column shows the results of the Relax conditions. You can see that when dissonance is high, the presence of an augmenting inference – i.e., I must really, really, have a lot of dissonance – led to even greater attitude change than normal, no-misattribution condition.

The misattribution paradigm that we invented in Zanna and Cooper (1974) is a robust way of showing that the arousal of unpleasant tension motivates the reduction of cognitive dissonance. In several studies we showed that if people have reason to believe that their arousal is due to virtually any stimulus other than their inconsistent cognitions, the need to reduce dissonance disappears. The lights in the room (Gonzales and Cooper, 1975), the heat and ventilation (Fazio, Zanna, and Cooper, 1977), as well as myriad pill opportunities, have all had the same effect on dissonance reduction: providing an opportunity to misattribute the arousal eliminates the need to reduce dissonance.

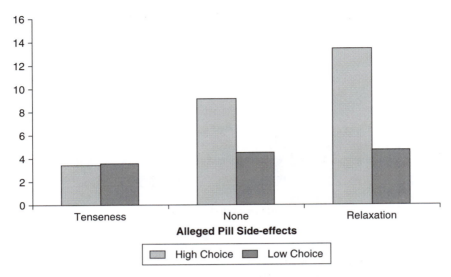

Figure 3.2   Attitude change toward position advocated (2)
Source: Adapted from Zanna and Cooper (1974)

Measuring dissonance arousal: is it really there?

The logical conclusion from the misattribution studies is that dissonance reduction must be driven by the need to reduce the unpleasant tension state. The results of the misattribution studies only make sense if people are motivated to reduce their discomfort – but of course it is futile to change cognitions in an attempt to reduce discomfort if that discomfort came from pills, bright lights, or stuffy experimental rooms. Nonetheless, if we want to be certain that dissonant cognitions cause tension and arousal, it would be best if we could measure it directly.

Robert Croyle was the first to measure physiological markers of cognitive dissonance (Croyle and Cooper, 1983). He reasoned that if dissonance were tension-arousing, as Festinger had speculated, then it should have a marker in physiological arousal. When a person's autonomic arousal is activated, there are several physiological markers. One that is ubiquitous and difficult to control consciously is increased perspiration, especially in the palms of the hands. The non-specific skin conductance response (SCR) is a measure of the body's increased production of skin moisture. Very small amounts of electrical current can be measured as they move between electrodes placed on the skin. The more perspiration there is, the quicker the electrical current flows. The fact that it is difficult to control the moisture on the skin makes skin conductance the primary measure of lying in the lie detector test. Lying causes stress and the stress is measured by the current passing through the electrodes.

Croyle and I wired university students to the polygraph. One of the lessons we learned was that worry about the machine causes increases in the skin's level of conductance. So, too, does any loud noise or the onset of a verbal command. Saying 'Hello!' to the students causes their SCR responses to spike. But by giving them ample opportunity to become accustomed to the machine, much of the startle response can be dampened.

While connected to the machine through their non-preferred hand, we asked some of the students if they would write a counterattitudinal essay taking a position in support of an alleged university proposal to ban alcoholic beverages (high dissonance). Other students were not given a choice and were instructed to write the attitude-discrepant essay (low dissonance). A third group was asked if they would be willing to write a pro-attitudinal speech opposed to such a ban (no dissonance).

In order to be sure that this procedure produced attitude change results that would be expected by dissonance theory, we had run a prior experiment only weeks before the current session. In that experiment, the same three conditions were run but no one was connected to a polygraph. After writing their pro-attitudinal or counterattitudinal statements, attitudes were measured. The results were as predicted: participants in the high-dissonance condition changed their attitude toward the allegedly proposed alcohol ban policy whereas participants in the other two groups did not.

Returning to the participants who were connected to the polygraph, we expected to find that the students in the high-dissonance condition would show more physiological stress as measured by the conductance in the skin than the students in either of the other two groups. Indeed, the groups differed in their physiological responding. At first, all groups of subjects showed spikes in their SCR scores, whether they were asked or told to write the counterattitudinal arguments or wrote pro-attitudinal statements. For low-choice participants whose magnitude of dissonance was low and pro-attitudinal subjects who experienced no dissonance, their SCR scores went back to baseline very quickly. Not so for high-dissonance participants. When they wrote their attitude-discrepant arguments, their non-specific skin conductance remained high. Dissonance, it appears, leads to heightened physiological arousal, just as dissonance theory had speculated.

Physiological arousal vs. psychological discomfort: bearing down more closely on the meaning of dissonance

We are not the only researchers to find evidence for physiological arousal consistent with the principles of dissonance theory (Elkin and Leippe, 1986; Losch and Cacioppo, 1990). Losch and Cacioppo's extension of our finding is particularly interesting because it raises another fundamental question based on Festinger's original formulation. As we know, Festinger wrote about the unpleasantness of the tension state of dissonance. This leaves open the question whether the active ingredient that prompts dissonance reduction is its arousal (tension) property or its negativity, or both. Croyle and Cooper (1983) had confirmed that arousal exists, but had not shown that attitudes change in order to reduce that arousal. The original misattribution studies (Zanna and Cooper, 1974) showed that people who attribute their arousal to an external source do not have a need to alter their attitudes in order to reduce dissonance.

The open question is whether it is the arousal that people are reducing when they reduce dissonance or the unpleasantness. Higgins, Rhodewalt, and Zanna (1979) had already pointed out that arousal can be independent of valence. Remember the pill, MC5771. It was described as causing unpleasant tension or agitation. Although those words were chosen to map most closely on Festinger's description, they interwove arousal with its negativity. It is possible for a pill to be arousing in a positive way. Similarly, a calming stimulus can have either positive (e.g., pleasant relaxation) or negative (e.g., unpleasant sedation) hedonic consequences.

Following the suggestion from Higgins et al. (1979), Losch and Cacioppo (1990) set out to replicate the finding that counterattitudinal behavior causes measurable physiological activity and also to determine if dissonance reduction is at the service of reducing that arousal, or whether it is the specifically negative aspect of the arousal that motivates attitude change. They combined the procedures of the misattribution studies (e.g., Zanna and Cooper 1974) with careful assessment of physiological arousal.

In their study, students were first asked to wear a pair of fascinating eye glasses in which the glass was actually a prism. The prism distorts light, turns objects upside down and inside out. The wearing of the prisms was soon to turn into a misattribution stimulus when the experimenter told the subjects that she would be returning in a few minutes to take the eye glasses off. In one condition, she told the subjects that when the glasses were removed, people often reported a sensation of 'pleasant excitement.' In a second condition, she substituted 'unpleasant tension' for 'pleasant excitement.' When the experimenter returned to remove the prism glasses for the next part of the experiment, she told the participants that the research team was studying reactions to the use of electric shock in experiments. Although most people are against the use of electric shock in research, the team was looking for strong and forceful arguments in favor of increasing the amount of shock that should be permitted in experiments in the psychology department. Participants in the high-dissonance condition were given freedom to decline to write. Participants in the low-dissonance condition were informed that it was a requirement of the experiment that they write arguments in favour of the proposal.

During the procedure, participants' electrodermal responses were monitored in a manner similar to that used by Croyle and Cooper (1983). They were connected to electrodes on their non-preferred hand that assessed their non-specific skin conductance (NSC). When the participants had finished writing arguments in favour of the electric shock proposal, they answered questions about their attitudes toward the use of electric shock.

This study had two major predictions. First, there would be measurable physiological arousal that followed from people performing an attitude-discrepant act, but only in high-choice conditions. That is, Losch and Cacioppo expected to replicate Croyle and Cooper's finding with a differ-ent population and a different issue (and much more updated equipment!). They were successful. They assessed NSC for three minutes following the dissonance procedure and found elevated arousal across the three-minute time span for participants in the high-choice condition compared to partic-ipants in the low-choice condition.

Their second prediction was based on the description of the prism glasses. Recall that some participants had been led to believe that removing the glasses would be pleasantly exciting; others had been told that it would be annoyingly irritating. Losch and Cacioppo predicted that the motivation to reduce dissonance specifically required the feeling of a negative state. If people only wanted to reduce arousal, then either pair of glasses provided an explanation for their arousal and they would not have to do the work of changing their attitude. However, if they want to relieve a negative state, then only the prism glasses that were alleged to produce a negative feeling should eliminate the need to reduce dissonance. The results of the attitude measure supported their prediction. As can be seen in Figure 3.3, partici-pants changed their attitudes most in the positive cue condition. There was a significant interaction between cue and choice such that participants in the high-choice condition who had the positive cue attached to the removal of the prism glasses changed their attitudes most. The negative cue, on the other hand, virtually wiped out the need for attitude change.

The singular conclusion from the Losch and Cacioppo study, as we com-bine it with the research that preceded it, is that people reduce dissonance in an attempt to reduce negative arousal. It is not just any arousal that people seek to reduce. From Zanna and Cooper's (1974) research, we learned that having a stimulus available to which to attribute arousal elim-inates dissonance. But it must be a stimulus that people realize is capable of having produced arousal. In the presence of a potentially relaxing stimulus, dissonance was exacerbated, not reduced. From Losch and Cacioppo (1990) we learned that the arousing stimulus must be specifically negative. In the presence of a stimulus that should have caused people to feel positively, dis-sonance was increased rather than decreased. The evidence clearly supports

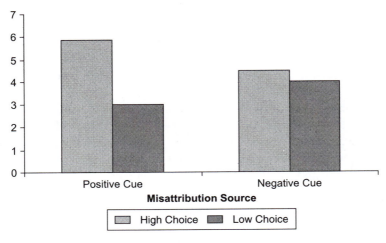

Figure 3.3   Attitude toward shock in psychological research
Source: Adapted from Losch and Cacioppo (1990)

this proposition: people change their attitudes to reduce dissonance because they need to resolve a state that is both arousing and aversive.

Why not just ask? The dissonance thermometer and the motivation to reduce dissonance

The process of dissonance arousal is difficult to see directly. As we noted, the first attempts to gain a glimpse of what was actually going on inside the mind and body of a person experiencing dissonance were indirect. Clever, but indirect. The reasoning was always in the form, 'If dissonance is really arousing, then the following should happen.' And that led to the research by Waterman and Katkin (1967), Pallak and Pittman (1972), and others. Only when measurement techniques finally became available were we able to gain more direct bodily indicants of the arousal that accompanies dissonance.

It is interesting that there were no reported studies in which asking participants how they felt was the major dependent measure. Identifying negative arousal via indirect means is certainly one approach, but asking people how they feel seems like a more direct means. There was no reported study using this method until Andy Elliot and Trish Devine (1994) conducted a study that provided additional evidence about the motivational basis of dissonance.

In addition to seeking a self-report measure of dissonance arousal, Elliot and Devine sought a descriptive account of what dissonance felt like. Dissonance has an arousal component, but it is also experienced as an identifiable affect. What does it feel like? How might people describe the affect? Much as Zanna and Cooper (1974) had done, Elliot and Devine combed Festinger's original description of dissonance. They decided that people's affective responses when they were experiencing dissonance would be some form of discomfort. They decided that the words *uneasy, uncomfortable*, and *bothered* would fit the description.

Here is the experiment Elliot and Devine conducted. They asked students at the University of Wisconsin to write essays on the issue of a possible large increase in the tuition rate the following year. All subjects were provided a high degree of choice to write their essay, but some were asked to write essays in favor of a tuition increase (high dissonance) while others were asked to write against it (no dissonance). Participants were then given a questionnaire in which they were asked about their attitudes and their affective experience.

The innovation in this experiment was the substance and timing of the affect questionnaire. The three items described above were included as part of the measure along with twenty-one other items that assessed a variety of positive and negative affective states (e.g., happy, sad, guilty). Half of the subjects in the high-dissonance condition received the affect scale before they filled out their attitude measure while the other half had their attitude toward tuition measured before receiving the affect scale.

The timing is important. If participants engage in a counterattitudinal act, they should experience dissonance. Their arousal should be high and so, too, should their experience of discomfort. After they reduce dissonance by changing their attitude toward tuition, their discomfort should be reduced. To assess this, Elliot and Devine compared the discomfort ratings of the subjects who were asked about their discomfort after they had the chance to reduce dissonance on the attitude scale with those subjects who filled out the affect scale before they changed their attitudes. Presumably, for the attitude-first/affect-second group, changing their attitude would lower their discomfort and return them to a more tranquil, comfortable state.

Let's look at the data by focusing on the measure that subjects answered first. If they responded first to the attitude questionnaire, as is typical of most of the experiments we have discussed so far, then we can see strong evidence for the classic dissonance prediction. Participants who wrote a counterattitudinal essay had a more favourable attitude toward tuition increase than participants who wrote a pro-attitudinal essay (or a baseline control group). For participants who had their affect assessed first, the prediction that the high-dissonance group would be able to identify themselves as uncomfortable, uneasy, and bothered was borne out (see Figure 3.4). They were significantly more uncomfortable than the pro-attitudinal group. The particular measures that Elliot and Devine guessed would map onto the experience of dissonance held up very well. The three measures correlated

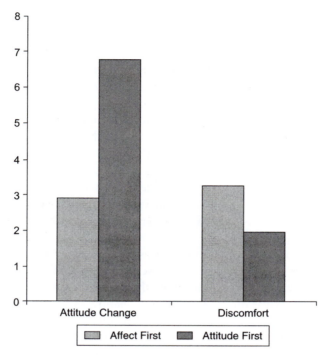

Figure 3.4   Ratings of attitude change and discomfort
Source: Adapted from Elliot and Devine (1994)

with each other but not with the other eighteen questions about affect.
Moreover, none of the other measures showed reliable differences as a function of condition. Participants in the high-dissonance group were not more
guilty, sad, or unhappy. They were not more angry or dissatisfied. They were
just more uncomfortable than the participants in the pro-attitudinal and
baseline control groups.

A most important finding is also displayed in Figure 3.4. The order of measurement made the difference that was predicted. If attitudes were assessed
first, then not only did attitude change occur, but psychological discomfort
did not. There was a statistically significant difference between the amount of
discomfort when it followed the writing of the counterattitudinal essay
(Affect First condition) than when it followed the attitude measurement
(Attitude First condition). Consistent with these results, there was a negative
correlation between discomfort and attitude change. The more attitude
change a participant expressed, the lower was his or her discomfort.

A second experiment, with many more participants, replicated the basic
effect. What was not replicated, however, was an intriguing and non
predicted finding in the original experiment concerning participants'

attitudes in the Affect First condition. When affect was measured first, participants' attitudes were lower than when attitudes were measured second. That is, giving participants the chance to express their discomfort reduced the need for attitude change. This finding was not statistically significant and was not replicated in their second experiment, so it should be taken cautiously. This unexpected result was found again in a study by Galinsky, Stone, and Cooper (2000) and raises the intriguing possibility that admitting to feeling uncomfortable from your actions lowers the need to do anything further.

The important lesson from the study by Elliot and Devine is that people can identify their affective reaction to dissonance and, consistent with Festinger's distinction, *discomfort* seems to be the best description. And their two studies also show that dissonance reduction is, at least in part, at the service of reducing the feeling of discomfort. Their study does not address whether attitude change also reduces arousal, although studies like Losch and Cacioppo's imply that it does.

A recipe for greater dissonance: add amphetamine and mix well

Suppose you could add or subtract physiological arousal to a person who has just committed a dissonance-producing, attitude-discrepant act. In a study aimed at the basic tenet of self-perception theory – that people are merely inferring their attitude without involving any internal states of affect and drive – Cooper, Zanna, and Taves (1978b) looked for a way to vary people's physiological arousal. We argued that if people behave in an attitude-discrepant manner, and if their ensuing attitude change is at the service of reducing arousal, then the more arousal they experience, the greater the change. Take away arousal, and the attitude-discrepant act should not produce attitude change. The absence of any experience of tension should eliminate the need for attitude change. Conversely, if the amount of tension is abnormally high, then there should be a great amount of change. Adding arousal should signal a very large need to reduce a very large amount of tension.

Mark Zanna, Peter Taves, and I decided to go after the question of arousal directly by giving people a substance that was known to increase autonomic system functioning, namely amphetamine (Cooper et al., 1978b). With a doctor's prescription and careful check of student health, some participants in our study were given amphetamine prior to writing a counterattitudinal essay. Other subjects were given a sedative, phenobarbital. Relative to a group of subjects who were not given any drug to raise or lower their arousal, we expected to see heaps of dissonance in the amphetamine group and very little in the group that took phenobarbital.

We asked students to volunteer for a study on the effects of three different drugs on people's short-term memory. We assured participants that we had pre-screened all of the health records to make sure that the drugs were safe for them to take. It was important for the participants to consent to taking the amphetamine or the sedative, but it was also important for them not to know which drug they had taken. In order to accomplish this, we told students that we would be randomly assigning them to one of the three drugs. One was an amphetamine, one was phenobarbital, and the third was a placebo. We asked for their agreement to take any of the three drugs that random assignment would assign them to. Following their agreement, the experimenter told participants, 'I am now going to give you a capsule that contains your drug. In order to keep the study controlled appropriately, even I do not know which of the three drugs you will be getting. You will know, because the paper in which your capsule is wrapped describes the drug to you.'

All of the participants received a capsule with a paper that told them that their drug was a placebo. For two-thirds of the participants, this was not true. One-third of the participants' capsules contained 5 mg of dextroamphetamine; one-third contained 30 mg of phenobarbital and one-third, true to our cover story, received a placebo. With this procedure, we were certain that all of the participants had voluntarily agreed to take the arousing or sedating drugs, but they all thought they were receiving only a placebo.

The dissonance-arousing procedure is, by now, familiar to the reader. While waiting for the alleged memory drug to take effect, the participants were asked to write a strong and forceful essay on a hot political issue of the day. President Gerald Ford had just issued a blanket pardon for all crimes that may have been committed by former president, Richard Nixon. Most students were upset by the pardon and disagreed with it. Nonetheless, they were either asked (high dissonance) or told (low dissonance) to write an essay favoring the pardon. Allegedly, prior to starting the memory experiment, the participants were asked to fill out a number of scales, one of which asked about their attitudes toward the pardoning of Richard Nixon.

The results are shown in Figure 3.5. The attitudes of the participants in the placebo condition are shown in the center column. They received neither an arousing nor a sedating drug, and they replicated the effect typically seen in induced compliance studies: high-choice participants were more in favour of the counterattitudinal position they had just advocated than were low-choice participants.

Participants who had taken phenobarbital had their arousal reduced by the drug. Even though they wrote counterattitudinal essays that should have caused dissonance, their level of arousal was low and they did not need to act on their cognitions in order to reduce that arousal. As can be seen in the left-hand column of the figure, participants in the sedative condition did not change their attitude after freely writing a counterattitudinal message.

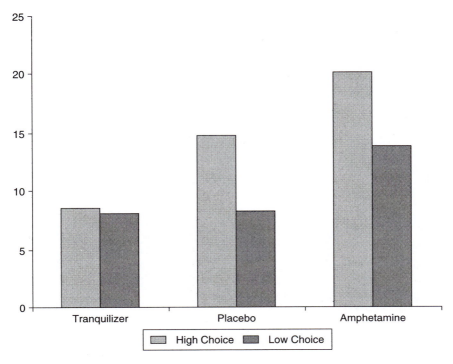

Figure 3.5 Attitude change as a function of pill condition
Source: Adapted from Cooper, Zanna, and Taves (1978)

The results of people in the amphetamine condition are interesting. We have two effects in this condition – one predicted and one not. With amphetamine, high-choice subjects changed their attitudes more than any other group in the experiment. When we added the arousal due to dissonance to the arousal due to the amphetamine, people flipped their attitude to the other side of the opinion scale (mid-point = 16). Confronted with the experience of that much arousal, they were motivated to make a major shift in their opinion to make it consistent with their behavior.

An intriguing and unpredicted phenomenon occurred in the low-choice amphetamine condition. These participants also showed attitude change, although not as much as the high-choice condition. The data reveal their predicament. They had behaved in a manner discrepant with their attitude about the pardon of Richard Nixon. They also had a cognition that they were told to do it by the experimenter. That cognition is usually important enough to eliminate the experience of cognitive dissonance. This time, it was not; they still experienced arousal. Probably based on their past experience with inconsistency, they used their level of arousal to decide how much change they needed to make in their cognition about their attitude. They

59

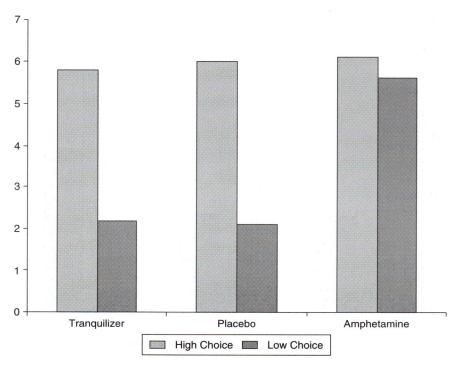

Figure 3.6   Perceived choice as a function of pill condition
Source: Adapted from Cooper, Zanna, and Taves (1978)

also used their level of arousal to decide, in retrospect, how much choice they must have been given. When asked about how free they had been to decline to write the essay, participants in the low-choice amphetamine condition rated themselves as having been free, even though they were not. Figure 3.6 shows the pattern. Despite the fact that the instructions to subjects in all three low-choice conditions were precisely the same, those who had taken amphetamine assumed that they had been given the freedom to decline. They must have reasoned, 'Why else would I feel tense and aroused unless I was responsible for writing this essay?' They attributed the choice to themselves and acted to reduce their tension.

Arousal, discomfort, and dissonance: a conclusion

In 1983, I had a chance to ask Leon Festinger what he thought about the motivational properties of dissonance when he was writing the theory. Did he believe that there was actually a drive and that people would feel discomfort, or was it a metaphor for how the system would work? He explained that that was not a question that would have arisen in the 1950s. Scientists built 'black box' models – models of how a system should work if it were to account for the data. A good 'black box' made interesting and novel predictions that could be confirmed by the data. As long as it accounted for the data, a scientist could continue to be proud of what he had put in the 'black box.' If data disconfirmed subsequent predictions made by the model in the 'black box,' then it needed to be changed or discarded. Because there was no real opportunity to view the contents of the box directly, there was little use in speculating about its existence.

The data that have accumulated over the decades using the induced compliance and similar procedures have given a lot of credence to what was in Festinger's black box. He observed the relationship between inconsistency and change. He inferred that there existed a state of cognitive dissonance and he put into the 'black box' the motivational concepts of arousal, tension, discomfort, and drive that could account for his observations of the dissonance state.

We now know that dissonance is uncomfortable. We know it because people will misattribute their reactions to counterattitudinal behaviour only to an uncomfortable, negative stimulus and not to a positive one. We know it because if we ask people, they will tell us. We know it because if we take away the discomfort, there is no dissonance.

We also know that dissonance is arousing. We know it because we can measure it physiologically. We know it because if we take away the arousal using a sedating chemical, the need to reduce dissonance disappears; if we add arousal with an agitating chemical, the need to reduce dissonance is enhanced.

Perhaps the expansion of technology that scans the body and brain will make us privy to other insights into how dissonance works on us humans. For now, however, the evidence is compelling that Festinger was correct in the motivational system he proposed. We change our attitudes and cognitions at the service of relieving the aversive, uncomfortable arousal state of cognitive dissonance.

Our analysis of dissonance will now take a U-turn and go back to the antecedent conditions that lead to the arousal state. Now that we can be confident about what the state of dissonance is, how sure are we that it is a function of inconsistency at all?

4

DISSONANCE IS NOT
WHAT IT USED TO BE

The New Look Model of Dissonance

During the infancy of research in dissonance, we've seen that interesting, novel and controversial predictions were made based on a simple principle of the need for consistency. Much of the work in the first decade was designed to shore up those findings to be certain that they were not due to artifacts of procedure or design and, in so doing, to extend the work into new areas. The primary advance in the second decade of research may well have been to identify the mechanism responsible for motivating change. Could dissonance reduction be shown to be based on the need to reduce aversive, unpleasant arousal? The work that began with Waterman and Katkin's (1967) study became a major focus of dissonance research in the 1970s and 1980s. As we concluded in the last chapter, the most likely resolution is that Leon Festinger had guessed correctly when he identified an unpleasant state of arousal as the consequence of dissonant cognitions and the desire to reduce that tension state as the basis for attitude change.

While accumulating data to accomplish these two major goals, a few problems emerged. The main thrust of the research was supportive of dissonance theory predictions, but a number of caveats began to develop. In my opinion, these were first viewed as small holes in the proverbial dyke; holes that needed to be filled but required no theoretical overhaul. After a while, however, it caused Russell Fazio and me to rethink what dissonance was all about (Cooper and Fazio, 1984). Even though dissonance produces negative arousal and even though the motivation is to reduce that arousal, perhaps we did not yet know precisely what provoked the dissonance. Perhaps it was not about inconsistency at all.

The 'but-onlys': the search for modifiers
raises theoretical questions

As researchers tussled with some of the early questions involving the arousal of dissonance, several limiting conditions were uncovered. Recall in

Chapter 1 that one of the first questions that received attention was whether Festinger and Carlsmith's (1959) original and provocative induced compliance study was replicable. Critics had worried about a number of artifacts that could have produced the inverse relationship between incentive magnitude and attitude change. Recall that Linder, Cooper and Jones (1967) identified decision freedom as a cognition that is necessary in order for dissonance to be aroused. It was a modifying condition. The inconsistency caused by advocating a position contrary to your attitude produces attitude change, *but only* when decision freedom is high.

The notion that freedom is important in dissonance fits nicely with dissonance theory, even though it had not been part of the original formulation. As I suggested in the first chapter, being coerced to engage in counterattitudinal behavior is a powerful cognition consonant with the behavior and brings the level of dissonance implied by the dissonance formula (see p. 9) to very low levels. Brehm's (1956) study using the free-choice paradigm is also consistent with this caveat. Choosing one consumer item over another causes increased attractiveness of the chosen item and decreased attractiveness of the rejected alternative. Giving an item as a gift without the choice being exercised by the research participants does not cause any change in the evaluation of the items. Choice matters; and it meshes with the general theoretical thrust of dissonance being a function of inconsistent cognitions.

The degree of *commitment* is another issue that appears to limit the ubiquity of dissonance. Several investigators argued that dissonance only occurs when a person feels committed to his or her attitude-inconsistent statements, such as when one is publicly identified with the statements (Carlsmith, Collins, and Helmreich, 1966) or when one cannot retract them at a later date (Davis and Jones, 1960). In the study conducted by Davis and Jones (1960), research participants were asked to evaluate another student (actually a confederate of the experimenter). As a way of inducing inconsistent cognitions, Davis and Jones had the participant rate the other student in a way that they did not truly believe. A perfectly nice and pleasant student was to be rated in a harsh and degrading manner. In some cases, the students were expecting to meet the confederate after the evaluation and thus could 'take back' what they said; in other cases, they could not. They were publicly committed to that evaluation and would not have an opportunity to withdraw it. Davis and Jones predicted that the attitude-inconsistent evaluation would cause changes in the participants' feelings toward the other student. As a way of reducing dissonance, they would come to believe what they had just said, *but only* when they were committed to their position. And that is what Davis and Jones found.

How can the importance of commitment be accommodated in a dissonance theory based on inconsistent cognitions? The task seems theoretically challenging and might have been construed as a reason to question the

63

assumption that inconsistency was the underlying event leading to dissonance arousal. That is, whether or not participants would see the confederate again does not bear directly on the inconsistency among their cognitions; the potential to retract the statement does not seem to have a clear role in the dissonance formula. Nonetheless, researchers seemed comfortable with the idea that behavior inconsistent with attitudes requires a commitment to that behavior. And the wagons moved on.

The role of the aversive consequence

The search for modifiers took a more far-reaching turn with the identification of the aversive consequence as an element necessary for the arousal of dissonance. Nel, Helmreich, and Aronson (1969) were the first to identify the importance of the unwanted consequence. They reported a study in which participants made counterattitudinal speeches favoring the use of marijuana for young people and made the speech to one of three audiences. One audience was alleged to believe firmly that marijuana was acceptable as a drug for young people; one was completely committed to the opposite position; and the third was an audience of young people who had not yet made up their minds. Participants' personal attitudes were against the use of marijuana for young people. The results showed that participants' attitudes toward marijuana changed in the direction of the counterattitudinal speech, *but only* for the audience that had the possibility of being convinced. The other two audiences were said to be firmly committed to their positions so the speech was not likely to have any effect.

Steve Worchel and I wanted to examine the consequence of counterattitudinal behavior more explicitly (Cooper and Worchel, 1970). We fashioned a pegboard and a spool board just like the boards used in the Festinger and Carlsmith (1959) experiment. We painted them gray and did all that we could do to make the experience of our subjects just as tedious and dull as the task had been in the original experiment and we repeated their experiment. What we wanted to see is whether there needed to be some adverse consequence to the participant's statement that the task was interesting and exciting.

What would constitute an unwanted or aversive consequence? As a participant in Festinger and Carlsmith's (1959) study, your statement that the task was interesting was made to a fellow undergraduate – someone just like you who might be convinced, just for one fleeting moment, to feel excited and enthusiastic about what was to happen during the next several minutes. You know you are not telling the truth; you know the fellow undergraduate is being duped; you know that his or her experience during the experimental task will be painfully dull and tedious. Creating such false momentary excitement in a fellow student is an unwanted consequence.

Reexamining Festinger and Carlsmith's procedure carefully, it seemed that the investigators had included such a consequence in their procedure. The confederate had been instructed to nod his head and agree with what the participant was telling him. Although it was only mentioned in passing and not manipulated as a variable in the original experiment, Worchel and I believed that this was an essential aspect of the dissonance process.

In our study, we decided to vary systematically how the confederate reacted. All of the subjects participated in the dull task and then, just as in Festinger and Carlsmith's experiment, they were offered a large or a very small incentive for agreeing to serve as the confederate who would tell the waiting subject that the task was fun. In the *convinced* condition, the confederate listened politely to the subject and then remarked, 'Thanks for telling me. All of the other psychology experiments I've ever been in have been dull and a waste of time. Now I'm really looking forward to this one. Thanks.' In the *unconvinced* condition, she also thanked the subject for her opinion, mentioned how dull she had found the other experiments she had participated in, but then continued, 'You're entitled to your opinion, but I don't expect that I will like this experiment any better than the others I've been in.' As a subject in the unconvinced condition, you did not dupe this fellow undergraduate. We predicted that we would replicate the induced compliance result for participants in the convinced condition, but there would be no attitude change for participants in the unconvinced condition.

There were two initial reasons for our prediction. The first was pure intuition. It just didn't feel right to think that we are in a state of dissonance when we just imagine saying something we do not believe. Have you ever taken a position on a topic, but strictly for your own benefit and strictly in your own head? For example, you might have considered arguments that you do not fully believe, or imagined what you would say to a potential romantic partner that exaggerates how much you like her or him. Have you ever imagined yourself taking one course of action over another, such as purchasing one attractive car rather than another? These imaginings could cause inconsistency, but it just does not seem convincing to think that they would cause actual changes of opinion and evaluation. Or, can you imagine a thought experiment in which you adopt a position you do not believe, make a speech on the topic, but say it only privately to yourself? It did not seem reasonable to us that these inconsistent cognitions would cause dissonance arousal and lead to attitude change. It is, of course, an empirical question, but that is how it seemed to us.

On a more theoretical note, we thought that if we were correct in our intuitions, then it would bear on the theoretical argument that was occurring at that time between Daryl Bem's (1967) self-perception theory and cognitive dissonance theory. If participants in our experiment made a

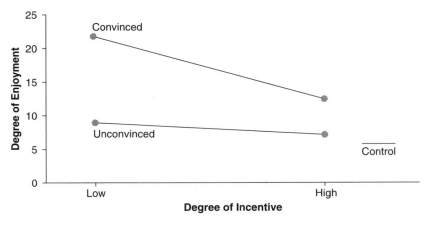

Figure 4.1 Evaluation of the boring task by participants who believed the confederate was convinced or not
Source: Cooper and Worchel (1970)

counterattitudinal speech for a small incentive but only changed their attitudes in a condition in which there was an aversive consequence, that would be a difficult finding for self-perception theory to explain. From the perspective of that theory, people observe their behavior (saying the task was interesting) and the stimulus conditions that provoked it (the experimenter's request and the magnitude of the incentive). In both the convinced and unconvinced conditions, participants could observe their behavior of agreeing to make the 'Wow, this was fun!' speech and notice that they had been offered only a very small incentive to comply. According to self-perception theory, they should both infer that their attitudes were quite favorable to the task. If our intuition was correct, however, subjects who made counterattitudinal statements without convincing the confederate would not manifest attitude change, regardless of the magnitude of the incentive.

When asked how much they enjoyed the task as the dependent measure of the study, the results supported our predictions. As can be seen in Figure 4.1, the inverse relationship between incentive magnitude and attitude change toward the task occurred only in the convinced condition. The interaction of incentive magnitude and whether the confederate was convinced was highly significant. There was no significant relationship between incentive magnitude and attitude change for participants who had not successfully duped the confederate. Moreover, a follow-up study showed that even successfully convincing a fellow student was not effective at producing dissonance if the participants disliked the fellow student. Only duping another person who was at least moderately liked created the aversive event necessary for dissonance (Cooper, Zanna, and Goethals, 1974).

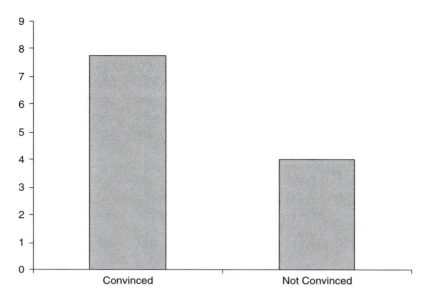

Figure 4.2   Attitudes as a function of whether the listener was convinced
Source: Adapted from Goethals and Cooper (1972)

Our conclusion from these data was that dissonance occurs following induced compliance, *but only* when an unwanted consequence ensues. Several follow-up studies showed how necessary it is to have some unwanted event occur following counterattitudinal behavior in order for dissonance to occur. For example, Goethals and Cooper (1972) used a counterattitudinal advocacy procedure much like that of Cohen (1962) and Linder et al. (1967). We argued that it is an unwanted consequence to convince someone to believe something you would rather not have that person believe. So, in our study, participants made a speech advocating that the voting age in the United States be raised to 21, a position with which the students were known to disagree. They were either given the freedom to decline the request (high dissonance) or not (low dissonance). Another student overheard the speech and announced that he was impressed by the speech and now agreed that the voting age should be raised to 21 (aversive consequence) or that he was impressed by the speech but still thought that the voting age should remain at 18 (no consequence).

Figure 4.2 shows the results. Attitude change occurred when people made their counterattitudinal speech under high-decision freedom conditions, *but only* when there was an unwanted consequence. We later discovered that the mere implication that an aversive consequence might occur also permits counterattitudinal behavior to lead to dissonance. In a study by Goethals and Cooper (1975), it was found that students changed their attitudes when counterattitudinal essays they had written were to be shown to a university committee that was in a position to make an unwanted change to a campus policy. However, no attitude change occurred when the speech was to be used for other purposes and would not be shown to the committee. Apparently, the *potential* for an aversive consequence is sufficient to allow dissonance to occur following counterattitudinal advocacy. Making it clear that the essay or speech will not be shown to anyone eliminates the dissonance. Showing it to a committee does not guarantee that anyone will be convinced by it, but the potential for the consequence to occur is sufficient for dissonance to be aroused.

You can't say you didn't know: the role of foreseeability

There is yet another contingency on the occurrence of dissonance following attitude-discrepant behavior. The points we have already developed tell us that dissonance will occur and will lead to attitude change if the attitude-discrepant behavior is freely chosen and if it has the potential to produce an unwanted event. We shall now add another.

Let's imagine that you are asked to assume the role of a debater and argue that spending money for the poor is ill-advised in modern society. You do not believe this position and hope that no one else does either. But this is solely for the purpose of debate and no one will hear it. Your debate coach asks if you will do it and you agree. After you make your stirring social Darwinism speech, you are told that the coach changed his mind and forgot to mention that he was sending all of the tapes to a high school class that was quite impressionable on this issue. You certainly can imagine the potential for an aversive consequence. The students might be convinced to believe in withholding support for the poor. All of the conditions we discussed so far seem to have been met. You developed arguments dissonant with your attitude, you freely chose to make your speech, and it had a potential aversive consequence. Nonetheless, we now know you will not experience dissonance in this circumstance.

Dissonance, it turns out, will occur *only* if the consequence of a freely chosen behavior was foreseeable when the person chose to commit the behavior. Surprise consequences that you could not have anticipated do not produce dissonance. I became particularly interested in this question for my PhD dissertation research at Duke University (Cooper, 1971). Let me describe the key elements.

The dissonance-producing procedure was a bit different from some of the more familiar paradigms of dissonance research. I aroused dissonance in participants by having them choose a partner for a game in which their goal was to make some money. Picking a good partner was consistent with that goal; picking a bad partner would be discrepant. Participants were paired with a partner and were told that the partner had a personality trait that could make him or her a bad partner for the game. Nonetheless, the experimenter requested (high dissonance) or required (low dissonance) that the participant remain with this partner. Indeed, as the game unfolded, the partner did exhibit the trait which the experimenter had hinted at, and it did cause the participant to lose the opportunity to win money.

I expected the participants to experience dissonance if they chose a partner whose trait made them lose money. The prediction was that if I asked participants after the game whether they liked their partner, they would use their liking as the way to reduce their dissonance. Similar to the subjects in Aronson and Mills's (1959) study who suffered embarrassment to participate in a boring group discussion, I expected my participants to justify their costly behavior by coming to like their partner. I also predicted that the worse the consequence, the more the liking. That is, the more money the partner caused the participant to lose, the more she would like her partner. And that is what I found. The arousal of dissonance was caused by freely choosing to work with a partner whose personality trait caused the subject to lose money.

There is one more caveat, however, and it is consistent with the point of this section. All of this happened if, and only if, the particular personality trait was foreseeable beforehand. Imagine that there were two traits, A and B, that would make partners less than ideal in this game. If I told you that your partner had trait A and you chose to work with her anyway, and then she cost you the opportunity to earn a prize, then the consequence of your choice was foreseeable at the time that you made it. But if she turned out to have trait B, despite my telling you that she had trait A, then the consequence of teaming with her would not have been foreseeable. You might reason, 'If I had only known she was a B, then I might not have chosen to work with her.'

The data showed that the dissonance effect was eliminated when the trait was unforeseeable. In the unforeseeable trait condition, the more the partner caused the subject to lose money, the less she was liked. Only in conditions in which the partner's trait was foreseeable and the participant freely chose to work with her, then the greater the aversive consequence, the greater the dissonance, and the more the participant came to like her partner. The conclusion we can draw from the study is that foreseeable aversive consequences lead to dissonance; unforeseeable consequences do not.

Status of the aversive consequence: a reprise

From the data presented in the prior sections, we now know that attitude-inconsistent behavior must lead to an unwanted consequence in order for

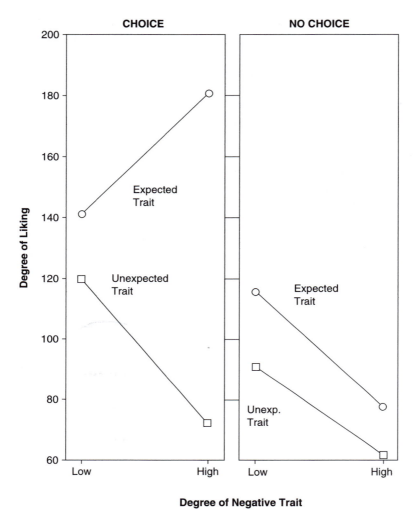

Figure 4.3   Mean liking as a function of expectancy and choice
Source: Adapted from Cooper (1971)

dissonance to be aroused and attitudes to change. We also know that the consequences need to be foreseeable when the decision to behave is made. It is worth pointing out that there is a difference between a consequence being foreseen and being foreseeable. Recall that in studies such as Goethals and Cooper (1975), Cohen (1962), and Linder et al. (1967), counterattitudinal essays were going to be shown to people who might or might not be convinced by the essays. The essay writers did not know, nor did they ever learn, whether the members of the various committees that were alleged to read the essays would ever be convinced. However, if they were to be convinced, that consequence would be foreseeable. An aversive consequence does not have to be explicitly foreseen in order to arouse dissonance; it just must be foreseeable that the consequence could occur as a result of the essay writer's counterattitudinal actions.

An explicit demonstration of the concept of foreseeability was provided by Goethals, Cooper, and Naficy (1979). We had participants write counterattitudinal essays about a potential change in a campus policy. Some participants believed that the essays were only for the eyes of the experimenter. A second group believed that the essays would be sent to a committee that could create the unwanted consequence. (This was typical of the conditions that aroused dissonance in the studies reviewed earlier.) And a third group was told that 'some other people' *might* be interested in reading it. In the end, everyone found out that the campus committee would read the essay. The first group had been explicitly instructed that only the experimenter would read the essay. For this group, the potential consequence of the committee reading the essay and implementing an unwanted policy was unforeseen and unforeseeable. For the second group, the consequence of sending the essay to the committee was explicit: it was both foreseen and foreseeable. The third group had not been told explicitly about the committee but, in retrospect, the committee was certainly a potential recipient for the essay. For this group, the consequence may have been unforeseen, but it was foreseeable. When attitudes were assessed, only the participants for whom the aversive event was unforeseeable at the time of the decision did not change their attitudes. The group that understood that the committee would see their essay (foreseen consequence) and the ones who should have been able to figure it out (foreseeable consequence) changed their attitude in the direction of the essay.

The good consequence

Let's turn now to the status of a good consequence in reducing cognitive dissonance and we will see that it works the other way too. An unforeseeable positive event does not reduce dissonance. Brehm and Jones (1970), for example, had participants rate a variety of music albums and then asked them to make a choice between two of them. Half of the participants were led to believe that if they chose the right album, they would receive two free movie tickets. The other half was not made aware of this extra gift. Brehm and Jones assumed that the bonus gift of the movie tickets would help the participants reduce any dissonance that was created by their choice. After all, the gift was described as an additional positive feature of their choice and should serve to reduce the need to spread the alternatives. When participants rerated the music albums, the results showed that the bonus gift did indeed reduce dissonance, but only if the gift was foreseeable.

When it was a complete surprise to participants and therefore unforeseeable, it did not alleviate the dissonance.

Cooper and Goethals (1974) conducted an experiment in which participants wrote counterattitudinal statements favoring an unwanted campus policy. Some participants were absolutely guaranteed that their statements would be sent to the committee. Other participants were told that *some* of the statements would be shown to the committee; a random draw after writing the essay would determine whether a particular essay was going to the committee or would just be discarded. After writing the essay, all of the subjects received the good news: their essay would not be sent to the committee after all. Those participants for whom such good news was foreseeable because they were advised of that possibility before deciding to write their essay did not change their attitudes toward the disliked campus policy. The good news had eliminated their dissonance. However, those subjects who chose to write their counterattitudinal essay thinking that it absolutely was going to be sent to the committee were not relieved of their dissonance following the good news. The unforeseeable nature of the good consequence did not allow these participants to be free of their dissonance and the need to change their attitudes.

Vietnam, the draft lottery, and foreseeable consequences: a field experiment

A study conducted outside of the laboratory contributes dramatically to the importance of the foreseeable consequence. In the late 1960s, the United States was enmeshed in the long and bloody war in Vietnam. Young men were drafted into the army by a lottery system. Birth dates were selected at random and assigned priority numbers. Men who had turned 18 and whose birthdays were selected in the first third of the lottery were virtually certain of being drafted into the military within the year; birthdays selected in the final third were almost certainly not going to be drafted; and birthdays in the middle third were uncertain.

The Army's Reserve Officers Training Corps (ROTC), which had been a bastion of training commissioned officers at colleges and universities since 1916, also became a program that people who wished to avoid being conscripted to Vietnam could use to delay their military service. Barry Staw surveyed ROTC cadets at four universities in Illinois (Staw, 1974). His focus was the impact of learning one's lottery number on satisfaction with the ROTC program. Consider the situation of people who had already signed contracts and were participating in ROTC primarily to avoid the draft. They knew, when they volunteered, that they were going to receive information that might create an aversive event. As soon as the draft lottery was held and birth dates were prioritized, some cadets would learn that their ROTC participation had been rewarded because their birth dates would otherwise have led to their being drafted within the year. However, other cadets learned that their ROTC participation was unnecessary. They were the ones who received high lottery numbers indicating that they would not be drafted.

The cadets were committed. They could not turn back and withdraw from ROTC. They volunteered for the corps knowing that they would later learn that their decision was worthwhile or that the effort was unnecessary. And perhaps more than just unnecessary, many of the cadets would not have joined the ROTC at all and would not have made any commitment to the armed forces if it were not for the possibility that it would protect them from the draft. These participants were in a high state of dissonance. A foreseeable consequence, a high degree of choice, and a commitment from which they could not withdraw caused the dissonance. Staw asked the cadets how satisfied they were with the ROTC. He found that the students who had the foreseeable consequence of discovering that their ROTC activities no longer served its original purpose were significantly *more satisfied* with ROTC than those cadets who received the information that they would have been drafted had it not been for their decision to join the ROTC.

One final note on Staw's study is that he also had a group of cadets who had not yet signed contracts committing them to remain in ROTC. When they received their randomly assigned lottery numbers, they withdrew from the corps as a linear function of their lottery number. Rather than increasing their satisfaction (like the committed members did), participants with birthdays that would have made it unlikely that they would be drafted were 82 per cent more likely to drop out of the ROTC than students with birthdays that made their being drafted virtually certain.

What causes cognitive dissonance?

Festinger's essentially uncomplicated version of dissonance theory took us a long way. It is, and always will be, convenient to think of dissonance in terms of what the words actually mean: a discrepancy among cognitions. Decades of research have supported Festinger's theory, generated and supported new hypotheses, and added many limiting conditions to the theory. I have referred to these as the *but only's*, and this would be a good time to summarize them.

Inconsistent behavior produces dissonance

- *but only* when decision freedom is high
- *but only* when people are committed to their behavior
- *but only* when the behavior leads to aversive consequences
- *but only* when those consequences were foreseeable.

Simply put, the research has shown a considerable number of modifiers for the basic proposition that inconsistent cognitions arouse the unpleasant feeling state of cognitive dissonance. Although some of the modifiers fit nicely within the cognitive dissonance formula, others do not. For example, it is difficult to see how to integrate the necessity for foreseeable aversive consequences into the dissonance formula without a great deal of theoretical shoving.

Dissonance begins with behavior

After reviewing approximately twenty-five years of dissonance literature from the late 1950s to the early 1980s, Russell Fazio and I concluded that the best straight line through the voluminous data was a new approach to what causes cognitive dissonance. In our New Look model of dissonance (Cooper and Fazio, 1984), we proposed a separation of the two aspects of dissonance theory: one that generates the dissonance arousal and the other that motivates people to change. The sequence of events that leads to dissonance arousal is shown in Figure 4.4. The elements of the model should cause no surprise because we have already seen the research that supports it. These, we proposed, are the events that lead to the state of dissonance.

The dissonance process begins with a behavior. People act. And as a result of those actions, consequences ensue. Those consequences can be positive, neutral, or aversive. As cognizant human beings, we typically assess the results of our actions and determine the valence of the consequences. We usually try to bring about situations that we like or find acceptable and most of the time we are successful at this. Most of the time we bring about events that are either positive or neutral, and most of the time we are not in a dissonant state. However, sometimes we notice that the consequences

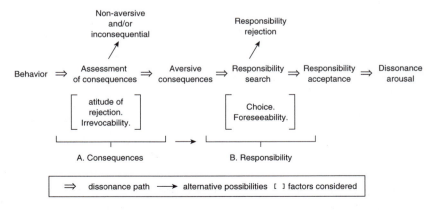

Figure 4.4   The sequence of events leading to dissonance arousal
Source: Adapted from Cooper and Fazio (1984)

of our behavior are unwanted or negative. It happens in the real world and, with proper stagecraft, can be made to happen in the psychology laboratory. Festinger and his students were successful at creating dissonance in participants because they were adept at developing laboratory scenarios that brought unwanted consequences to the fore. They were also adept at recognizing the unfolding of such events in the real world, as crystallized in the prophecy of the doomsday cult that had predicted the cataclysmic end of the Earth (Festinger, Riecken, and Schachter, 1956).

With very few exceptions and regardless of the particular research paradigm, successful dissonance studies have included unwanted, aversive consequences. The adults in Mrs Keech's doomsday cult suffered unwanted consequences when their failed prophecy came shatteringly close to ruining their lives. In the free-choice studies, Jack Brehm's research subjects, once they had made a choice between two consumer items, could no longer have the attractive features of the rejected item and were stuck with the unattractive features of the chosen item. Aronson and Mills's (1959) participants suffered the embarrassment of a sexual screening test and the children in Aronson and Carlsmith's study never got to play with their attractive robot. And, as we have discussed on several occasions above, the participants in the induced compliance experiments (e.g., Festinger and Carlsmith, 1959) were confronted with the knowledge that they had duped a supposedly naïve fellow student into thinking that he or she was going to have a fun-filled experience in a psychology experiment. In each case, the participants acted inconsistently; in each case, too, their behavior brought about an unwanted consequence. It is the unwanted consequence that begins the dissonance process.

There are two caveats that need attention before the progression to dissonance continues. One is that there is a continuum of what is acceptable as a behavioral consequence and what is not. Not all outcomes are perfectly beautiful and not all outcomes are perfectly evil. On that continuum, people have a 'latitude of acceptance' and a 'latitude of rejection.' In the former is a series of possible outcomes that vary in how positive they are but which people find basically acceptable. Similarly, in the latitude of rejection is a series of outcomes that people find unacceptable. Bringing about an outcome that lies in a person's latitude of rejection is the key element to start the dissonance process (Fazio, Zanna, and Cooper, 1977).

The second caveat is that the consequence needs to be irrevocable. It is far easier to wait to see if a consequence occurs than to do the cognitive work of adjusting your attitudes to relieve dissonance. If there is a possibility that you can 'take back' what you did (Davis and Jones, 1960) or that you will ultimately find out whether a committee will or will not read your attitude-discrepant essay (Goethals and Cooper, 1975), then dissonance can be forestalled. So, bringing about an irrevocable consequence that lies within a person's latitude of rejection fulfills the first step in the New Look model of dissonance arousal.

Who is responsible?

The next question that is asked in the process leading to dissonance arousal is who is responsible for this unwanted consequence? Dissonance occurs when an individual feels personally responsible for bringing about the aversive event. This is why decision freedom is so important in the lead-up to dissonance.

Imagine that you are in an induced compliance study and acted in a way that duped that poor undergraduate to believe she was about to have a great time in the research. Imagine that you consider that outcome to be in your latitude of rejection – a consequence that you wish you had not brought about. It would be so easy at this point to decide that you were not the person responsible for this outcome. How can that happen? Well, if you were in a no-choice condition, then you would not have to feel responsible. If you were forced or coerced, then you could hardly feel responsible for the action. The experimenter, or whoever coerced you, would be responsible and the dissonance process can end there.

Formally, we defined personal responsibility as *the attribution that the locus of causation for an event is internal*. Informally, it's the conclusion that, 'I did it; I brought it about.' Choice is not the whole story when it comes to responsibility. Choice needs to be combined with foreseeability. Choice may be necessary, but it is not sufficient. Imagine that you chose to buy a book at the local bookstore. It seemed interesting; you did not know anything about the author, but you thought you would give it a try. You pay your money and put your book away to read later. On your way home, you read in the newspaper that the book you bought is the subject of a feature story. It seems that the author is donating all of his profits to the American Nazi Party. You are devastated because you just contributed money to an organization you despise. Is there dissonance? You chose to buy the book and you caused the unwanted event of making a monetary contribution to the Nazis. I believe that, despite the consequence and the freedom, the answer is no. The consequence had to be foreseeable when you made that choice. In this case it wasn't, and you will be able to absolve yourself of personal responsibility.

In general, people will be able to absolve themselves of responsibility for an aversive consequence if they believe they had no choice but to behave as they did and/or the consequence was unforeseeable when they made that choice. People are motivated to seek avoidance of responsibility for aversive consequences. Dissonance is unpleasant and the result of needing to reduce dissonance is usually the work of changing attitudes. If responsibility can be denied, the process is over.

Recent empirical evidence supports the use of responsibility denial as a way to put an end to the arousal of dissonance. Gosling, Denizeau, and Oberle (2006) had participants at the University of Paris write counterattitudinal essays about the university's admission policy. The degree to which the participants viewed themselves as responsible for having written their essays was made intentionally ambiguous. In one condition, students were provided with a rating scale that asked them about their degree of responsibility. By absolving themselves of responsibility, the students could alleviate their dissonance and did not need to alter their attitudes about the admission policy. Gosling et al. (2006) found that, as predicted, the students who were provided with a scale that gave them a convenient way to say they were not responsible, immediately seized the opportunity. They used the scale to claim they were not responsible for the essay they had written, nor were they even responsible for choosing to participate in the study. When asked about their attitudes after denying responsibility, these participants showed no change of attitudes toward the admission policies. However, when other students were asked for their attitudes *before* filling out a responsibility measure, they showed the familiar, dissonance-induced attitude change toward the admissions policy, bringing their attitudes into line with their essays.

In conclusion, if responsibility cannot easily be denied, if the essay-writing behavior was freely chosen and the consequence was foreseeable, then responsibility is accepted, and the state of cognitive dissonance is aroused.

From arousal to motivation: what is accomplished when attitudes change?

The state of arousal begins a chain of events that will likely lead to attitude change as a way of reducing the arousal. Figure 4.5 shows the steps that take place before people do the work of changing their attitudes. It makes sense that people have to put a cognitive label on their emotion. Recall Schachter and Singer's (1962) two-factor theory of emotion that was the basis for the misattribution work discussed in Chapter 3. When people feel autonomic arousal, they seek to put a label on it. When they feel the excitation due to dissonance, they need to put a label on it. Is it a positive or negative emotion they feel? What is it due to? As Schachter and Singer would have suggested, they assess the situation they are in and quickly make an inference.

It is possible that the dissonance arousal can be labeled either positively or negatively. Fazio and I speculated this was the case on the basis of Schachter and Singer's theory, although the evidence is slim and several scholars disagree (e.g., Elliot and Devine, 1994). Still, there is some evidence suggesting that under the right circumstances, the dissonance arousal could be considered a positive emotion, which in turn would end any need for attitude change.

Rhodewalt and Comer (1979) had subjects perform an induced compliance task under conditions of high choice. Prior to their agreeing to write their

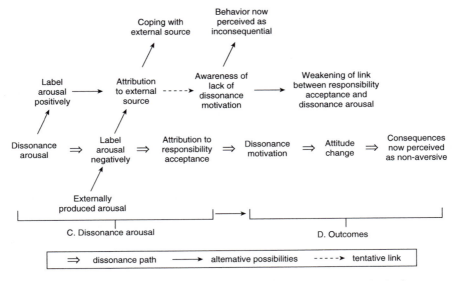

Figure 4.5 The sequence of events leading from dissonance arousal to attitude change
Source: Adapted from Cooper and Fazio (1984)

counterattitudinal statements, electrodes were attached to the participant's face, allegedly to assess physiological activity. Their faces were placed in positions that simulated either frowns or smiles, allegedly to allow the electrodes to record more reliably. Both pieces of information were part of the cover story. There was no physiological activity being recorded and the fixing of the facial musculature as a smile or frown was designed to cue positive or negative emotional states. Rhodewalt and Comer found that participants only changed their attitude when their face had been in the form of a frown. This seemed to assist the participants to label their arousal negatively. The interesting group consisted of participants whose face was in the form of a smile. They showed no attitude change following their counterattitudinal behavior. Rhodewalt and Comer speculated that the smile enabled the participants to label their dissonance arousal as a positive state, thereby relieving any need to change attitudes.

In another study, Cooper, Fazio, and Rhodewalt (1978) asked participants to write counterattitudinal essays under high-choice and low-choice conditions. Based on much previous research, we can be confident that this procedure produced dissonance arousal in the high-choice subjects. We borrowed a finding from an older study by Schachter and Wheeler (1962) who had shown that injections of epinephrine (which caused undifferentiated autonomic nervous system arousal) made subjects believe that a humorous film was funnier than other subjects rated it who had not had epinephrine. If dissonance arousal is as labile and flexible as epinephrine, then participants in the high-choice conditions of our experiment should be able to attribute their arousal to a cartoon, find it funnier, and not have any further motivation to change their attitudes. Our results supported this prediction. When subjects in the high-choice condition saw and rated a cartoon immediately following their counterattitudinal behavior, they rated the cartoon as funny and did not change their attitude on the issue they had written about. In the other high-choice condition in which subjects wrote their essay, then rated their attitudes, followed by the cartoon, they changed their attitudes on the issue but did not rate the cartoon as funny.

The results of these two studies suggest that it is possible for people to make a positive emotional attribution to their arousal. In most cases, however, the default is to make a negative attribution – to feel discomfort and tension. People search their environment and their immediate past behavior to find a reason for their tension. Could I be uncomfortable because of some fleeting aspect of my environment? Is the room too hot, the lights too bright, or are these the side effects of the drug I have taken? If so, then as we saw in the previous chapter, attributing their arousal to an external stimulus conveniently ends the process (e.g., Zanna and Cooper, 1974). There is no reason to go through the process of changing my attitudes and cognitions. I simply need to wait for the pill's effects to diminish, leave the hot room, turn off the lights, or in some way act on that aspect of the environment to which I have falsely attributed my arousal.

In the absence of an obvious external source to explain my arousal, I must recognize that I have been responsible for bringing about an unwanted event and that is a sufficient explanation for my uncomfortable tension. Although I may not have the words for 'I feel that I'm in a state of cognitive dissonance,' that is functionally what I have now done. I am now motivated to reduce that state of uncomfortable tension we call dissonance.

The function of attitude change

Dissonance motivation is the state of arousal that Festinger described and that has received support in the work of Elliot and Devine (1994), Losch and Cacioppo (1990), and Croyle and Cooper (1983). It is negative, uncomfortable, physiologically arousing, and needs to be reduced. In the New Look view, dissonance does not occur because of inconsistency per se, and attitude change is not in the service of restoring consistency. Rather, *attitude change occurs to render the consequences of behavior non-aversive*. If it was a negative outcome for me to have duped a fellow student to believe a dull task was going to be interesting, then I can change all of that if I believe that the task was fun. It cannot be aversive to convince the next student that the task will be fun if it really is fun. Similarly, it cannot be an aversive outcome to convince a committee at my university that tuition rates should increase if I think that a rise in tuition is a good idea. Thus, attitude change has a direct functional value for the person who has been responsible for bringing about an aversive event: it renders that event non-aversive and thereby reduces the dissonance.

On the status of the two views of dissonance

What happened to inconsistency?

In the exposition of the New Look in Figure 4.4, the word *inconsistency* never appears. Dissonance, we have argued, has precious little to do with inconsistent cognitions but rather is driven by the perception of unwanted consequences. Festinger's formulation was perhaps more elegant, but it was the anomalies and exceptions that accumulated in the decades of data collection that led us to see that the original formulation was no longer the best explanation for the phenomenon (Cooper and Fazio, 1984). When it comes to the reduction of the motivational state (Figure 4.5), the two versions of the theory are substantially the same. There is a difference between the two models in the analysis of what is accomplished by attitude change, but that attitude change occurs as a way of reducing the uncomfortable tension state is the same.

What role does inconsistency play in dissonance? In the first three chapters of this book, the concept of inconsistency was used in the analysis of dissonance and its concepts were used to make the predictions that revolutionized social psychology. Inconsistency is still an important concept but more as a heuristic than as an accurate representation of the cognitions that arouse dissonance. It is easy to use the inconsistency rule as a quick way to analyze and understand the conditions that lead to the uncomfortable tension state. The reason that the heuristic usually works to make accurate predictions is that acting inconsistently usually produces an aversive consequence. The typical methods that produce inconsistency – e.g., espousing a position that you don't believe, suffering to accomplish a mediocre goal, refraining from engaging in enjoyable activities, or making a choice between two choice alternatives – also produce unwanted consequences. Typically, then inconsistency can serve as a *proxy variable* for the unwanted consequence. There is much overlap in the two variables so that, most of the time, when we think of situations in which there is cognitive inconsistency, we are also thinking about situations in which the unwanted, aversive consequence is produced.

Nonetheless, there are occasions when the two concepts do not overlap and it is through an analysis of those situations that the unwanted consequence formulation can seem to be the more accurate one. There are two types of non-overlapping circumstances that can provide critical tests. One is when people hold inconsistent cognitions but there are no unwanted consequences. The other is when there are unwanted consequences without inconsistent cognitions. In both cases, the evidence favors the unwanted consequence position.

We have already examined a number of empirical studies in which people acted inconsistently with their attitudes but their actions did not produce aversive consequences. One of those studies was the induced compliance experiment of Cooper and Worchel (1970), in which we found that people changed their attitude toward a dull spool-turning task if they acted counterattitudinally by telling a waiting subject that the task was interesting. As you recall, this only happened when the waiting subject believed, rather than disbelieved, the participant. That is, this only happened when an unwanted consequence developed from the behavior. Note how important the inconsistency is in this research. It was because the behavior was inconsistent with the subject's attitude that it set in motion a consequence that was aversive. Nonetheless, it is the consequence that is the necessary condition to produce the effect.

A caveat for inconsistency: action orientation

It would be an overstatement to say that dissonance researchers have *never* produced attitude change in the absence of an aversive consequence. Harmon-Jones, Brehm, Greenberg, Simon, and Nelson (1996), for example, showed that people changed their attitude about the sweetness of a horrible tasting drink after making a counterattitudinal statement about how good it was, without any apparent consequence occurring. Moreover Dickerson and her colleagues found that people changed their behavior toward conserving water during a drought emergency in California without producing an aversive event (Dickerson, Thibodeau, Aronson, and Miller, 1992).

Harmon-Jones (1999) has pursued the inconsistency argument further by suggesting a mechanism that would explain *why* people are upset by inconsistency. Recall that for Festinger, it was as though people were 'hard-wired' to be aroused by inconsistency. Just as surely as food deprivation leads automatically to the hunger drive, inconsistent cognitions lead to the drive-like state of dissonance. Harmon-Jones presents a different stance on the role of inconsistency. He suggests that people acquire a stance toward the world that makes it adaptively better to act on the world without ambivalence and conflict. Inconsistent cognitions interfere with our action tendencies and thus create a negative emotion, motivating us to rid ourselves of the inconsistency. From the action orientation point of view, it is not inconsistency per se that causes us to be upset, but rather the effect that inconsistency has on our need to have an unequivocal stance toward action in the social and physical environment.

The action orientation position is interesting in that it links inconsistent cognitions with a reason for feeling upset, tense, and aroused. That position does not require an aversive consequence or unwanted event for dissonance to occur. However, the empirical fact is that, in the vast majority of studies in which consequences were systematically varied, the weight of the evidence strongly supports the idea that inconsistency is not sufficient to produce cognitive dissonance. Rather, the aversive consequence is a necessary ingredient for dissonance.

The sufficiency of the aversive consequence

Although the aversive consequence may be necessary for dissonance to occur, is it also sufficient? There are far less data bearing on this question, but it is important for several reasons. As we have noted, the sequence line in Figure 4.4 is silent about inconsistency. A behavior that produces an aversive consequence leads a person to experience dissonance arousal. In principle, this does not have to be an attitude-inconsistent behavior, but in all of the research discussed thus far, consequences have occurred in the context of inconsistency. In nearly all of the work on cognitive dissonance theory, the typical research subject is asked to do something that is inconsistent with his or her attitudes. We know now that dissonance requires an unwanted consequence, but the consequence in most research nonetheless follows attitude-inconsistent behavior.

If dissonance arousal requires the combination of attitude-discrepant behavior and an aversive consequence, then the New Look theory would simply be a limitation on the older one. That does not make it wrong, but it limits the scope of the theory by limiting the conditions to which dissonance is applicable. It provides a newer, and arguably more accurate, way of viewing one of the major *but-only's* we have discussed in this chapter. (Interested readers can pursue a discussion of this point in an exchange between Berkowitz and Devine [1989] and Cooper and Fazio [1989].) On the other hand, if dissonance also occurs when attitude-*consistent* behavior produces a foreseeable aversive consequence, then the newer version of the theory is an expansion of the theory by expanding the types of situations to which dissonance applies.

Steve Scher and I set out to construct a situation in which a foreseeable unwanted consequence occurred from attitude-*consistent* essay-writing behavior (Scher and Cooper, 1989). Our design permitted us to vary orthogonally whether the attitude-relevant behavior was pro-attitudinal or counterattitudinal and whether it led to an unwanted or a desired consequence. We asked university students to write a strong and forceful essay about a fee increase at their college. They were told that we were studying how committees make decisions when they read forceful essays. We informed them that our research findings thus far had shown that only the first few essays and the last few essays seemed to be effective.

In order to make both wanted and unwanted consequence seem foreseeable, the participants were told: 'The first couple of essays a committee reads seem to have the opposite effect of the way they were written. What I mean is that the first essays produce a boomerang effect. If they were written to support one side, they tend to convince the committee to take the other side.' They were told that the last few essays tend to be effective in a more straightforward way, convincing committee members in the direction they were intended.

Participants were then asked to write an essay on increasing college fees. The essays would be shown to the Dean's Committee on Policy, which was in charge of setting the fee structure at the college. All of the participants were given high-choice instructions. Half of the students were asked if they would be willing to write a strong and forceful essay taking the (pro-attitudinal) position that there should be no rise in the college fee. The other half was asked to take the (counterattitudinal) position that the fee should be raised.

When the essays were completed, the experimenter told the participant that the committee would read fifteen of the essays that he collected in his research. He said he could tell the subject whether her or his particular essay would be used by the committee. He checked a list on his clipboard and said, 'Yes, your essay will be one of the fifteen.' In the *straightforward* instructions, he continued, 'In fact, I can tell you that your essay will be read fourteen, which,' he reminded them, 'means that the essay will probably have a straightforward convincing effect on the committee.' In the *boomerang* instructions, the experimenter observed that the participant's essay would be read second, and reminded them that it would probably cause their essay to contribute to a boomerang effect on the committee.

In this 2 (pro-attitudinal vs. counterattitudinal essay) x 2 (boomerang vs. straightforward persuasion) design, the likelihood of aversive consequences occurs in two conditions: When a pro-attitudinal essay written against a fee hike proposal is likely to boomerang and when a counterattitudinal essay written in favor of the fee hike is likely to lead to straightforward persuasion. There are three possible predictions that can be derived from the various perspectives that we have examined so far.

- The New Look version of dissonance theory predicts that aversive consequences lead to dissonance. Therefore, any behavior that will lead the committee to believe in an unwanted position – regardless of whether the behavior itself was pro- or counterattitudinal – will lead to dissonance and attitude change.

- The inconsistency version of dissonance theory predicts that counterattitudinal behavior leads to dissonance. Therefore, the two conditions in which participants wrote essays contrary to their beliefs will lead to dissonance and attitude change.
- The inconsistency with a *but only* modifier holds that attitude-inconsistent behavior leads to dissonance, but only when an aversive consequence is produced. This compromise view would predict the arousal of dissonance only in the condition in which counterattitudinal behavior (the pro-fee hike essay) was expected to cause the committee to believe in raising the college fees.

The instructions in the study were complex, so great care was taken to make sure that the participants understood what the outcome of their essay writing was likely to be. Checks on the manipulations showed that the students understood. They were then asked for their own attitudes on fee increases. The results of the measure of attitudes are presented in Figure 4.6. The strong main effect for the valence of the outcome clearly supports the predictions of the New Look approach.

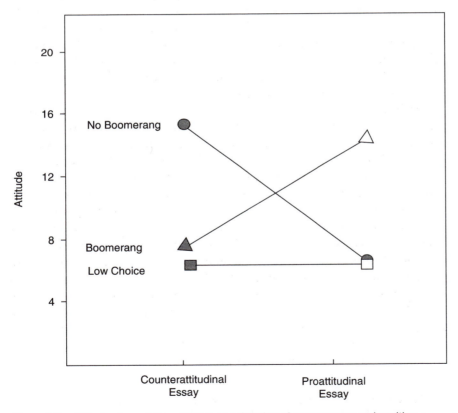

Figure 4.6   Attitudes toward the proposal as a function of consequence and position
Source: Adapted from Scher and Cooper (1989)

Relative to low-choice control conditions, participants became more supportive of fee hikes when they wrote counterattitudinal essays that would convince the committee to raise fees and when they wrote pro-attitudinal essays but believed that the boomerang effect would cause the same unwanted outcome of the committee raising fees. It was the outcome that determined attitude change. When the outcome was unwanted, dissonance occurred and attitudes changed in the direction of that outcome, regardless of whether the behavior itself was consistent or inconsistent with the participants' attitudes.

Dissonance, it seems, is propelled by responsibility for consequences rather than by inconsistency.

Motivated reasoning: the process of attitude change following dissonance arousal

How do people actually go about changing their attitudes following cognitive dissonance? We now know *why* they do it: they seek to make the consequences of their behavior acceptable and non-aversive. We still do not know *how* they do it. What process do people engage in to accomplish the goal of attitude change? Festinger (1957) indicated that people will change any cognition that is least resistant to change. Because attitudes are private constructions, they are often easy to change, at least easier than publicly committed behavior. Yet, it strains credibility to think that we can simply declare a new attitude willy-nilly, with no regard at all for the attitude we had even minutes before. Granted we are motivated to change our attitude, but it requires a few steps to understand how we go about the process of accomplishing it in a psychologically reasonable way.

Ziva Kunda's (1990) theory of motivated reasoning presents a compelling view of how people change attitudes in the service of a desired state (see also Pyszczynski and Greenberg, 1987, for a similar position). Kunda maintained that when people are motivated to hold a particular attitude or a particular view of themselves, they engage in a process whose outcome is partially determined by their motivation. We know the attitude that we desire to have, and we engage in a search of our past behaviors, statements, and opinions to find evidence that the new attitude is really one we have had all along. For example, participants in the high-dissonance conditions of Scher and Cooper's study knew that they could render the consequence of their behavior non-aversive if they supported tuition fee hikes. Rather than merely adopting a new position, Kunda's analysis would suggest that the participants searched their memories for occasions in which they were supportive of increased tuition. Perhaps it was an idle comment to a friend, perhaps it was the absence of an objection when the fee was hiked on a prior

85

occasion. Armed with these observations, they were prepared to believe that they really supported tuition hikes all along. Their essays in favor of tuition hikes caused no damage because they always were in favor of tuition hikes.

Reality, however, has a habit of getting in the way. Participants knew that only moments before, they had felt that tuition hikes were a bad idea. In many studies, the participants are even asked prior to their essays or speeches whether they agree or disagree with the position they are about to espouse. So, in the end, the new position is a compromise. Changes in the original attitude occur because people search their autobiographical memories for any evidence they can marshal to suggest that they are in favor of the position they supported, but constrained by their realization of their original attitude.

A study about self-concept helps us see the process unfold (Sanitioso, Kunda, and Fong, 1990). Participants were asked to generate autobiographical memories about whether they were introverts or extroverts. When participants had been led to believe that introversion was better than extroversion, the participants generated more memories of themselves as introverts compared to participants who were led to believe that extroversion was a more desirable trait. These differences in recall were constrained by participants' actual traits. People who really were introverts (as previously measured on personality scales) still rated themselves as introverts and people who were really extroverts still rated themselves as extroverts. Nonetheless, the degree of introversion and extroversion was dependent on the outcome of the motivated autobiographical search. The effects of the manipulation that motivated people to see one trait as more desirable than another resulted in self-views consistent with that motivation, but constrained by prior self-knowledge.

The motivated reasoning view of the attitude change process is similar to what Kunda (1990) found for the estimation of traits. The motivation to have an attitude that renders the consequence of a behavior non-aversive causes a biased autobiographical search, but one that is constrained by prior knowledge of their true attitudes. This process results in attitudes that are more like the positions advocated in their speeches and essays than they had held originally, but not completely isomorphic with it. And this fits the data of dissonance experiments very well. People who state that tuition hikes are wonderful come to believe that such hikes are okay – i.e., they are more in favor of tuition hikes at the end of the study, but they are not nearly as extreme in their attitudes as their essays suggest. Students in Cohen's (1962) study at Yale University who wrote essays extolling the actions of the New Haven police did not come to believe that the police were the paragon of diplomacy and restraint – it is just that they were more understanding and positive to the police than they had been previously. We have no direct evidence that the motivated reasoning approach underlies the process of attitude change following the arousal of dissonance. However, the approach has been used in a variety of areas to understand the process of change. It seems a promising mechanism for understanding how people change their attitudes such that potentially unwanted consequences are converted into acceptable ones. And it also shows the likely limitations of that change.

Speculations about the ontogeny of dissonance

Where does dissonance come from? Why do we suffer an unpleasant tension state when, for example, we convince someone to believe in an issue that we do not believe, suffer to achieve a goal, choose a course of action, or perform any of the behaviors that research has shown lead to cognitive dissonance? We have no firm answer to this question but it is interesting food for thought.

One possibility is that dissonance occurs as part of the unfolding of human development, part of the hard-wired system embedded in the phylogeny of the species. As I mentioned earlier in this chapter, Festinger (1957) simply asserted that the drive for consistency existed, but not why or how. In his earlier theory of social comparison he had taken the same stance by arguing, 'There exists in the human organism a drive for social comparison.' Perhaps this is all that needs to or can be said about the emergence of cognitive dissonance.

Another intriguing possibility is that dissonance is not automatically present in people but, rather, that it is learned in childhood as part of the sequence of development that we call growing up. We know that children as young as 5 have been shown to reduce dissonance, at least in the forbidden toy research that I described in Chapter 1 (Aronson and Carlsmith, 1962; see also, Freedman, 1965; Lepper, Zanna, and Abelson, 1970). We have not seen it with younger children and it seems intuitively plausible that dissonance becomes observable in children at approximately that age.

Let's imagine a scenario of a young toddler who is learning to interact with her social environment. The goal of the example is to see if we can glean some of the roots of dissonance development that are consistent with the New Look approach. In this approach, we ask not where learning to abhor inconsistency comes from, but rather we ask why children learn to become upset when they cause unwanted events to occur.

Our young toddler is in her living room with her parents. One day, while playing in her room, she innocently knocks over the floor lamp. Her mother is angry or worried. She responds negatively. Perhaps she yells, or gets upset, or just communicates her discomfort in some empathic way. The little girl gets the message. She feels bad because of her mother's reaction. It doesn't require a pathological reaction on mom's part nor does it require a spanking. It only requires the communication of the negative emotion for the little girl to feel bad. And, of course, something like it will happen again, and again, in the toddler's life space. So, eventually, the child learns that whenever she produces an unwanted event (i.e., one the parent considers negative), then the parent will respond with a discomfort-producing emotion. As time progresses, the child can anticipate what those events are that form the category of 'negative or unwanted events' and will also learn to anticipate the parents' emotional reactions to them (Sullivan, 1953). These negative events are to be avoided. A healthy self will not want to endure the parents' negative reactions.

Children also learn that the falling lamp does not *always* lead to the negative emotional reaction. There are certain conditions that the child learns cause a disruption in the negative emotional feedback. Imagine that the little girl, who experienced her mother's annoyance at knocking down the lamp, is pushed by her older sister and the lamp falls again. The adult is annoyed and steps toward the child. But this time, the negative response is directed at the sister rather than the child. Before too long the girl realizes that a negative emotional response is not encountered when one had no choice but to engage in the unwanted act. Being pushed is one such instance. The responsibility for the behavior is the sister's, not hers. She is the one to whom the anger is directed. The younger sister is off the hook.

This enables the child to realize that bringing about unwanted events brings a negative emotional reaction, but not if the behavior was forced by someone else. The parallel to dissonance in older children and adults is clear. Bringing about an unwanted event signals unpleasantness, but only if you are the one responsible for its occurrence. We can take this metaphor a bit further and the parallel continues. A little boy takes a chair from its place under the kitchen table. That action begins a chain of events that leads to the lamp falling down. Unbeknownst to the child or anyone else in the house, the father had placed the chair in a position to hold up the table because the table leg was broken. Pulling the chair caused the table to wobble which pushed a broom handle that fell into the lamp and caused it to come crashing down. The little boy chose to take the chair from its position by the table and for that he was responsible. But he could not have known what would happen next. He could not foresee that the lamp would fall because he neither had enough knowledge of physics nor did he know that his father had used the chair to hold up the table. His parents do not respond to him with anger, anxiety, or any other negative emotion. Because he could not foresee the aversive consequence when he pulled the chair, no one holds him responsible and the negative emotional state is avoided.

The point of these stories is this: it is very possible that cognitive dissonance is a learned secondary drive. The emotional response to negative events is aversive and upsetting. It should be avoided and, if it occurs, it needs to be resolved. However, the child also learns that actions that produce negative events do not produce negative emotional states if those actions were forced or if the consequences of the behavior were unforeseeable. This may be the beginning of how dissonance is learned.

Although I know of no evidence that addresses this conjecture, the story at least provides one possible mechanism that can help us see how dissonance develops and the story is consistent with the principles we know are important for dissonance arousal. There is some evidence that dissonance can be *unlearned* and that by using principles of secondary learning, people can learn to become less aroused by dissonance procedures (Cooper, 1998). However, what is needed at this point are some novel research techniques that can delve more deeply into the ontogeny of dissonance in young children.

5

THE SELF-STANDARDS MODEL AND
THE EMERGENCE OF THE SELF
IN DISSONANCE THEORY

The role played by the self has become increasingly prominent as a field of study in social psychology (Baumeister, 1999; Kihlstrom and Cantor, 1984; Leary and Tangney, 2003; Sedikides and Gregg, 2003). Questions about how the self affects – and is affected by – what we do and think have moved to the forefront of social psychology. Analyzing the role of the self has also played an increasingly important role in the understanding of cognitive dissonance.

Self-affirmation: dissonance as a part of the self-system

A good case in point is the theory of self-affirmation developed by Claude Steele and his colleagues (Steele, 1988; Steele and Liu, 1983). Steele proposed that a motive high on people's priority list is the protection of the integrity of their self-systems. We like to think of ourselves as good and honest people. And most of the time we are. We set high standards, have good values, and generally live up to them. However, there are times when we act in ways that we find problematic. Imagine that we had a few drinks at a party and then drove home without a designated driver. Or we did not do as well as we would have liked on a chemistry test. Or we did not return to the shop to tell the cashier she had given us five cents too much change after we had paid the bill. Taking cognizance of these behaviors may compromise what we think of ourselves. Shouldn't honest people have rectified such errors? Don't good people refrain from driving while even slightly under the influence? Are we really as good and as honest as we would like to believe we are?

The theory of self-affirmation suggests that we are indeed motivated to see ourselves as good and honest people and any evidence to the contrary will upset our equilibrium. We will need to rationalize our activities, to distort or add information about ourselves in order to preserve the integrity of our ideas about ourselves. If we did something wrong, i.e., something that

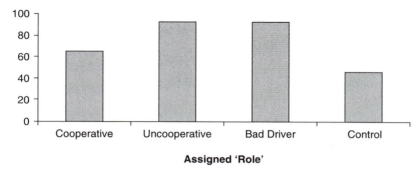

Assigned 'Role'

Figure 5.1 Housewives' willingness to help by assigned community reputation
Source: Adapted from Steele (1975)

good and honest people would not have done, then there must have been a good reason. Alternatively, the 'something' that we did might not have been that wrong. People will distort their cognitions about themselves in the service of protecting their self-system. And that motivation, according to self-affirmation theory, is the primary influence that motivates the attempts to reduce cognitive dissonance.

Imagine that you were a homemaker in a closely knit neighborhood in Salt Lake City, Utah, in the mid 1970s. If you had been chosen to be in a study that Steele (1975) conducted, you would have received a phone call from a pollster who was conducting a telephone interview. During the course of the interview, the pollster would have made it clear that you were known in the community to be a person who was uncooperative with community projects. This label was intended to be threatening to the woman's view of herself as a cooperative and helpful person. Other women in Salt Lake would have received different information during the phone call. Some were randomly assigned to be told that they were known to be very cooperative while still others were told that they were known to be careless and unsafe drivers.

Two days later, another stranger called asking the participants if they would be willing to help in a baking project that would benefit the community. Steele had expected the women who had been called uncooperative to volunteer more often for the baking project than women who had been labeled as cooperative. He expected them to use the second occasion to repair any damage to their sense of self by showing that they could and would help the community when asked. The data in Figure 5.1 show that this occurred. Participants who were accused of being uncooperative agreed to help in the baking project. What was surprising in the results depicted in Figure 5.1 was that women who had been labeled as reckless drivers were also more willing to help with the bake sale compared to women who had received the positive label or no label at all.

Steele concluded that threats to the self-system can come in many varieties and can also be repaired in quite flexible ways. Participants whose views of themselves had been threatened by challenges to their cooperativeness or to their driving skills found that they could restore the integrity and goodness of their self-systems by volunteering for the baking project. Bolstering their cooperativeness with the baking project fended off attacks to their self-system, regardless of whether the attacks were about their degree of coop-erativeness, or about something entirely different – their driving skill.

Self-affirmation meets cognitive dissonance

The general form of Steele's argument is that people need to affirm the integrity of their self-system when that system is threatened. Threats occur whenever information, certainly including the information contained in our own behavior, makes us feel less than worthy, honest, or capable. Through this lens, Steele argued that the dilemma in which people are placed in cog-nitive dissonance research creates a threat to their sense of self. When people say things that they know not to be true, when they make difficult choices, or when they endure effort or embarrassment, they will have suf-fered a threat to their self-systems. Good and honest people do not dupe another student nor do they write essays whose positions they do not believe. Good and competent people do not voluntarily suffer embarrass-ment or effort to get into dull and worthless groups. In the high-dissonance conditions of all of the extant dissonance experiments, people have man-aged to threaten their own sense of worthiness, moral rectitude, or compe-tence. How can they make it right?

According to self-affirmation theory, they can do almost *anything* to make it right. The problem is not one of rectifying the specific wrong, but in finding some way to affirm the global integrity of the self. As we have noted, one way to restore the self-system after writing a counterattitudinal essay is to convince yourself that you really agreed with the position in the first place. But, in the self-affirmation theory view, there are many other ways to affirm the self-system. A person can volunteer to give blood to the blood donor drive or to make a cake for the bake sale. A person can remind himself that, even though he may have written an essay he does not believe, he nonetheless gave to charity last week, or will give to char-ity in the future. He may even concentrate on how competent a tennis player he is. Any of those cognitions has the potential to affirm the self-system and repair the damage done by the decision to write a counteratti-tudinal essay.

It only remains to ask why participants in cognitive dissonance experi-ments change their attitudes. And self-affirmation theory's answer to this question is that, within the context of the experiment, attitude change is the only way available for the participants. They are asked what their attitudes are about a boring task, tuition policy, or classes that are held at 7:00 am, but they are not asked about their contributions to charity, their cherished values, or the skills at which they are competent. They are only asked what they thought about the boring task, tuition policy, and so forth, so that is the route they must use to affirm their self-systems.

Steele and Liu (1983) created an ingenious research paradigm to establish an empirical basis for their reasoning. They established an induced compliance research procedure – with a twist. Participants at the University of Washington were asked (high dissonance) or were told (low dissonance) to write an essay favoring increased tuition rates at their school. Prior to writing their essays, the students had filled out a value assessment questionnaire and were known to be either very strong or not so strong on their political/economic values. Then, after writing their counterattitudinal speeches favoring tuition hikes, the participants were given a political/economic subscale from a different values questionnaire. On this subscale, participants had the opportunity to affirm how strong their interest was in political and economic issues and how much they enjoyed engaging in activities in support of those values. For students who had strong political and economic values, filling out item after item on this scale would be self-affirming. It would remind them of issues and activities that were important and fulfilling to them. For students who were not high on such values, the items would not affirm important aspects of their self-systems because of the low importance that economic and political activity held for them.

After filling out the values scale, participants indicated what their attitudes were toward a tuition hike. The results for participants who had not been self-affirmed (i.e., those who did not have high social/political values) followed the typical result shown in dissonance experiments. Relative to the low-dissonance condition, participants who were low in political and economic values changed their attitudes toward tuition to make them consistent with their essay-writing behavior. As predicted, though, this did not happen for the participants high in economic/political values. For them, filling out the scale apparently affirmed their self-system. They were now able to see themselves as good and worthy people, rendering attitude change unnecessary. The average attitude of this group did not differ from the low-choice subjects.

In a similar study, Steele, Hopp, and Gonzalez (1986) had participants make a choice between two music albums. Recall that this is the paradigm first used by Brehm (1956) to show that people spread apart the choice alternatives following a decision as a way to reduce their dissonance. In the Steele et al. study, participants had been selected for the research because they were either high in science values (as measured by a values questionnaire) or

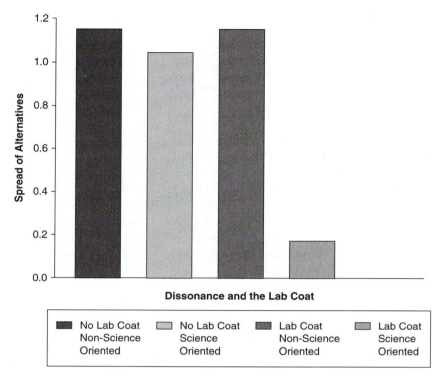

Figure 5.2   Spread of decision alternatives following a choice
Source: adapted from Steele (1988)

high in business values. Half of the students chose their music album after donning a white lab coat, while the other half were normally dressed. Steele et al. reasoned that all of the participants making a difficult choice between the albums would suffer a threat to their self-system. However, those who were science oriented and who wore a lab coat would have symbolic affirmation of their core value. They would not need to adjust their evaluation of the choice alternatives because their self-system would have been affirmed by their lab coat. The rest of the subjects – i.e., those not wearing a lab coat and business-oriented students who had a lab coat – would need to change their evaluations of the music in order to reaffirm their threatened self-system. The results, depicted in Figure 5.2, show that, as predicted, the spread of the music alternatives did not occur for science-oriented participants who were wearing the lab coat.

There are at least two fascinating issues raised by Steele's approach relative to inconsistency reduction and the New Look. The first is about what motivates change following an attitude-discrepant act. Self-affirmation and the New Look agree on what dissonance is *not*. Both agree that dissonance reduction is not about restoring consistency. For Cooper and Fazio (1984), the motivation for people to change a cognition is to make an unwanted consequence less aversive. For self-affirmation, it is restoring the integrity of the global self-system.

A second issue put into focus in self-affirmation is whether repair of the compromised system needs to be specific or global. For Festinger, dissonance reduction required restoring consistency about the specific cognitions that were discrepant. Similarly, for Cooper and Fazio (1984), the repair for bringing about an unwanted event requires repair at the local level – i.e., it is the specific consequence that has to be rendered non-aversive. Self-affirmation takes a radically different approach. As Steele has commented, it's the war, not the battle, that has to be won. If a specific, attitude-discrepant behavior threatens the self-system, the repair can be made at either the local or the general level. If need be, the attitudes compromised by a particular behavior can be left intact, and the individual can find a way to bask in the glory of his or her other achievements, goals, and accomplishments. It is the overall composite of the self-system that needs to be bolstered by self-affirmations.

Being what you expect to be: self-consistency as the motivation for cognitive dissonance

Self-affirmation was not the first theory to implicate the self in the arousal of cognitive dissonance. Perhaps the initial emphasis on the importance of the self-concept was offered by Elliot Aronson (1968). Aronson had been a graduate student of Leon Festinger's while dissonance theory was in its infancy. His research is among the most imaginative of the work in dissonance theory and he has continually been a proponent of the importance of dissonance in social psychology. His work departed from Festinger's in one important respect. For Festinger, two discrepant cognitions were the fuel to begin the cognitive dissonance process. Any cognition would do. In his 1957 book, Festinger posited several predicaments of inconsistency that he thought would provoke dissonance. Let's look at two of them, because they will highlight the different emphasis that Aronson thought was important:

1 You are standing in the rain and you are not getting wet.
2 You read information that smoking is bad for you but you continue to smoke.

The first of these, based on your past experience with being caught in the rain, creates inconsistency between the cognition 'water is falling from the sky' and 'I remain dry.' The second creates inconsistency between the information you read about the adverse effects of smoking and your behavior of lighting up yet another cigarette. For Festinger, both of these incidents would arouse dissonance. For Aronson's self-consistency view (Aronson, 1968), only the latter would create dissonance.

Self-consistency theory (Aronson, 1968; Thibodeau and Aronson, 1992) emphasizes the need for the self to be involved in dissonance arousal. Like Steele's self-affirmation view, self-consistency theory holds that people have a need to see themselves as good, competent, and moral people. If someone smokes after learning of the health crisis created by smoking, that person can hardly think of him or herself as competent. It is the discrepancy between a person's behavior and his view of himself as moral, rational, and competent that creates the dissonance. In the classic experiments on cognitive dissonance, the self was always compromised by the participant's behavior. What kind of competent and moral person would dupe a fellow student? How competent could it have been to engage in an effortful and embarrassing screening test in order to get into a dull group? How competent can a person perceive herself to be if she accepted a kitchen blender despite knowing all of the attractive features of the toaster she could have chosen? In each case, the person's behavior called into question the competence, honesty, or wisdom of the actor.

Aronson put it this way: 'At the very heart of dissonance theory, where it makes its strongest predictions, we are not dealing with just any two cognitions; rather, we are usually dealing with the self-concept and cognitions about some behavior. If dissonance exists, it is because the individual's behavior is inconsistent with his self-concept' (Aronson, 1968: 23). The fact that people usually try to see themselves as good, honest, competent, and moral people makes their negative behavior discrepant with their self-esteem. Most participants in research studies are college students who generally have high regard for their intelligence, competence, and integrity. Getting them to behave in ways that threaten that self-concept (as is usually the case in cognitive dissonance studies) is the reason their behavior leads to the arousal of dissonance and the need to change their attitudes.

Festinger's smoking example certainly fits the description of a person whose behavior compromises her or his generally high view of himself. But standing in the rain without getting wet does not. You would certainly be perplexed if the rain were falling on you but you were nonetheless dry. It is not that you would accept this situation without trying to figure out why, but you would not experience cognitive dissonance. In the self-consistency view, without the involvement of the self-concept, there would be no dissonance.

Turning the self upside-down

Most of the time, Festinger's notion of inconsistency and Aronson's emphasis on the self make similar predictions and Aronson rarely drew sharp distinctions between the two models. The essence of the similarity is that people usually feel good about themselves, expect that they will do good, competent, and moral things, and then feel dissonance when their behavior violates those expectations. There is at least one classic study that turned self-concept on its head and provided interesting evidence for the self-consistency view.

We have already had occasion to review this study in this book (see Chapter 1). Recall the study by Aronson and Carlsmith (1962) in which they created the expectation that students were either really competent or really incompetent at being able to select which of two photographs was that of a schizophrenic. When people who believed they were good at this skill did poorly, they suffered cognitive dissonance. But so did people who had a negative self-view with regard to this skill and who found that, in a critical final trial, that they had actually done well. When given an opportunity to change their behavior and confirm their poor ability, or stick with it and experience success, they did the former. They changed their successful performance to failure in a presumed attempt to behave consistently with their negative self-concept.

Although this study has proven somewhat difficult to replicate (see Shrauger, 1975), it is an interesting example of how violations of what people expect of themselves can create dissonance. In a study that is consistent with Aronson's view, Cooper and Scalise (1974) showed that people who consider themselves introverts experienced dissonance when they acted in extroverted ways whereas people who considered themselves to be extroverts experienced dissonance when they acted in introverted ways. In other words, the very same behavior caused dissonance only when it violated people's self-concepts. Extroverted behavior caused dissonance for introverts but not for extroverts; introverted behavior caused dissonance for extroverts but not for introverts. One's view of oneself – i.e., a person's self-concept – establishes expectations whose violation, in turn, leads to the arousal of dissonance.

Differences in approaches using the self

Aronson's self-consistency view and Steele's self-affirmation theory share some fundamental assumptions. Both theories see the reduction of dissonance to be intimately involved with a person's self-conception. Both take as a starting point that we generally have a healthy sense of self-esteem and that we feel threatened by anything that interrupts that view. When we act in a morally questionable way or when our competence is called into question by our actions, then we are motivated to take steps to defend against the threat.

But there is a major difference between the two approaches as well. The self, in Aronson's formulation, creates an expectation of how I should behave. If I fail to act in accordance with that expectation, there is an inconsistency between my behavior and my view of myself. In principle, valence does not matter. People with low self-esteem suffer dissonance if a behavior is good and competent; people with high self-esteem suffer dissonance if a behavior is incompetent or morally suspect. It is just that most people have reasonably high self-regard, so the former case rarely occurs. Nonetheless, dissonance is a matter of inconsistency, much like Festinger said it was. The major difference is that, in Aronson's self-consistency view, the inconsistency *must* involve some expectation regarding the self.

Self-affirmation theory, by Contrast, takes a unidirectional approach to dissonance and sees dissonance as a subset of occasions in which people attempt to protect their self-integrity. Expectations are not the issue. Seeing oneself as good and moral is the objective. And inconsistency per se is not the motivator for change. Inconsistency is simply a vehicle that can create a threat to the self-system and the person takes measures to protect it.

One implication of this difference is the way people can go about satisfying their motivation to protect their sense of self. In the self-consistency view, the repair must be directed at the specific inconsistency that caused the problem. We can change our view of ourselves as moral and competent people or, more typically, we can change our attitudes or other relevant cognitions to make ourselves feel more worthy. For self-affirmation, the repair can be general. As I pointed out earlier, anything that reaffirms the integrity of the self-system will do. If it is more efficacious to change a cognition such as an attitude, that will do. If it is easier to think of other ways that you are a worthy and competent person, then you can take that approach, not bothering to repair the specific inconsistency that challenged your self-view in the first place.

The New Look approach to dissonance shares with self-consistency the idea that dissonance needs to be alleviated by cognitions relevant to what caused the dissonance in the first place. For Cooper and Fazio (1984), dissonance can only be resolved by some change of cognition that renders the consequence of behavior non-aversive. For self-consistency, the goal is to make yourself feel less unworthy or in Aronson's colorful terms, less like a 'schnook' than your behavior would imply. Of the three approaches, only self-affirmation makes the prediction that dissonance can be resolved by the bringing to bear of any cognition that makes a person feel good about him or herself.

Does self-affirmation work? Yes and no

Can any information that makes you feel good alleviate the unpleasant tension of dissonance? This is a key element of the way in which the self is regarded in self-affirmation theory. Does it work? The evidence has been mixed, but from that mix a more accurate picture may emerge of how the self-concept affects dissonance.

Steele and Liu's (1983) research, which we reported at the beginning of this chapter, is consistent with the self-affirmation approach. People who were highly committed to economic and political values apparently had their dissonance reduced by filling out a questionnaire that asked them about their political and economic interests – this case is consistent with that approach (see Figure 5.2). However, a nagging problem with that research is that people filling out a values questionnaire may have been distracted from their dissonant cognitions. We know from several other studies that distraction allows people to avoid dissonance (e.g., Zanna and Aziza, 1976). People who have more genuine interest in the activities being asked about on the questionnaire may have been more distracted than people whose interests in economic and political issues were minimal.

Joshua Aronson, Hart Blanton, and I designed a research study in which people wrote dissonance-producing counterattitudinal essays and then were given an easy opportunity to see themselves in a positive light (Aronson, Blanton, and Cooper, 1995). Princeton University students were asked to write essays for a Dean's committee advocating the reduction of funding for handicapped students at the university. All versions of dissonance theory would agree that this situation would arouse dissonance and lead to attitude change. The self-affirmation approach takes the position that attitude change toward funding for handicapped services only occurs because there is not a more direct means of self-affirmation available for the participants. They elect to change their attitudes because that is the most available and accessible means to self-affirm.

So we decided to make it easy for students to self-affirm if they so desired. The aspect of their self-system that participants had compromised by writing a grouchy essay against services for the handicapped was their sense of their own compassion. What kind of person would write such an essay? Only a person deficient in altruism and human compassion. The good news for our participants was that they had just taken a personality test as part of a supposedly unrelated study. Before filling out the attitude-dependent measure, we told students that the results of the personality test were now available and that they could read paragraphs about the personality dimensions on which they had scored outstandingly high. Some of the dimensions, like 'compassion,' were related to the aspect of themselves that had been compromised by their writing the essay against handicapped facilities.

Did the participants want to read about how compassionate they were? If they did, they could immediately affirm a dimension that had been called into question by their essay. They knew that they had scored high on this dimension and they could choose to bask in the glory of their high degree of compassion. But they didn't. Compared to participants in low-choice

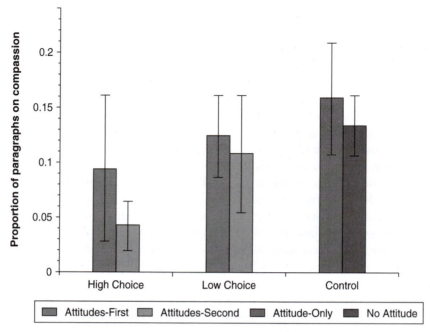

Figure 5.3   Interest of participants after compassion task in reading
about their compassion levels
Source: Aronson, Blanton and Cooper (1995)

control conditions who did not experience dissonance, the subjects in the
throes of high dissonance actively avoided any information about their compassion. Given an opportunity to affirm themselves directly on the challenged dimension, the participants avoided it. Instead, as predicted by the
New Look model of dissonance (and any of the other models that suggest
that dissonance is remedied at the level of the cognition that caused the difficulty), participants in the high-dissonance condition changed their attitudes to be less in favor of handicapped funding.

On the other hand, we (Aronson et al., 1995) observed an interesting
finding when we looked at students' interest to see reports extolling aspects
of their personality that had *not* been compromised by the attitude-discrepant essay. For example, the subjects in the high-dissonance condition
really wanted to read about how creative they were, even as they shunned
the paragraph about their compassion. We thought it was possible that self-
affirmation works best when people can affirm aspects of themselves that
are not relevant to the aspect of their self-concept that had been compromised by their behavior.

In a follow-up study, we tested this possibility directly by systematically
varying the kind of feedback students could receive (Blanton, Cooper,

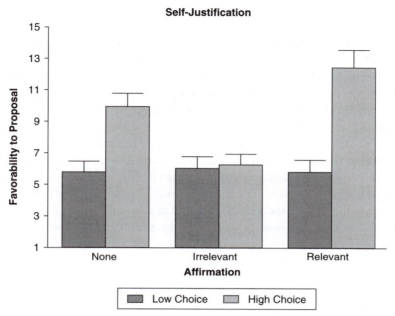

Figure 5.4 Exacerbation of dissonance due to relevant affirmation
Source: Blanton, Cooper, Skurnik and Aronson (1997)

Skurnik and Aronson, 1997). In a procedure similar to the one just reported by J. Aronson et al. (1995), students wrote a counterattitudinal essay arguing against funding for the handicapped. Then, instead of being asked what feedback they would like to see from the personality test, they were assigned feedback that either extolled their creativity (an irrelevant personality dimension), their compassion (a relevant personality dimension), or in a third condition, received no-feedback at all. The results show that attitude change as a means of reducing dissonance occurred in the no-feedback condition and was exacerbated in the relevant feedback condition. Not only did students *not* want to know about their compassion but, when shown how compassionate the personality test revealed them to be, it actually increased their dissonance arousal and subsequent attitude change. Only in the irrelevant condition, when students could read about how creative they were, was dissonance reduced by affirmation rather than attitude change.

The 'duelling banjos' of the self-concept

Earlier in this book, we talked about how much is gained when theories make diverging predictions. Theorists then argue with each other and

THE SELF-STANDARDS MODEL

experiments are designed as critical tests that will determine the issue. In the most productive of cases, there is a consensual winner, or there is a dialectical process that results in a new approach that subsumes the various points of view. The studies by J. Aronson et al. (1995) and by Blanton et al. (1997) were conducted to suggest that the New Look model of dissonance could predict what would happen when people were given an opportunity to self-affirm directly on a compromised aspect of the self. We predicted that direct self-affirmation would not reduce dissonance but that only a change of attitude toward funding handicapped facilities would be effective at reducing the aversive consequence. To some extent we were right. But the reduction of dissonance when participants affirmed irrelevant aspects of their self-concepts was unexpected. Was it merely distraction that accounted for less attitude change in that condition? Eventually we would come to see that this finding could lead to an integrated view of how the self is implicated in the dissonance process – a view we called the Self-Standards Model (Stone and Cooper, 2001).

First, however, there is another intriguing issue that places self-affirmation theory and self-consistency theory on opposite sides of a fascinating argument. What is the role of self-esteem in dissonance reduction? If we think of self-esteem as the general regard that people have for themselves, people differ in terms of the valence of that regard. Put more simply, people vary along a continuum of high to low self-esteem. Although self-affirmation and self-consistency see the integrity of the self as the foundation of dissonance arousal, the two theories play radically different songs on their respective banjos when the role of self-esteem is considered. The question may be put this way: Do people who think highly of themselves, i.e., have high self-esteem, experience more dissonance than people with low self-esteem when they engage in attitude-inconsistent behavior?

For Aronson's self-consistency view, the self is a set of expectations. People with high self-esteem expect that they will do good and moral things, will not hurt others, and will act with honor in any given situation. People with low self-esteem have a different set of expectations. Relative to their high self-esteem counterparts, they expect to make poor judgments and it does not surprise them when they act in ways that throw their honor and morality into question. Aronson and Carlsmith's (1962) experiment, in which people's expectations about how well they performed the task of picking schizophrenics, was consistent with this notion. The general form of Aronson's argument is that people with chronically low self-esteem are like the participants in the Aronson and Carlsmith's experiment whose expectation for failure was manipulated by the experimenter. People chronically low in self-esteem typically have low expectations for themselves. Therefore, it is a clear prediction from the self-consistency model of dissonance that people with high self-esteem will be upset by the recognition that they chose to dupe a fellow student or write an essay that convinces someone to believe a disliked position. People with high self-esteem generally think they make good choices and act honorably. They should experience a great amount of dissonance when they act in a way that violates their expectancy.

However, people with low self-esteem do not have the same expectancy about how they will behave. By the definition of low self-esteem, these individuals are not surprised when they agree to dupe someone or write arguments against their positions. They behaved like a 'schnook' because that is what they believe themselves to be. When considering their behavior and its unwanted consequences, their expectations have not been violated. They have acted consistently with the kind of person they believe they are and very little dissonance should ensue.

For self-affirmation theory, preserving a high sense of self-worth is people's primary goal. When threatened by, let us say, behavior that might bring about an unwanted policy or that may dupe a fellow student, people can search for other ways to affirm themselves. They can conjure up cognitions about other things they are good at, or bask in the expression of their important values. Here is where self-esteem enters the picture. High self-esteem serves as a resource that can help you with your self-affirmation. The more aspects of your life you believe you are good at, the more aspects you can bring to bear to affirm your goodness. And the more aspects you believe you are good at, the higher is your self-esteem. People who feel very poorly about themselves, by contrast, have no positive aspects to bring to bear. If their self system is threatened by duping a fellow student, they have no reservoir of valued attributes to think about that can help them buttress their self-system. The derivation from self-affirmation theory is that people with low self-esteem will be more inclined to change their attitudes following dissonance-producing behavior. It is the low self-esteem people who will need to change their attitudes as a way of convincing themselves that they did not compromise the integrity of their self-system.

Because self is a resource for self-affirmation theory, high self-esteem buttresses us against the experience of dissonance. Because the self is an expectation for self-consistency theory, high self-esteem exposes us to a greater amount of dissonance after attitude-discrepant behavior. Empirical research on the issue has yielded mixed results. Steele, Spencer, and Lynch (1993) found evidence that when people of high and low self-esteem are primed to think about their positive and negative attributes, high self-esteem individuals change their attitudes less than people with low self-esteem, a result consistent with self-affirmation theory. On the other hand, criticisms of this research (see Stone, 1999) make it more likely to say that we crossed into the twenty-first century without a definitive answer to the self-esteem controversy. Stone and Cooper's (2001) Self-Standards Model (SSM) attempted to address some of the issues in a model that will be described presently.

And, lest it go unnoticed, the New Look was silent about the role of self-esteem in dissonance arousal. Being responsible for an aversive outcome is sufficient to arouse dissonance, regardless of the level of a person's self-esteem. Self-esteem has little or nothing to do with it.

Fitting the pieces together: the Self-Standards Model of dissonance

Jeff Stone and I (Stone and Cooper, 2001) wondered whether the empirical and philosophical differences between the New Look and the analyses based on the self were, indeed, surmountable. We wondered if there was not common ground even between self theories that made such diametrically opposed predictions about the role of self-esteem. We considered the possibility that each theory had captured a piece of the larger puzzle and that each is correct in its own domain of applicability. The key to unlocking the larger puzzle is to see when, and in what contexts, the self plays a role in dissonance arousal and, when it does, whether its role is one of resource, expectation, or both.

Stone and I attempted to create an integrative outgrowth of the New Look that captured a role for self-esteem. As in the earlier New Look model, we believe that the events leading to the arousal of cognitive dissonance begin with behavior and a consideration of the behavior's outcomes. When we act, we usually have an impact on our physical and social environment and it makes sense to begin with an assessment of the impact. What happened as a result of my behavior? Was it a desired outcome or an undesired outcome? Did I do a good thing for myself and others or did I bring about something unwanted? In asking these questions, the SSM takes the same stance as the New Look approach (see Figure 4.4 in the previous chapter).

In the New Look, we were intentionally positivistic about the meaning of aversive consequences. In that paper, we considered a behavioral consequence to be aversive if it led to a state of affairs that the actor would rather have not brought about. It was a positivistic definition in the sense that its occurrence depended on the meaning that the actor attributed to it. There was no a priori definition of what makes a consequence aversive. It may, but it may not, include bringing harm to another person. Rather, a consequence is aversive if you, the actor, find it aversive. A person behaving in a counter-attitudinal manner who duped a fellow student may well think that he would rather not have done that. A person who experienced embarrassment in order to join a group might wish she had not embarrassed herself. Of course, the odd individual who thinks it's cool to dupe a fellow student or to be embarrassed will not have brought about an unwanted event and, for that person, an aversive consequence would not have occurred.

Nonetheless, the positivistic approach masked a number of possibilities that have became important in the development of dissonance theory during the last two decades. Most significantly, it left out how the self can be involved in the assessment of the consequences. Let's consider the question of how a consequence may be aversive by using less of a 'whatever it means to you' approach and consider what the possibilities are. In order to assess consequences, you would necessarily have to compare those consequences to a standard of judgment. If I asked you if a person you see running on a track is running fast, you might ask, 'Fast, compared to what?' You check your watch and note that he is running at a pace of four miles per hour. 'No', you might answer, 'he is running quite slowly compared to an average runner who runs on this track.' Then, remembering that you saw the same person running on the track yesterday, you think 'Yes, he is running fast … compared to yesterday's run.'

The assessment of the runner's speed takes its meaning only from a comparison with a standard of judgment. In the case of the runner, comparing his speed with his prior speed provides one answer to the question, but comparing his speed to a championship runner's speed provides a different answer. The same is true for the assessment of behavioral consequences. To answer the question of whether the outcome of behavior is unwanted or wanted, aversive or positive, requires comparison to a standard of judgment. And not all standards are the same.

Inspired by the work of Higgins on self-discrepancy theory (Higgins, 1989), Stone and I argued that there are two major categories of standards that a person can use to assess the meaning of the consequences of his or her behavior – normative and personal. There are some kinds of outcomes that we can effect in the world that most people would agree are of a particular valence. Most people would agree that contributing to charity or helping a roommate study for an exam are positive events. We know there may be occasions in which the help provided to the roommate and/or the contribution to the charity may have complicated mixed motives, but by and large, such actions are considered positive. Similarly, there are consequences that most people would agree are negative or undesired. For example, running into someone on the street and knocking him down would be generally aversive. So, too, is lying to someone, especially when the person believes and is influenced by your lie. Granted, there may be some odd times when those outcomes are positive, but, typically, most people would agree that they are negative.

When a standard of judgment is based on a perception of what *most people in a culture* perceive to be foolish, immoral, or otherwise negative, then we can say people are using a *normative standard of judgment*. Note that the culture may or may not be as broad as a society but may also be as small as a person's family, neighborhood, or community. The main thrust of the definition is that the standards are based on a shared understanding of good and bad, wanted or unwanted, foolish or clever (cf. Higgins, 1989).

The other broad category of standards of judgment are those that are based on the unique characteristics of the individual. We will call these *personal* self-standards because they refer solely to the judgments people make when they consider only their own values, judgments, or desires. Personal standards may or may not be similar to normative standards. Consider a casual runner who runs a mile in 4.5 minutes. By the standards of most casual runners, this is an extraordinary achievement. We may be surprised to learn that our runner is depressed. His own personal expectation was that he would run the mile in closer to 4 minutes. His high expectation of himself caused him to judge the outcome of his efforts negatively, despite its being quite an achievement to most people who try to run.

Let's return to the person who has successfully lied to a fellow student in a cognitive dissonance experiment such that the student is now supposedly looking forward to an exciting time. Most participants would judge their disingenuous behavior as something negative and aversive, but some might not. They may put a substantial weight on their acting ability and find it quite affirming that they were able to convince their audience (i.e., the waiting subject) of the veracity of their act. Thinking of themselves as thespians, they may be proud that they met their own expectations. Another person might believe that, in general, he is a deceitful person with few moral scruples. It does not surprise him that he agreed to tell the student the experimental task was interesting and he has duped a fellow student. Believing he is usually callow and typically expecting to make such choices, he is not disappointed. He has compared his behavior to a personal standard of judgment – perhaps a strange and depressing standard – but the result of the comparison is not negative at all.

Another person in the same study may believe that she is the most honorable person among her peers. She may believe that she is the kind of person who would never foreseeably act to dupe a fellow student. But she has. She agreed to help the experimenter and now has successfully duped a fellow student. Compared to her personal standard of super-integrity, her behavior has not just brought about an unwanted event, it has led to the supernova of all aversive outcomes and she judges herself very poorly indeed.

Figure 5.5 shows the arousal of dissonance schematically. It makes more explicit and detailed the 'assessment of consequences' that formed part of the New Look model. In the SSM, we suggest that people assess their behavior along two possible pathways. Pathway 1 of Figure 5.5 is an assessment

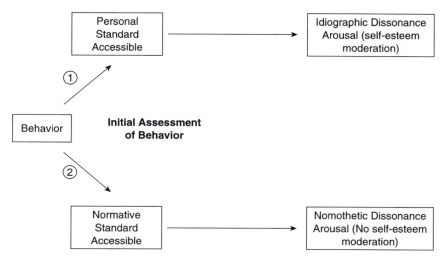

Figure 5.5   The Self-Standard Model of dissonance arousal (1)
Source: Stone and Cooper (2001)

against a personal standard of judgment. Issues of self-concept and self-esteem matter. When making a judgment based on reference to a personal standard, the issue is very much one of where a person thinks he or she stands on a particular dimension. 'I am always honest' or 'I am never honest' determine how a person will judge a particular episode of dishonesty. In a more global fashion, a person's personal standard may be based on a global consideration of his self-esteem. He thinks, 'I am a person who usually does the right thing; I have many good attributes; I am usually moral and wise.' That person will have high expectations for his behavior and will be disappointed by anything that falls short.

If people use personal standards to judge their behavioral outcomes, and if those outcomes are judged to be unwanted, then they will experience dissonance arousal. Just as the various self-theories (Thibodeau and Aronson, 1992; Steele, 1988) would predict, the magnitude of that arousal will be affected by what people think of themselves – i.e., by their self-esteem. We refer to dissonance that occurs by comparing behavioral outcomes to personal standards, *idiographic dissonance*.

If people use normative standards to judge the outcomes of their behavior, then individual differences in self-esteem are not involved at all. When judgments are based on normative standards, dissonance occurs because the consequence of behavior falls into a category that people realize is consensually negative. For instance, it is bad, and people know it is bad, to dupe a fellow student. It is bad, and people know it is bad to convince a Dean to adopt a policy that you think is unwise. It is foolish, and people know it is

THE SELF-STANDARDS MODEL

foolish, to suffer needless embarrassment to join a dull and boring discussion group. These are judgments that can be made quickly and confidently by referring solely to the consensus (or norms) in the culture. Such judgments lead to *nomothetic dissonance* and self-esteem plays no role.

Determining the standard to use

It remains to ask what determines whether people will use personal or normative standards of judgment when they assess the acceptability or aversiveness of the behavioral outcomes. The answer is determined by the accessibility of the standard. By accessibility, we mean the ease with which a particular cognition (in this case, a standard of judgment) can be called into consciousness. The more accessible something is, the more quickly it comes to mind.

Standards can become accessible in two major ways. One is that they are made accessible by some cue in the environment. For example, if I show you a photograph of various writing implements and then ask you to quickly fill in the missing letter in the sequence **p _ n,** you will be more likely to use **e** than **i** or **a.** Even though pin, pen, and pan are all common words, the photograph would make you think more quickly and fluently of pens rather than pins or pans. Similarly, in a dissonance situation, anything that makes you think of culture, groups, society, or other people will make normative standards more accessible and more likely to be used as your standard of judgment against which to compare your behavioral outcomes. On the other hand, anything that reminds you of your unique characteristics should make your personal standards more accessible. Seeing yourself in a mirror or writing your name should make it more likely that you will use personal standards when assessing your behavioral outcomes – and those are the situations in which your self-esteem is likely to affect the magnitude of your dissonance.

The other broad category that makes one standard more likely than another is *chronic*. People vary in how likely they are to use particular standards in the absence of any pushing or prodding from events in their environment. For reasons unique to their own developmental histories, some people are more likely to think of themselves and their unique histories, while others are more likely to carry with them the views and norms of their society and culture. At the extremes of this dimension, we all know people who cannot refrain from talking about anything or anyone except themselves and view all occurrences as though they were only happening to them. At the other extreme are people who never think of themselves and only think that the world exists in terms of general rules and norms. These people have chronically accessible standards. The former will almost always use personal standards and, when they experience dissonance, it will almost always be idiographic. The latter will almost always use normative standards and, when they experience dissonance, it will almost always be of the nomothetic variety and their self-concept plays no role.

Reducing dissonance with the Self-Standards Model

When dissonance is aroused, the fun begins in figuring out the best way to reduce it. As in the prior models, we see the experience of dissonance as an unpleasant tension that must be reduced. As in the New Look model, when people make the attribution that their arousal is due to their having produced aversive consequences, they are driven to reduce it. But by considering how people integrate their unique, personal expectations and ideas they have about themselves, we not only see additional routes to creating the dissonance arousal, but also additional avenues that can assist or hinder its reduction. Figure 5.6 presents a schematic of the possibilities.

Once dissonance is aroused, either nomethetically or idiographically, the reduction again depends on accessible cognitions. Consider Path 1 in Figure 5.6. This is the path that is typically followed in most of the classic experiments we have discussed in this book. After dissonance was aroused, people went straight to the task of reducing the dissonance. Most typically, their dissonance motivation was reduced by justifying their behavior. They

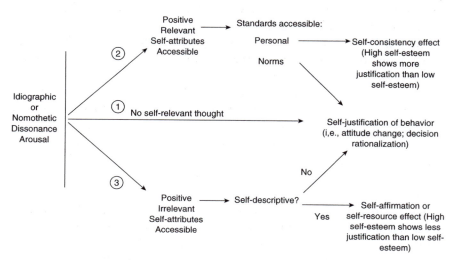

Figure 5.6 The Self-Standard Model of dissonance arousal (2)
Source: Stone and Cooper (2001)

changed attitudes, justified their choices, and rationalized their expenditure of effort to render the consequences of their behavior non-aversive. Paths 2 and 3 are more special cases and incorporate what we have learned from the theories of self-consistency and self-affirmation. While in the throes of dissonance, suppose a person's self-concept is made accessible by having her think about her positive self-attributes. She can remind herself that she is a good person, honest, moral, and generous to a fault. How will that affect dissonance? Recall that self-consistency theory considers positive self-attributes to be a set of high expectations that exacerbates dissonance. If you think of how you are usually an honest and moral person, then, for example, having duped a fellow student is particularly outrageous and leads to even more dissonance. For self-affirmation theory, these positive attributes are a resource that a person can focus on to restore self-system integrity, thereby reducing dissonance.

Our position is that it all depends on the standard of judgment being used. If the standard of judgment was normative, then the attributes that you now marshal in support of yourself play no role. They do nothing to relieve a cognitive dissonance that was not based on personal standards in the first place. On the other hand, if the dissonance was based on personal standards, then thinking about your own personal characteristics will matter. But how will it matter? Recall the studies I presented earlier in this chapter by J. Aronson et al. (1995) and Blanton et al. (1997), in which people wrote counterattitudinal essays that implied they were not compassionate. Based on the results of that research, the SSM predicts the effect of marshaling positive self-attributes is completely determined by whether the attributes are *relevant* or *irrelevant* to the unwanted consequence you produced. Recall that in those studies, people who had had their dissonance aroused by writing uncompassionate essays did not want to think about evidence that they were indeed compassionate people. They did not want to see that they had a high degree of the particular positive attribute that had been compromised by their essays. Not only did they not want to see the evidence, but when they were forced to do so, it increased rather than decreased their dissonance. For that reason, we proposed that positive self-attributes that are made accessible and that are *relevant* to the aversive outcome of behavior increase dissonance as self-consistency theory predicts.

The positive personal qualities that decrease dissonance are those that are accessible and *irrelevant* to the aspect of self that was compromised by the attitude-inconsistent behavior. The predictions of self-affirmation theory are most likely to occur when people think about good qualities that are not relevant to their behavior. The participants who wrote counterattitudinal essays in the study by Blanton et al. (1997) felt better, experienced less tension, and found less of a need to change their attitudes, if they were told how creative they were. Since their high creativity was not related to their uncompassionate essay, it worked along the third path to dissonance reduction, as expressed in Figure 5.6.

A key question: Is there a default?

Thus far, in the SSM, we have talked about the paths to dissonance arousal and dissonance reduction as a function of which standards of judgment are made accessible. The accessibility of normative standards brings about dissonance independent of the self-concept whereas dissonance is affected by self-concept considerations if personal standards are accessible. When people seek to reduce their dissonance, self-esteem becomes important if personal standards have been made accessible. The standard that is used as the measuring stick is a matter of situational or chronic accessibility.

Can we determine which path will be followed if there is no situational cue that makes the normative or the personal standard particularly accessible and if a person is near the middle of the normal continuum of chronic accessibility? What standard do people typically use?

The SSM (Stone and Cooper, 2001) did not specifically deal with this question. I think, though, that people usually measure their behavioral outcomes by the measuring stick of the normative standard. I think that when people commit behavioral acts, they typically judge their behavior against shared community values. We will see some tentative support for this proposition in research that will be described presently.

Research on the Self-Standards Model I: priming personal and normative standards of judgment

Let us now look at a few studies that support the major propositions of the Self-Standards Model of dissonance. The first study systematically varied the standards that were accessible to people prior to their writing a counterattitudinal essay (Weaver and Cooper, 2002). It was our first attempt to show that when personal standards were easy to bring to mind, the self-esteem of the essay writer could play a role in the arousal of dissonance. However, if normative standards were accessed instead, then self-esteem would not make any difference for the arousal of dissonance.

Participants had their self-esteem measured earlier in the semester by use of a scale developed by Rosenberg (1965). When they arrived at our study, we told them we had two projects for them to complete. The first was a 'cognitive task' in which the participants were to try to unscramble a set of words and to make a sentence from all but one of the words provided. Unbeknownst to the participants, the real purpose of the scrambled words task was to prime the standards that we hoped the subjects would use later on after they completed a counterattitudinal essay task. For half of the participants, the words were relevant to norms, consensus, and society. A sample trial for subjects in this condition would ask them to use the words *follow, should, people, cat, standards*, and *ethical*. From these words, a participant could make the sentence, 'people should follow ethical standards.' The other half of the participants saw trials like the following: *things, many, unique, chair, make*, and *me*, from which they could make the sentence, 'many things make me unique.' In this way, participants had their personal standards primed and were more likely to use a personal standard to evaluate their behavior. But this gets us ahead of our story.

After completing the scrambled word task, the participants were taken to another room where they were asked or told to write an essay for a Dean's committee on our (now familiar) issue of opposing additional funding for handicapped services. The essay was counterattitudinal, had the consequence of potentially convincing the Dean to effect an unwanted policy, and also called into question the integrity and morality of the participant for agreeing. We predicted that if normative standards were accessible and likely to be used as the standard for assessing the behavior, the consequence of the essay would lead to dissonance arousal and attitude change. According to the SSM, and contrary to the predictions of any of the self-theories, self-esteem was not expected to make a difference for these participants. Once the meaning of behavior is inferred by comparison with normative standards, aspects of self neither diminish nor enhance the dissonance. On the other hand, when personal standards are accessible and more likely to be used as the standard of judgment, then self-esteem will moderate dissonance.

Figure 5.7 shows the results of the study. A low-choice control condition shows people's general attitudes toward the reduction of funding for handicapped services. As predicted, in the condition in which normative standards were primed, there was no significant difference between the attitudes of high and low self-esteem participants. Relative to the low-choice control group, the typical prediction of dissonance theory was confirmed: people changed their attitudes toward handicapped funding. The level of self-esteem made no difference. However, when personal standards were primed, then self-esteem did make a difference. As predicted, participants who had high self-esteem were apparently able to use their self-esteem as a resource to protect themselves against the experience of dissonance.

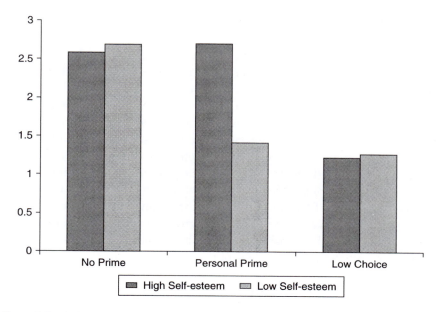

Figure 5.7   Attitudes regarding handicapped facilities as a function of primed standards, level of self-esteem, and choice

It is also interesting to look at the bars at the left side of Figure 5.7. In this condition, participants wrote their counterattitudinal essay without priming any standard. Participants changed their attitude regardless of their level of self-esteem. This is why I suggest that the normative standard is the default comparison. Without making personal standards particularly accessible through a situational intervention (e.g., by priming), people compare the outcome of their behavior against a normative standard and the self does not moderate cognitive dissonance.

These findings are compatible with data reported by Stone (1999). Using the methodology of the free-choice paradigm, Stone asked high and low self-esteem students to make a choice between two music albums. Half of the students were primed to make their personal standards accessible and half were primed to make their normative standards accessible. Stone found that participants in the normative prime condition confirmed the disso-nance theory prediction and spread apart the decision alternatives, regard-less of their level of self-esteem. Self-esteem only moderated the level of dissonance if personal standards were specifically made accessible by the priming procedure. Then and only then did dissonance differ as a function of their level of self-esteem.

THE SELF-STANDARDS MODEL

Research on Self Standards II: The relevance of self-attributes

In the SSM, we predicted that after dissonance is aroused, its reduction can be moderated by aspects of a person's self-esteem – if and only if a person's self-concept were made accessible through an intervention such as priming. Both idiographic and normative dissonance, once aroused, can be affected by a person's level of self-esteem provided it is made accessible. Moreover, the direction of the effect will be diametrically different depending on whether the self-attributes that a person brings to mind are relevant or irrelevant to the aspect of self that was compromised by the behavior.

Stone and Cooper (2003) had students at the University of Arizona write a counterattitudinal essay on the handicapped funding issue under conditions of low or high choice. Presumably, the high-choice subjects experienced dissonance from writing their essay. Some of the high-choice participants were then given a scrambled word priming task to solve which made them think about their particular personal attributes. For one group of participants, positive attributes that were highly relevant to the essay they had written were made accessible. Like the subjects in the Blanton et al. (1997) and J. Aronson et al. (1995) research, these subjects were primed to think of attributes such as compassion, thoughtfulness, and kindness. Another group was primed to think about other important attributes – but ones that were not relevant to their uncompassionate essays. Self-concepts such as creativity, intelligence, and imagination were primed. In a third group, neutral words primed some unimportant aspects of personality: 'I try to be quiet' is an example of a neutral concept.

The predictions of the study were that, when self-attributes were primed that were relevant to the behavior the participants had committed, then the self-concept would function as an expectancy: the higher the self-esteem, the greater would be the dissonance and the more attitude change that would occur. Priming a person's compassion and kindness would make the participants who had higher expectations about their compassion (i.e., those with high self-esteem) experience more dissonance as a function of their counterattitudinal essay. By contrast, when the attributes were irrelevant – when the participant simply thought about his or her intelligence and creativity, then the moderation would operate in the other direction. People with higher self-esteem could use their self-esteem as a resource to buttress themselves (or, possibly, to distract themselves) from the experience of dissonance. Figure 5.8 shows that this is exactly what happened.

Once again, it is interesting to look at the left-hand bars of Figure 5.8. When neutral, unimportant attributes like 'quietness' were primed, self-esteem did not moderate cognitive dissonance at all. This is another illustration of how, in the absence of making important self-attributes accessible, individual differences in self-esteem play no role in dissonance.

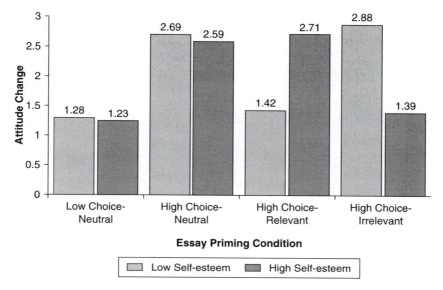

Figure 5.8   Interactions between self-esteem and priming on dissonance magnitude
Source: Stone and Cooper (2003)

Conclusions about the role of self

The Self-Standards Model of dissonance (Stone and Cooper, 2001) allows us to continue the metamorphosis of dissonance theory. It expands on the New Look model (Cooper and Fazio, 1984) which suggested a radically different motivational basis for dissonance from the one Festinger had introduced in 1957. We continue to believe that dissonance is created by believing that you have created an aversive event. However, we now have a better understanding of how and when the important concept of the self plays a role in dissonance. The seminal contributions on the role of self contributed by Steele (1988) and by Aronson (1968; 1992) have led us to see that the self is a potential standard of judgment that we use to assess whether a behavioral consequence is aversive or not. Some people are predisposed to rely on personal standards as their measuring stick and some are predisposed to rely on normative standards. Most often, the standard that people use is determined by what is primed by the social situation that provoked the dissonance.

Although the SSM delineates the occasions that dissonance is affected by the self-concept and outlines the processes by which that occurs, research has nonetheless found that the playing field is not even. It seems to be tilted in the direction of reliance on the normative standard. It is more typical for dissonance to occur nomothetically. That is, people are inclined to measure the outcome of their behavior against commonly and consensually agreed benchmarks for what constitutes unwanted behavior. In the wake of deciding that their behavior was indeed an unwanted event that contradicted the culturally shared norms, dissonance occurs and is reduced by changing attitudes to render the consequence non-aversive. Self-esteem affects dissonance, and is an important part of the process, but mainly in those special circumstances in which thoughts about self have become particularly accessible and salient.

6

VICARIOUS COGNITIVE DISSONANCE

Experiencing Dissonance
Through the Actions of Another

In this chapter, we will begin an excursion through some newer issues in dissonance research. They are not as fully woven into the fabric of dissonance development and controversy as the issues presented in the prior chapters. These issues hold considerable potential for the further development of theory and research in dissonance. The first of these is a phenomenon known as *vicarious cognitive dissonance* (Cooper and Hogg, 2007; Norton, Monin, Cooper and Hogg, 2003).

Can people experience cognitive dissonance by observing *other people* act inconsistently with their own attitudes? If so, it raises the possibility that cognitive dissonance affects us in our daily lives more than we have previously believed. We already know that dissonance is pervasive, because it affects us every time *we* make a choice and every time we engage in effort to achieve a goal. Imagine, though, if dissonance also occurred when *other people* made choices or when others acted in a way that brought about an aversive event. If this happened, it would multiply the occasions in which we experienced, and needed to reduce, dissonance.

Current research tells us that it does happen, at least under certain conditions. This chapter will present the evidence for the existence of a state called vicarious cognitive dissonance, defined as experiencing dissonance through the actions of another person. We will review the evidence and examine the conditions that facilitate and limit its occurrence. In Chapter 7 we will revisit vicarious dissonance to understand how dissonance is experienced in other cultures. Then, in Chapter 8, we will make use of the phenomenon of vicarious dissonance to accomplish behavioral change that can have a positive bearing on people's health.

Cognitive dissonance and the social group

Vicarious cognitive dissonance is based on common group membership between you and a particular target person. For the purpose of explaining how and when vicarious dissonance occurs, allow me to make you a member of the British Labour Party. Imagine that you are attending a gathering of civic leaders at a London hotel. The Labour MP goes to the platform to answer questions from the audience. He is asked about his view on the privatization of industry and you cannot believe you heard his answer correctly. You believe you heard him say he was in favor of it, a position with which you, he, and the Labour Party disagree. You understand that he was drawn into the position by relentless questioning from Conservative members of the audience. Nonetheless, he not only took the Conservative position, but he even agreed that he would write a letter to that effect for publication in the newspaper. As a left-leaning member of the Labour Party, you know your MP has always been for more social control and government ownership. So are you. But you just heard him disagree with a position that was the essence of his and your membership in the Labour Party. How does it make you feel?

You fidget in your chair. You experience a number of emotions. You imagine how uncomfortable the MP must feel at the moment, having been nudged into a position with which you know he disagrees. You may also be angry that he took the bait and ended up advocating the position of the other party. However, you feel close to your MP and realize he is a good party member, just as you are. Now you feel tense, uneasy, and uncomfortable, too. In this scenario, you would be experiencing vicarious cognitive dissonance.

Everything we have written thus far about cognitive dissonance would lead us to predict that your Labour parliamentarian friend will experience dissonance arousal. He was responsible for his behaviour, could foresee the aversive consequence it would have, and nonetheless answered the question in a Conservative and counterattitudinal manner. The MP would experience arousal and would be quite likely to change his attitude about privatization, or find some other cognition to change, in order to reduce his discomfort. The new question is, what about you, the observer? How will you feel and what will you do when witnessing the MP's dilemma?

We will present a view of this dilemma that suggests that the observer, too, will experience an unpleasant tension state and the observer, just like the actor, will be motivated to change his or her attitude. Witnessing the counterattitudinal behavior can lead to attitude change to reduce vicarious cognitive dissonance.

Social identity creates common bonds

Observers are more likely to share in the emotions of people to whom they feel close. A family member might feel the pain or joy or embarrassment of another family member. A team member might experience the frustration of his teammate's missing a goal in the soccer match or the exhilaration of a late inning home run in the baseball game. Relationships in which people feel closely identified with one another help to activate the empathic transmission of emotions.

One powerful reason that causes people to feel close to one another is common membership in important social groups. When we share group membership with someone, we take on part of that person's identity and they take part of ours. We are connected by common membership and common fate. It is not just that we get to wear the same team hats or carry similar membership cards. Our membership in social groups affects our very identity as human beings and puts us in unison with others who share that identity.

The theory of social identity and social categorization

One of the fundamental features of human social experience is the categorization of people into groups. There are groups we are in and groups we are not in. Ours is the in-group while the other is the out-group. Decades of research in social identity and social categorization show that we identify with our in-groups and, amongst other behaviors, favor in-group members to the detriment of out-group members. This occurs whether the groups are formal or informal, and whether they are long lasting or short-lived. Sports teams can provide an illustration of what I mean by formal and informal groups. Consider the New York Football Giants, a team playing in the National Football League. Players on the New York Giants Football team are official. They have contracts and uniforms (especially contracts!). They are easy to identify when they don their uniforms and know that they are formally members of the team. Others of us are football fans. We have no formal membership, no card, no uniform. Yet, as an ardent fan of the New York Giants, I know I am a group member and, on any given Sunday in the Fall, I feel very close to my compatriots in New York and elsewhere who suffer or glow with me as the game unfolds.

According to social identity theory (Tajfel, 1982), people gain much of their personal identity from their group membership. Our evaluation of ourselves comes partly from our unique personal experiences and partly from the experiences in the groups to which we belong. And just as most of us are motivated to think of ourselves as good and competent individuals, we are also motivated to see our groups in a favorable light as well. The group can be formal or informal, and it can have a long or a short duration. Whenever people are classified into groups and their group is made salient, they will be motivated to favor their in-group to the detriment of an out-group.

Tajfel and his colleagues conducted several studies that showed that people's in-group favoritism occurred even when the group was informally created on the most minimal pretence that the experimenters could devise. In one of their classic experiments, participants were shown a massive array of dots on a sheet of paper. They were instructed to estimate the number of dots. They were then told that people could usually be relied on to overestimate or underestimate the number of stimuli they perceive (such as dots on a page). Some were told that they had overestimated the dots; others were told they had underestimated.

Tajfel and his colleagues found that people who were told that they were overestimators preferred others who were overestimators; underestimators preferred other underestimators. In other words, people liked their in-group members better than they liked out-group members. When given an opportunity to divide resources between overestimators and underestimators, people gave more of the resources to members of their in-group. The basis for dividing people into in-groups and out-groups had been completely bogus trivial; nonetheless, their alleged tendency to overestimate or underestimate dots led to in-group favoritism and out-group derogation.

Another aspect of social identity is that people tend to see their group as more similar to a prototypical member of the group than they really are. People's individuality becomes blurred and members are seen to have more of the qualities of the group prototype. This causes group members to see themselves as fused with other members of the group. Their preferences, values, attitudes, and emotions are perceived to be more similar to each other. And so, each individual member of the group feels identified with the other members; their separate identities, attitudes, and values become less individualized as their experiences meld.

We all have multiple identities. This is not to suggest we are schizophrenic, but rather to say that sometimes we think of ourselves as unique individuals and, at other times, we think of ourselves as members of a group. In addition, we are all members of many overlapping groups. Our tendency to think in terms of social categories and to feel at one with the members of our group depends on at least two factors. The first is whether a particular group is salient in our thinking at a particular time; the second is the degree to which we feel attached to, or identify with, a particular group. It is particularly when a group with which we identify becomes salient in our thinking that we fuse with the members of the group and use the group as a source of our own identity.

For example, although I may be a New York Giants football fan, I do not normally think of that group in my daily life. On several Sundays in the Fall, however, I become extremely aware of my group identity. I would think of the other fans who are also watching the Giants. Even though I do not know any of them, I would have a tendency to think that they are very much like me and I am very much like them. I will feel their pain if we lose; I will feel their joy when we win. The degree of salience of the group and the degree to which I identify as a group member are key factors in social identity.

Social identity meets cognitive dissonance

When I observe someone acting to produce an aversive outcome, I may very well feel his tension and discomfort. This will happen to me if

1 he and I share a social identity caused by our belonging to the same social group;
2 if the group is salient to me at the moment; and
3 if I am attracted to the group.

I may feel his pain, experience his discomfort, and be motivated by his tension. Just like that group member, I may be motivated to change my attitudes and cognitions. The experience of the dissonance is vicarious, because it was not *my* behavior that produced an unwanted outcome. Indeed, I haven't 'behaved' at all. However, my witnessing a fellow group member engaging in the behavior causes me to experience a vicarious emotion and will result in a change of cognition to deal with the tension. This is what is known as vicarious cognitive dissonance. That is why, if you were a member of the British Labour Party in the scenario I presented earlier in the chapter, you would experience dissonance vicariously and would be motivated to change cognitions in order to reduce it.

Diane Mackie and Eliot Smith (1998) make a similar point from the perspective of what they call intergroup emotions theory. They say, 'when membership in a group is salient, events that happen to fellow group members, even if not directly to the self, can trigger emotional reactions' (p. xx).

In-groups, out-groups, and vicarious dissonance

Let's examine some data from a research paradigm crafted to study vicarious dissonance in the controlled environment of the laboratory (Norton et al. 2003). We created a story that would permit Princeton University students to witness a student from their own group, or from another group, making a decision to write an essay that could lead to adverse consequences at Princeton.

We created an intriguingly complicated cover story designed to allow students to overhear a group member advocate a position with which the group member disagreed. All Princeton University freshmen and sophomores are assigned at random to one of five residential colleges. Each student lives and eats in one of the colleges and each college has its own social and academic activities. We used the existence of the several colleges to manipulate whether participants in our study believed they were witnessing an interaction with a student from his or her own college (in-group member) or from a different college (out-group member).

Participants arrived for a study in 'linguistic subcultures' in groups of two, although they were taken to separate rooms, each equipped with two-way mirrors. We told them that the purpose of the study was to investigate the way that group cultures create slight, but measurable, differences in speaking patterns. For example, we know that someone living in Arkansas develops a different pattern of English speech than someone living in New York. The experimenter continued by explaining that the purpose of the current study was to see if these speech patterns occur in microcosms – i.e., small groups within a larger context. We told the students that, in this study, we wanted to see if the speech patterns of students in one residential college at Princeton University differed from the speech patterns at another college, and whether we can measure them. We explained that one of the two students, selected at random, was going to write and then deliver a speech on a given topic and the other student was going to listen carefully and then respond to several questions about the speaker's pattern of speech.

In this way, students had a credible, although completely fabricated, story that allowed them to overhear a speaker's decision to write a speech on a controversial topic. Each participant was told that, by the luck of a random draw, he or she was assigned to rate the speech, while the student in the other room was assigned to give the speech. The procedure allowed us to make the student's residential college group salient and manipulate systematically whether the speaker's residential college group was the same (in-group) or different (out-group) from the participant's. The participant was asked which residential college he or she lived in, and then was told that the other participant was from the same or a different college. The lights were briefly turned on so that the participants could see that there genuinely was another student in the room behind the two-way mirror, but at a sufficiently low illumination that the student's identity could not be discerned.

The experimenter left the room, ostensibly to instruct the other participant about the speech he or she was to make. During the intervening period, participants filled out various measures, including measures of how much they liked and felt identified with their residential college. In a few minutes, the experimenter returned with a tape recording of the completed speech. On the tape, the participant heard the experimenter explain the 'linguistic subculture' story to the other student. The experimenter also explained that he was fortunate to be able to combine two studies into one. The Dean's office had asked for a study trying to assess student opinion about the possibility of raising tuition fees by a more than typical amount. Similar to the cover story developed by Linder et al. (1967), the experimenter asked the student to write a strong and forceful speech advocating a spike in tuition fees. He explained that this would be the speech that the other subject (i.e., the real participant) would rate for its linguistic features and that it would then be sent on to the Dean's office.

At the conclusion of the speech, the experimenter asked the participant to fill out a few measures about his own feelings and reactions prior to rating the communication itself. The measure contained questions about the participant's feelings and his or her attitudes toward the question of whether tuition fees should be increased.

Our prediction for this study was that people who heard an in-group member express counterattitudinal opinions would feel dissonance vicariously and would change their attitudes in the direction of the communication. We did not expect this to occur if the speaker was an out-group member. Moreover, we expected the effect to be moderated by the level of a student's identification. The more the student felt close to, and identified with, his or her group, the greater should be the vicarious dissonance and the more attitudes should change.

Figure 6.1 shows the results of this study. The difference in the slope of the regression lines tells us that when the speaker was a member of the in-group, stronger identification with the group led to more attitude change. For out-group members, the effect was reversed. As predicted, people who were strongly identified with their residential college changed their attitude in the direction of the speech when the speaker was an in-group member but not when he or she was a member of a different college. We concluded from this study that people are likely to change their attitude from someone else's counterattitudinal behavior, but only when the behavior is from an in-group member and only when the individual feels strongly identified with the in-group. Apparently, social identity matters.

Does it quack like the proverbial duck?

In order to label what we found in our first study as dissonance, the data should have the properties usually associated with dissonance. There is a saying that, 'If it looks like a duck, and quacks like a duck, then it's a duck.' Is the vicarious dissonance effect really dissonance? If so, it should parallel the conditions that we know are essentially important for the arousal of personal dissonance. For example, if we make an attitude-discrepant statement but were forced to do it, the absence of responsibility would eliminate dissonance. If we make a speech that has no foreseeable unwanted consequences, then we would not experience dissonance. Does vicarious dissonance work in the same way? That is, if we witness a group member make a counterattitudinal speech but the member was required to make it and/or was certain that no adverse consequence would occur, then is our vicarious dissonance eliminated?

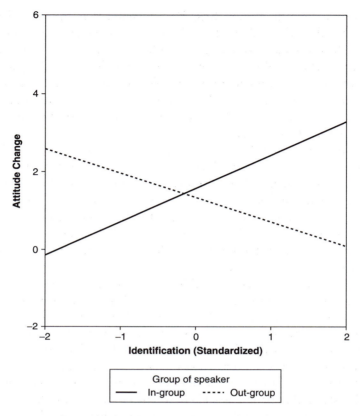

Figure 6.1   Attitude change based on vicarious dissonance: in-group vs. out-group speaker
Source: Norton, Monin, Cooper, and Hogg (2003), Study 1

I will describe another study that examined these questions (Norton et al., 2003, study 3). We assessed the hypothesis that vicarious dissonance occurs when a person witnesses a fellow group member act in a way that can lead to potentially aversive consequences and observes that the behavior was committed as an apparent act of free choice. Of course, as in the first experiment, we predicted that this would only occur if the group member who witnesses the behavior is highly attracted to the group.

Another facet of this research was to close some alternative explanations of the first vicarious dissonance study. It is certainly possible that the speech that the fellow group member allegedly made that led to the data of Figure 6.1 actually had persuasive value. And it is also possible that participants who thought the speech was made by a member of their own residential college and who liked their residential college paid more attention, and were more persuaded. Indeed, Mackie, Worth and Asuncicn (1990) have shown that people attend more carefully to the arguments of in-group members than out-group members when reading or listening to a persuasive message. Therefore, a few changes were made in the procedure of the experiment to be more certain that the vicarious experience of dissonance was responsible for the results.

Once again, participants came to the laboratory, allegedly with another student from their university. This time, the study was conducted in Australia and the in-group was the University of Queensland. Students' level of identification and liking for the University were measured. As in the original study, the students believed they were participating in a 'linguistic subculture' study assessing differences in speaking patterns between students at the University of Queensland compared to students from other universities in the state of Queensland. The participant always believed that the other student was a fellow student at the University of Queensland.

As before, the participant was always selected as the student who would hear the speech and the 'other student' was the one who would make the speech. All 'conversations' occurred via written communication on computer screens. The real participant believed that he or she was witnessing the written correspondence between the 'other University of Queensland student' and the experimenter. The experimenter explained that the topic of the talk was the imposition of upfront fees at the university. This was a very unpopular idea among students. It had been the policy of the Australian government to collect tuition fees for students at public universities after the completion of the degree. The new proposal called for fees to be paid upfront, prior to the education. It violated decades of tradition of public expenditures for higher education and was anathema to most students. It made for a very suitable issue for our study. The participant heard the experimenter tell the 'other student' that he was to write a strong and forceful essay advocating the collection of upfront fees at the University of Queensland. The 'other subject' always made it clear that he or she was strongly against the collection of such fees; the experimenter always made it clear that the direction of the remarks was to be in favor of the upfront fees.

Half of the participants heard the fellow student given freedom to decline to write the speech. The other half heard the experimenter make it clear that there was no choice. Half of the students witnessed the experimenter assure the fellow student that the speech would only be used for its linguistic features, and would then be destroyed (no consequences); the other half discovered that the speech was going to be sent to the Dean who needed them to craft his own policy statement about the upfront fees issue (a potentially negative consequence).

We expected that vicarious dissonance would be experienced by students who liked their in-group – i.e., liked being at, and felt attached to the University of Queensland. We predicted that they would be the ones most likely to experience vicarious dissonance and most likely to change their attitudes in the wake of witnessing another UQ student act in a

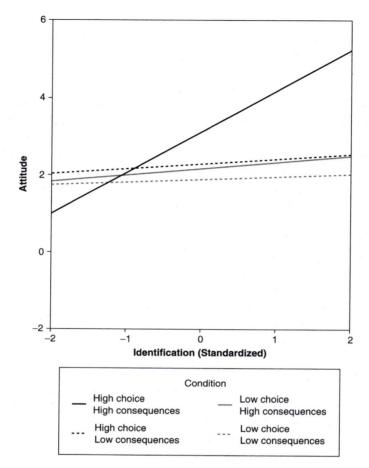

Figure 6.2 Vicarious dissonance: attitudes toward upfront fees as a function of choice, consequence, and group identification

Source: Norton, Monin, Cooper, and Hogg (2003), Study 3

counterattitudinal fashion. However, this prediction is qualified by confining it to those conditions in which, as the Self-Standard and New Look models of dissonance predict, the speech writer was responsible for the potential aversive consequences of his behaviour.

Figure 6.2 shows the mean attitude toward upfront tuition fees for all of the conditions in the study (Norton et al., 2003, study 3). At the left of Figure 6.2, attitudes are depicted for students who did not feel attached to their in-group. In the absence of the attachment, none of the conditions caused attitudes to change in the direction of the speech. However, on the right side of Figure 6.2 are the attitudes of students who did feel attached and identified to the university. You can see that the condition that differs from all other conditions in the study is the condition in which participants observed a fellow group member agree to make the counterattitudinal statement (1) freely and (2) with knowledge that it would be sent to the Dean. That is precisely the condition in which an individual would be expected to experience personal dissonance. Apparently, then, vicarious dissonance 'quacks like the duck' of personal dissonance. As long as people are highly identified with their group, they changed their attitudes when the group member acted freely and with knowledge of foreseeable aversive consequences.

The experience of vicarious dissonance

We know that personal dissonance is experienced as tension and has measurable physiological indicants of stress (Croyle and Cooper, 1983; Losch and Caciopo, 1990). People report feeling tense, bothered, and uncomfortable (Elliot and Devine, 1994). What do they report when observing someone else behave inconsistently?

We asked our student participants about their emotional state after they saw their fellow student agree to write the essay, and we asked it in a number of ways. We asked them how tense, bothered, and uncomfortable they were at that moment. They reported no particular degree of tension or discomfort. The experimental conditions did not differ from each other nor did discomfort correlate with attitudes in any of the conditions. However, when we questioned them about their *vicarious affect* by asking *how they thought they would feel* if they were in the speechwriter's position, the participants responded in a very interesting way.

The results of the vicarious affect measure are presented in Figure 6.3. You can see that the vicarious affect results parallel the attitude results in Figure 6.2. Participants said that if they were in the speechwriter's position, they would experience a high degree of discomfort in the condition in which they felt highly attached to their group, and their fellow group member wrote freely with the possibility of producing aversive consequences.

We also examined the functional question of what is accomplished by attitude change in vicarious dissonance. A fascinating component of the study by Elliot and Devine (1989) that was reported in Chapter 3 was that the investigators systematically varied the order in which they assessed the dependent variables of affect and attitudes in a personal dissonance experiment. Sometimes they collected the attitude data first; sometimes the affect reports were collected first. They found that when attitudes were assessed first, the reports of discomfort and tension dropped. It seems that, by changing attitudes, there was no residual psychological discomfort. As Festinger (1957) would have predicted (but did not test) a half-century ago, changing attitudes has the effect of lowering the experience of discomfort.

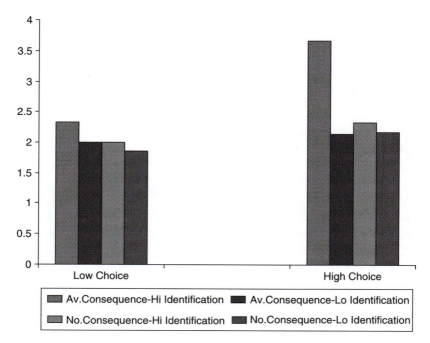

Figure 6.3 Vicarious Discomfort as a function of choice, consequence, and identification
Source: Adapted from Norton, Monin, Cooper and Hogg (2003)

In the Norton et al. (2003) study, we found that changing attitudes reduces vicarious discomfort in very much the same way. When attitudes were assessed before vicarious affect, there was no residual vicarious discomfort. The reports of vicarious discomfort shown in Figure 6.3 are exclusively for students whose vicarious discomfort was assessed first. When attitudes were assessed first, thus giving people the opportunity to change their attitudes as their way to reduce dissonance, vicarious discomfort disappeared. The vicarious discomfort of students in the high-dissonance condition (i.e., the highly identified students whose fellow student agreed to make a counterattitudinal statement with high choice and high consequences) was no greater than in any other condition of the experiment. This strongly suggests that changing attitudes to reduce vicarious dissonance is at the service of reducing vicarious discomfort. And it is apparently successful.

Vicarious dissonance and the prototype

In social identity theory, which we believe is at the root of the experience of vicarious dissonance, group members feel a unity with prototypical members of their group. The Sunday football fan who cheers for the New York

Giants is more likely to feel identified with a prototypical member – the person who represents the group norm in attitudes and behavior. As one of those fans, I'm not likely to feel as fused with the group member who only watches one game per year as the fan who, like me, watches almost every game. Similarly, I am unlikely to feel highly identified with the few fans on the rabid, lunatic fringe who paint their bodies blue and red and attend football games shirtless in January. My intersubjectivity – that is, my loosening of personal identity in favour of the group and my fusing with my fellow group members – is more likely to occur in the presence of the prototypical member (Hogg, 2001).

If vicarious dissonance occurs because of social identity and intersubjectivity, then it should occur more in the presence of a prototypical group member and less for a member who is on the fringe of the group. It should also occur more if the individual who is witnessing the attitude-discrepant behavior believes that he or she is a prototypical member of the group.

We conducted another study at the University of Queensland, using a procedure similar to the studies I described above (Hogg and Cooper, 2006). Students heard a fellow Queensland student agree to make a statement about upfront fees under conditions of high- or low-decision freedom. In this study, the consequences were always set high – that is, the written speeches were to be sent to the Dean. What we varied was the presumed prototypicality of the speaker and the participant. At the beginning of the experimental session, before the linguistic subculture cover story was explained, all of the participants filled out an extensive battery of questions. The battery included the now-familiar questionnaire that assessed how much the students liked and felt identified with their group. The battery also included scales that inquired about their attitudes, behaviors, and values. We never actually looked at the answers to these questions; its purpose was to make credible what was about to happen.

The linguistic subculture cover story was explained and the participant understood that he was going to be rating the speech given by a fellow University of Queensland student. Prior to learning anything about the topic of the speech or the choice and consequence conditions, the experimenter informed the participant and his partner that the results of the values, attitudes, and behavior questionnaire had been analyzed and the data were now entered into the larger data file that comprised all of the students at the University of Queensland who had taken the test. The experimenter continued that she knew that most people wanted to know their results. She told them that she was prepared to give them an analysis of where their profiles were in the context of all of the other UQ students.

The experimenter showed them a scatterplot graph. She explained that each dot represented a student's score. Anyone with a dot near the center of the array was a very typical UQ student. In order to emphasize this point, the student was shown a computer screen with a red circle drawn tightly in the center (see Figure 6.4a). People with scores within the center could consider themselves typical; people with scores around the fringe (see Figure 6.4b) could consider themselves as not very typical of their group. Each participant was then shown his or her score and the score of the alleged other student (the speechwriter). What was systematically varied was whether the speechwriter and the partner were placed in the center of the circle and were therefore prototypical or placed at the fringe of the circle and therefore non-prototypical. The procedure of the study then continued in a similar fashion to the other vicarious dissonance studies. The group member agreed to make a counterattitudinal speech favoring upfront fees under conditions of high-choice and high-potential aversive consequences. The major dependent variable was the participants' attitudes about upfront fees. Under what conditions did they change their attitudes?

The results, shown in Figure 6.5, again show that compared to a low-choice control condition, subjects changed their attitudes toward upfront fees, but especially when they believed that they, and the fellow group member, were both prototypical members of the group. In that circumstance, the subject – having been shown that he is a prototypical group member – seemed to identify more closely with his prototypical partner and experienced vicarious dissonance.

We also found that the degree of identification with the group moderated the results, as it had in the previous study. For all but one condition, the attitudinal effect of vicarious dissonance was greater for people who felt identified with the university group than by those who did not.

The one interesting exception to that finding was for students who found that they and the speaker were at the periphery of the student group *and* who did not feel attached to their group on the individual difference measure of group attachment. These subjects also experienced dissonance when the speaker agreed to write the counterattitudinal essay. In a way, this group of participants helps make the case for a social identity explanation of vicarious dissonance. It is as though the combination of disaffection established the conditions for a small and cohesive dyad. The individual participant did not care for his group; indeed, the values/behavior feedback seemed to confirm that the participant was at the periphery. He or she also learns that the partner is at the periphery. The participant probably assumed that the speaker, like the participant, was disaffected by his university. After all, the subject's score at the periphery was consistent with his or her feeling about the university. The subject then reasons that the very same disaffection is true of the partner. It's a perfect little group. As a result, the participant feels close to his new group member, with the group being 'those people who do not like the university.' Vicarious dissonance then became greater as the participant's identity fused with the partner, and attitude change ensued.

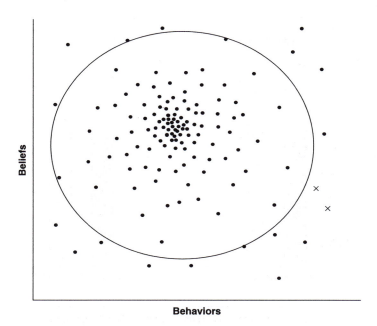

Figure 6.4a   Information shown to participants to have them believe they were non-prototypical University of Queensland students

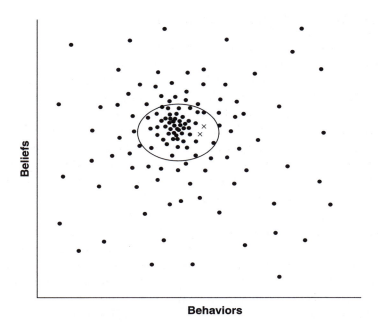

Figure 6.4b   Information shown to participants to have them believe they were prototypical University of Queensland students

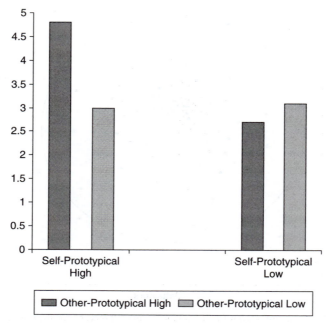

Figure 6.5   Effect of self and other prototypicality on attitude change

What vicarious dissonance is and is not

Vicarious dissonance is an intriguing phenomenon, yet the reasons that underlie it are not as transparent as in personal dissonance. Research in this area is in its infancy, and only a little is known about its causes, its limits, and its mediators. I have been describing vicarious dissonance as a group-based phenomenon that has its roots in the social identity among group members. Research supports this idea, but questions arise. Is there anything else that could lead to vicarious dissonance? One possibility is that friendship or other form of close relationship can produce the same effect. If a friend of mine behaves in an attitude-discrepant way with all of the ingredients that usually lead to dissonance, will I experience dissonance vicariously? Or suppose it is a relative or a romantic partner? One could argue that any dyad is a group, so that two friends are in a friendship dyad, two lovers are in a romantic dyad, and so forth. However, there seems to be a difference worth exploring between membership in a group such as football fans, university students, and residential colleges compared to a friendship between two individuals who share no common memberships.

Another way of thinking about the causes of vicarious dissonance is that it is the expression of people's ability to show empathy for another. Empathy is an individual's ability to feel and intuit the experiences of another (Davis,

1994). It is not based on social factors such as group membership. We all have the ability to do it; some of us more and some of us less. Various scales have been developed to assess individual differences in empathy. In some of our studies (Monin, Norton, Cooper and Hogg, 2004), we administered Davis's measure of empathy (Davis, 1983) and found that it did not correlate at all with the attitude measures of our vicarious dissonance studies. In a word, empathy did not predict the amount of vicarious dissonance.

An intriguing challenge for vicarious dissonance is the prospect of specifying the motivational basis for attitude change following an episode of vicarious dissonance. We know that after observing counterattitudinal behavior under the right circumstances, people report vicarious negative affect and they also change their attitudes. The more vicarious affect they acknowledge, the more they change their attitude. We also know from the studies by Norton et al. (2003) that once people change their attitudes following vicarious dissonance, they cease to report vicarious discomfort. Attitude change, I have noted previously, seems to be at the service of reducing the negative affect.

However, the reasons for the link in vicarious dissonance are not entirely transparent. In the New Look model of personal dissonance, it seemed reasonable that personal dissonance should be reduced when attitude change renders a consequence non-aversive. It's done, finished; there is no longer an aversive event to cause troubling and disquieting discomfort. However, in vicarious dissonance, the negative affect is something participants acknowledge only by indicating how they would feel if they were in the speaker's shoes. The participants have not acknowledged their own sense of arousal and discomfort. Moreover, one can ask what changing one's own attitude accomplishes if it was your group member arguing against his or her own position.

A possible resolution to these issues is that people feel they know what the group member is going to do after engaging in the counterattitudinal speech writing. Participants may reason that the group member will probably change his or her own attitudes and therefore the participants will switch, too, in order to conform to what the group member is likely to do. We looked for evidence for this approach in a study by Monin, Norton, Cooper, and Hogg (2004). Princeton University students experienced vicarious affect after watching a fellow student make an attitude-discrepant speech advocating the unpopular position that parents of university students should have unlimited access to students' health records. As in the previous research, we found evidence to support the arousal of vicarious affect and we found attitude change in the predicted conditions. However, in this study, we also asked what the participants thought the speaker's attitude was both before and after he wrote his essay supporting unlimited access. The results showed that the participants remembered correctly that the speaker was against the position prior to writing his speech. In fact, the more the subject believed the speaker was hostile to the position in the essay, the more vicarious attitude change the participants showed. And, when asked whether the speaker changed his or her attitude after having written the speech, the participants said, no. There was no systematic change reported by our participants in their belief about the speechmaker's new attitude. Apparently, conformity to the speaker's new position does not underlie the vicarious dissonance effect.

The other way to understand the motivational basis for attitude change in vicarious dissonance is to assume that the attitude change alleviates a tension-arousing dilemma *for the witness* rather than the witness trying to be sympathetic to the plight of the actor.

As background for this possibility, let me describe some of my own television habits. Some years ago, at the beginning of the Iraq War, I was watching a forum on television in which student leaders at various universities were discussing President Bush's decision to send troops to topple Saddam Hussein's government. When the student leader at my university spoke, she supported the sending of troops. I thought that position was discrepant from the attitudes of most students on campus and it made me uncomfortable to watch. How much easier it would have been if I had agreed with her. It struck me that changing my attitude based on the student's behavior would have created some greater degree of comfort for me. The situation is not entirely parallel, but the lesson from the example is that the shared social identity put pressure on me to find a way to alleviate my own predicament.

In vicarious dissonance, as in the television example, it is the group member who caused a potentially aversive event to occur. Because of your relationship with the actor, you feel as though you did it. You know, of course, that you are not really the person who brought about the event and, if asked, you know the difference. Still, it feels as though you were partially responsible for it, as you and the actor are fused together by a common social identity. You then take whatever steps you can take to make the action not as bad as it seems. You engage in changes of your least resistant cognitions to make the consequence non-aversive. It is non-aversive (for you) if the actor's arguments are actually more in line with your own private position. Consequently, you change your attitude in the direction of the actor's counterattitudinal remarks.

Vicarious dissonance broadens the scope of cognitive dissonance in our lives. We know it is rare that we advocate positions we do not believe, yet that is the experimental paradigm in which most dissonance phenomena have been studied. By dint of sheer numbers, it is less rare that people in our various social groups occasionally act in ways that are attitude discrepant and may lead to unwanted consequences. Similarly, when we expend effort or suffer embarrassment to achieve a goal, we are motivated to reduce dissonance, but that motivation will occur so much more frequently when we experience dissonance from the behavior of the members of our social groups.

7

CULTURE, RACE, AND COGNITIVE DISSONANCE

The group of faculty gathered around me was impressive. It was the day of my final oral exam for the PhD in Psychology. In a building still ingloriously called 'Building 9' at Duke University, I braced for questions about my doctoral thesis. I anxiously thought about my statistics. Did I really understand the analysis of variance? What did Festinger say in his final chapter of *A Theory of Cognitive Dissonance?*

Jack Brehm asked me the first question. He stared at me for a few seconds and asked, 'Do you think that sanitation men experience cognitive dissonance?' Nothing in my studying and cramming had prepared me for this question. Nor did I know what he meant. I was certain that Jack did not have an abiding interest in the sanitation department, yet I did not think his question was in jest. It has taken social psychology a long time to catch up with the conundrum that underscored his question. Social psychology considers itself to be the study of how most people react to social situations but it bases its conclusions on the responses of mostly young, predominantly white, middle-class students at colleges and universities. How, then, can we be certain of our ability to generalize our findings to that phantom collective called 'most people'?

Here is the experimental philosophy that everyone working with samples of participants knows. We conduct our research on a sample of participants typically drawn from the population of students at our universities, we look for differences based on our experimental manipulations, and then conduct our statistical analyses to see if the pattern of data we found in our samples is applicable to the population from which the sample is drawn. Technically, this permits us to generalize to the university population who were potentially available to participate in the study. We know that the metaphorical ice becomes thinner as we extend our conclusions to populations that we did not test. However, to restrict our conclusions in this way would seem highly self-defeating and unnecessary. If I collect data at my home institution from students at Princeton University, can I generalize my findings to students at neighboring Rutgers University? Can I generalize to students anywhere in New Jersey or the northeast? How about citizens of any age in New Jersey? Generally, we ignore these questions and assume that our findings have generality across artificial boundaries such as geographic region, socioeconomic status, and age.

Sometimes we are wrong. Gender, for example, was ignored for decades in social psychology research. We now know that gender frequently makes a difference. Boys and girls, men and women, often respond differently to social situations such that a conclusion based on one gender cannot automatically be generalized to the other. As an illustration, research on the impact of aggression in the media was based almost exclusively on the responses of boys to violent film episodes. Subsequent research showed that the responses of girls were not identical to those of boys. Researchers are much more careful in the current era to test for gender similarities and differences before reaching a general conclusion about how 'most people' respond to a social situation.

There has never been a single rule that tells researchers how and whether to restrict the conclusions of their studies. Generally, it seems wise to consider whether there is any logical reason to suspect that there will be differences in the populations we tested compared to populations we did not test in the phenomenon under study. We cannot test for every possible difference and be finished within a single lifetime. If one of my graduate students finds an interesting result working with Princeton students, I am not likely to ask him or her to replicate the study in Pennsylvania or Oregon. Neither is the editor of the journal to which the findings are sent, nor are the readers of the manuscript if it is published. But is it reasonable to assume that findings based on Princeton students will occur in similar ways in India, East Asia, or Africa?

That brings my anecdote back to its beginning. The underlying question I was asked was whether dissonance was a phenomenon experienced by everyone, everywhere; or was it the response to inconsistency experienced predominantly by relatively young and affluent college students in the United States? The world of the young researcher seems limitless and it would have been deflating to think that our research findings would be limited by occupation, geography, or culture. However, we have learned that major demographic and social variables such as class, race, and culture do impact the experience of cognitive dissonance. Far from being a limiting factor, such differences have allowed us to understand the dissonance process more fully and have also shed light on our understanding of those social constructs.

Culture and the psychology of cognitive dissonance

Culture is a set of shared, symbolic rules and norms that characterize a social group (Bodley, 1994). It includes the group's values, ideals, and rules for living and is passed on from generation to generation within the group. The cultural rules help determine the way in which people in a culture act, feel, and think. While most human cultures share much in common, differences also abound. And those differences create subtle distinctions in the way people in different cultures perceive themselves and others.

Joan Miller (1984) drew a distinction between cultures in which people are viewed as agentic and responsible for their own outcomes and cultures that are more holistic, viewing outcomes as a joint function of interrelationships, roles, and social obligations. She observed that in North America and Western Europe, culture tends to be agentic. People see themselves as controlling their own actions and responsible for their own behavior. When people in agentic cultures make attributions for behavior, they assume that the traits and dispositions of the actor are the reasons for the behavior. In East Asia and India, cultures are more holistic, with people viewing their behavior as embedded in their relationships with significant other people.

As an example, Miller (1984) asked Hindus living in Mysore, a city in southern India, and Americans living in Chicago, to make attributions for people's behavior in a variety of scenarios she created. In one scenario, Miller described a vehicle accident in which the driver of the vehicle – an attorney – dropped off his injured passenger at a hospital without making sure that proper care was being administered. The attorney continued on to court in order to meet with a client. Miller found that Hindus, whose culture is holistic and interdependent, were far more likely to see the cause of people's actions as residing in their roles and social obligations than did Americans. For example, a Hindu participant explained the attorney's action by saying, 'It was the attorney's duty to be in court for the client whom he is representing … and the passenger might not have looked as serious(ly injured) as he was.' By contrast, an American participant explained, 'The driver is obviously irresponsible … and aggressive in pursuing his career success' (Miller, 1984: 972). The American, having been socialized in an agentic culture, was more likely to assume that people's behaviors were a product of who they were i.e, the traits that made them unique individuals.

Independence and interdependence

'I said what I meant, and I meant what I said,
An elephant's loyal 100 per cent.'
Dr Seuss

This noble sentiment was expressed by Horton the elephant in Dr Seuss's classical tale of an elephant who went to great lengths and endured all kinds of hardships in order to stay true to his promise to Mayzie the lazy bird to keep watch over her egg. Horton will never allow his behavior to deviate from what he promised. Is it possible that Horton's admirable consistency between his promissory statement and his behavior was a product of the agentic, individualistic culture of his creator, Dr Seuss?

In a seminal contribution to our understanding of cross-cultural differences in social psychological processes, Hazel Markus and Shinobu Kitayama sharpened the consequences of the two types of cultures on a person's self-concept (Markus and Kitayama, 1991). In Western cultures, they argued, people feel an independence from their social and physical environment. In Western cultures, people are given credit for acting in accordance with their own unique beliefs, values, and goals. Our 'selves' are characterized by our internal traits – i.e., our beliefs, attitudes, and dispositions. It is a mark of maturity and mental health to actualize one's self (Rogers, 1961) and to act according to the person you 'really are.' Some traits may occur through genetic predispositions that we often call temperament, while others are learned through interaction with our parents, peers, and other socializing agents. In the West, we are certainly concerned about other people in our lives, but we see our true self as an entity that interacts with others. We do not think of others as being part of our self-concept. Our traits are our own; we take responsibility for who we are and what we do. We assess our self-worth by evaluating the goodness of our dispositions, traits, and values.

By contrast, in interdependent culture, people view themselves not as separate entities but rather in relation to others. Similar to Miller's concept of how people in holistic cultures view their social world, Markus and Kitayama (1991) view the interdependent self as intrinsically connected to others. Individual traits are important aspects of the self, but no more important than the quality of relationships. The ability to create harmony in relationships and to act for the good of the people with whom you are connected is as important to the interdependent self as any personal belief, attitude, or trait. The self-concept of people in interdependent cultures is based on a joint function of the worthiness of their individual dispositions and their ability to maintain pleasant and harmonious relationships with others they are connected to.

Dissonance and interdependent selves: a conceptual question

In the Western cultures that feature independent selves, it is considered virtuous (like Horton) to say what we believe, to believe what we say, and to take responsibility for our actions. In interdependent countries, according to Markus and Kitayama's (1991) analysis, saying what one believes and believing what one says are more complicated. There is considerable self-defining value in creating harmony in relationships.

Markus and Kitayama cite research by Iwao (1988) who asked respondents in the United States and Japan to evaluate the appropriateness of potential responses to a set of scenarios. In one scenario, a daughter was said to have brought home a potential fiancé who was of another race. One of the possible responses that was provided for the parent in the family was: 'he thought that he would never allow them to marry but told them he was in favor of their marriage' (p. 241). American respondents thought this was a terribly inappropriate response. In Western culture, we eschew (at least in principle), not saying what we believe, even if dissimulating does allow the immediate interpersonal situation to proceed smoothly. Only 2 percent of Americans chose this scenario as appropriate, whereas 48 percent thought it was the worst thing the parent could do. By contrast, 44 percent of Japanese respondents thought it was the best response in the situation and only 7 percent thought it was the worst. Westerners are supposed to act consistently with their inner thoughts and feelings; in the Far East, the harmonious flow of interpersonal interaction is an equally important aspect of the self.

If a focus on interpersonal relationships takes precedence over expressing one's innermost feelings and beliefs, then Markus and Kitayama (1991) raised the question of whether the motive for cognitive consistency is as important for people in interdependent cultures as it is for people in independent cultures. As we know from Chapter 1 of the current book, the original version of cognitive dissonance theory (Festinger, 1957) was one among many theories (e.g., Heider, 1946; see also, Abelson et al., 1968) that assumed that people prefer consistency among their behaviors, attitudes, and beliefs and are distressed when they are confronted with inconsistency. Markus and Kitayama (1991) suggested that dissonance reduction may not be a universal motivation after all, but rather may be a phenomenon restricted to the agentic, individualistic cultures of Western Europe, Australia, New Zealand, and North America.

Dissonance and culture: the research trail

Markus and Kitayama (1991) thus boldly raised the question of whether dissonance is culture-specific. It is as though they had been present at my doctoral oral several years before and observed me struggling with the question about the sanitation workers. The cultural issue is a broader version of that question. Are there groups of people for whom dissonance is particularly aversive and others for whom it is not an issue? Earlier in the chapter, I remarked that not every division among people (e.g., occupation, geography, age, gender) can be tested and it is not practical to unnecessarily limit the generalization of research findings to the particular demographic locale in which a study is conducted. However, Markus and Kitayama set

CULTURE, RACE, AND COGNITIVE DISSONANCE

the question at a cultural level and presented an interesting theoretical rationale to consider it seriously. Is dissonance culturally specific? This question piqued the interest of many researchers and continues to be a matter of ongoing debate.

Do the Japanese experience dissonance? No, yes, and sometimes

Steven Heine and Darrin Lehman (1997) were the first investigators to examine Markus and Kitayama's (1991) question empirically. They conducted a study in which they requested participants from independent and interdependent cultures to make a choice between music CDs. That is, participants from the two cultures participated in the free-choice paradigm of dissonance that has been a robust method for producing cognitive dissonance among Western participants since it was introduced decades ago by Brehm (1956).

The study was run in Vancouver, Canada. Canadian participants were drawn from the student population at the University of British Columbia. Japanese participants were recruited by advertisements in Japanese language newspapers requesting participation by Japanese who were in Canada temporarily on short-term visas. For the Japanese sample, the study was run in Japanese by a Japanese researcher and, for the Canadian sample, run in English by a Canadian researcher. They asked Japanese and Canadian students to make a choice between two desirable music CDs. Participants were first asked to rate a series of forty music CDs. Later in the study, the experimenter told the participants that they could choose one CD to take home with them. Allegedly because of 'limited stock,' the participants were allowed to choose between two available CDs. The choice for all participants was between his or her fifth and sixth ranked CD. At the conclusion of the study, the participants reranked all of the CDs. As in previous research using this paradigm, the measure of dissonance reduction was the spreading apart of the two alternatives: the chosen alternative should become more attractive and the unchosen alternative should become less attractive.

Heine and Lehman's (1997) results suggest a difference in the way Japanese and Canadian samples responded to the dissonance-invoking dilemma. As Figure 7.1 demonstrates, Canadian participants significantly spread the attractiveness of the choice alternatives, confirming the typical prediction of cognitive dissonance theory. Japanese participants did not.

There was another interesting independent variable in Heine and Lehman's study. In addition to giving the participants a choice of CD albums to take home, they also provided an opportunity for the participants to self-affirm. Recall from Chapter 5 that Claude Steele and his colleagues (e.g., Steele

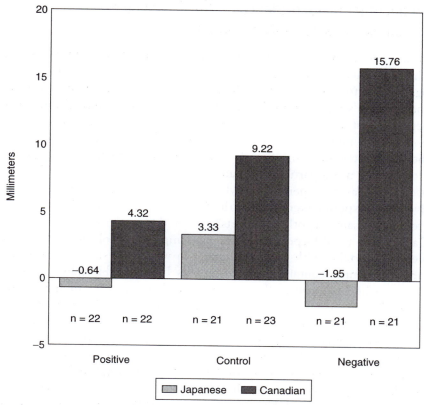

Figure 7.1 Spread of alternatives as a function of culture and personality test feedback

Source: Heine and Lehman (1997)

and Liu, 1983; Steele, Spencer, and Lynch, 1993) found that giving people positive information about their very important qualities reduced the need to spread the choice alternatives. Similarly, providing people with information that attacked their confidence in their good qualities enhanced the need to deal with their dissonance when given a choice between CDs. Heine and Lehman ran two additional conditions to the one depicted in Figure 7.1. In one, they used the self-affirming information and in the other they used information attacking the participants' personal qualities. Canadians performed precisely the same way as the participants in Steele et al.'s studies: positive information about the self reduced the spreading of alternatives whereas negative information enhanced it. Japanese participants did not spread apart the choice alternatives, regardless of whether there was self-enhancing or self-derogating information.

On the other hand: evidence for the existence of dissonance in a collectivist culture

What conclusions can we draw from Heine and Lehman's (1997) study? The experiment was not an easy one to design and the issues that the investigators had to solve were difficult. The results were consistent with Heine and Lehman's expectations based on their analyses of cultural differences between East and West. Nonetheless, it is risky to draw confident conclusions from a null finding. That is, the Japanese participants did not spread the choice alternatives significantly – certainly not as much as the Canadians. However, if more participants had been run, would the spreading have occurred? Was the experimenter who ran the Japanese participants as effective as the experimenter who ran the Canadian participants? Were the two groups the same in other respects? All of the participants were run in Canada. The English-speaking, Canadian sample were college students who were comfortable with the environment in which the study was run. The Japanese sample contained some students but were basically visitors to Canada who had been in the country from between four months to five years. They were less comfortable in Canada and less comfortable with experimentation in a college environment. This is not in any way to demean Heine and Lehman's study, but results based on nothing happening (i.e., the small bar in Figure 7.1) are always subject to alternative explanations.

The Japanese social psychologist, Haruki Sakai, was not seeking to examine the influence of culture when he embarked on a set of studies at Sapporo University in Hokkaido, Japan, in the 1980s. Rather, he was investigating important issues in dissonance theory based on the existing literature at the time – a literature based on North American and European samples. For example, in one study, Sakai (1981) found that being asked to make a speech contrary to one's attitudes produced more attitude change when it was made publicly than when it was made privately. In another, Sakai and Andow (1980) supported the idea that personal responsibility for an attitude-discrepant speech was important for cognitive dissonance (cf. Cooper, 1971). Perhaps because these studies were published in Japanese language journals, they escaped the attention of North American and European investigators. Nonetheless, they show evidence that cognitive dissonance was aroused in Japanese students and, in a manner similar to participants from agentic, independent cultures, they resolved their dissonance by changing their private attitudes toward the topic of their speech.

An interesting difference between Sakai's findings and those of Heine and Lehman is that Sakai used a dissonance procedure that is essentially interpersonal whereas Heine and Lehman used a procedure that is far more intrapersonal. In Sakai's studies, participants were explicitly aware that their essays were going to be shown to a group of their peers. By contrast, in the free-choice paradigm that Heine and Lehman used, people were asked to make personal choices between two music CDs. They did not anticipate making their choices public to any other students nor was there any anticipated interpersonal interaction. Although in North America and Europe these two research paradigms have been used interchangeably to arouse dissonance, perhaps the cultural differences intrinsic to interdependent, holistic cultures make the two approaches quite different.

The return to the Self-Standards Model

The essential difference between dissonance in independent and interdependent cultures rests on what people in each culture consider an aversive consequence. Readers will recall that in Chapters 4 and 5, we concluded that dissonance occurs when people believe their actions have brought about an unwanted event. We saw that in agentic, Western cultures, people compare the outcome of their behavior against a standard of judgment. Sometimes the comparison standard is based on what a person thinks of him or herself (i.e., one's self-concept) and sometimes it is based on the normative standards of society. I suggest that the same underlying process is true for people in interdependent cultures. What differs between cultures is the content of the standard. As Markus and Kitayama (1991) pointed out, in interdependent cultures, there is special emphasis on preserving interpersonal harmony. Anything that upsets the harmony is a prime facie instance of an aversive consequence. In Sakai's (1981) study, cognitive dissonance occurred especially when a person was publicly identified as the one who made a statement that was contrary to the attitudes of his or her group and delivered the statement to the group members. It is quite possible that the anticipated disruption in the smooth flow and harmonious interactions in the group was the source of the aversive consequence and thus, the source of dissonance arousal. By contrast, there was no interpersonally based, aversive consequence in Heine and Lehman's study and thus dissonance was experienced only by Canadian and not by Japanese participants.

The essential point is this: if there is a reliable difference between Japanese and North American students, it is not because there is a difference in the underlying structure of cognitive dissonance. Rather, it is because the events that people in interdependent cultures find aversive are interpersonal in nature, whereas in independent cultures, aversive events may be more evenly distributed between interpersonal and intrapersonal outcomes.

This logic received support in an experiment by Kitayama, Snibbe, Markus, and Suzuki (2004). They reasoned that the Japanese would experience cognitive dissonance, even when choosing among music CDs, as long

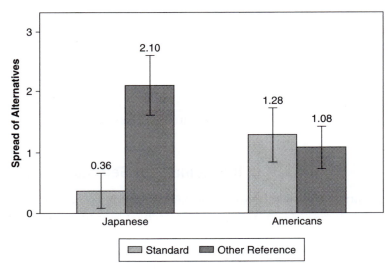

Figure 7.2   Spreading of choice alternatives as a function of reference and culture
Source: Kitayama, Snibbe, Markus, and Suzuki (2004)

as they were thinking about people in their social group when they made their choices. In one of their experiments, Japanese students at Kyoto University were asked to rank ten music CDs according to their own preferences. As in many experiments using this design, the students were then given a choice of two of the CDs to take home, after which they reranked the CDs. Kitayama et al. (2004) predicted that the students would not show a spreading apart of the choice alternatives that is the hallmark prediction of dissonance. And, indeed, that was what they found: no dissonance effect for the Kyoto students in that condition.

In a second condition, Kitayama et al. asked the students to rank the CDs as they thought *most Kyoto students* would rank them. In this condition, having students think about the preferences of their fellow university peers was expected to place the decision in a more social and interdependent context. Kitayama et al. predicted that when they subsequently chose between the CDs, Kyoto students would experience dissonance and spread the choice alternatives. The results, depicted in Figure 7.2, show that this is precisely what occurred. In the standard condition, without any reference to the opinions of their peers, Japanese students showed no dissonance effect. When the preferences of their peers were primed, Japanese students significantly spread the attractiveness of the CDs, consistent with the predictions of dissonance theory.

The right side of Figure 7.2 shows the results of the very same study in which the participants were undergraduates at Stanford University. There

American students showed a significant spreading of the choice alternatives, regardless of whether they thought about the other students' preferences. For the American students, it was not necessary to think about others' preferences, nor did thinking about others modify the dissonance they were experiencing. They spread the alternatives by merely thinking about their own choices.

The interpersonal nature of cognitive dissonance was made still more explicit in a set of innovative experiments reported by Hoshino-Browne, Zanna, Spencer, Zanna, Kitayama, and Lackenbauer (2005). They asked participants at the University of Waterloo in Ontario, Canada, to participate in a study in which they would help to evaluate the menu in a new Chinese restaurant opening near the university. The researchers amplified the importance of the task by indicating that the university administration was considering allowing students to use their university cards at the restaurant, depending on the feedback they received on the menus.

In the *friend* condition of the research, the task was made highly interpersonal. The experimenter explained that, on the basis of past research, it was believed that the survey would be most meaningful if the respondents pictured themselves making the decision not for themselves, but for another person. The experimenter continued, "We would like you to picture a close friend, someone whose food preferences you feel you know fairly well, and respond as you make the decision for your friend' (p. xx). The experimenter provided the participants with a list of twenty-five menu items. They were asked to think of their friend and make a list of what they thought their friend's ten most preferred entrees would be and to rate how much they thought their friend would enjoy each of them. Finally, they were told that, for their helpfulness, they would be able to present their friend with a coupon for one of the meals on the new menu. They were given a choice between the menu items they had ranked fifth and sixth. After a few minutes' delay, they were asked to rate the items on the menu once again.

In the *self* condition, participants were led through a similar procedure, but the sole focus of the ratings was to be on the their own preferences for menu items. They were asked to rate the items based on their own preferences and, when the coupon for a future meal was mentioned, it was a coupon that the participant could use rather than one that a friend could use. Otherwise, the menu choices and description of the research was identical for the *friend* and *self* conditions.

Approximately half of the participants were of European descent, all of whom were born in Canada. The other half were Asian Canadians who were born in Asian countries such as Hong Kong, the People's Republic of China, Vietnam, Taiwan, Japan or Vietnam. Hashino-Browne et al. (2005) assumed that the European Canadian students would replicate the typical dissonance effect and spread the attractiveness of the chosen and

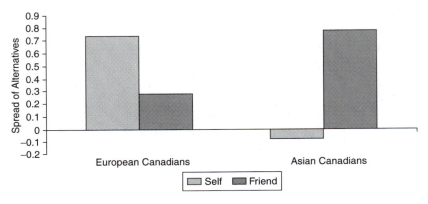

Figure 7.3   Spread of the attractiveness of choice alternatives for European and Asian Canadians when choosing for themselves or for a friend
Source: Hoshino-Browne, Zanna, Spencer, Zanna, Kitayama, and Lackenbauer (2005)

non-chosen menu items when making a decision for which meal coupon to secure for themselves. However, Hoshino-Browne et al. expected Asian Canadians would not spread the choice alternatives. For the Asian Canadians, there was no need to justify their choice since the consequences of the decision were solely an intrapersonal matter. On the other hand, making a decision for a friend is more complex for the Asian Canadians. As Markus and Kitayama (1991) had suggested, important decisions for people from interdependent cultures are the ones that involve relationships among people. In the *friend* condition for Asian participants, the consequence of not knowing a friend's tastes and preferences is far more aversive than not being sure of one's own preferences. For European Canadians, raised in an independent culture, the more aversive consequence is making the wrong choice for oneself rather than a friend. Hoshino-Browne et al. expected European Canadians to spread the choice alternatives when making choices for themselves more than when they made the choices for someone else, even a close friend.

The results of the spreading apart of the alternatives is shown in Figure 7.3. Each bar represents the degree of difference between the alternatives before and after the choice. On the left, we can see that Europeans showed significant spreading of alternatives when deciding for themselves. There was some spreading of the alternatives when deciding for a friend, but that magnitude was not statistically significant. For Asians, the pattern was reversed. Asian Canadians showed significant spreading of the attractiveness of the menu items when deciding for a friend, but none whatsoever when deciding for themselves.

Another interesting feature of Hoshino-Browne et al.'s (2005) data was the impact of the degree to which Asian Canadian participants identified with their Asian heritage on the degree of dissonance reduction. The Asian students were asked to indicate how much they identified with their country of birth. The more strongly they identified with their Asian birthplace, the more post-decisional dissonance they showed in the *friend* condition and the less dissonance they showed in the *self* condition.

Overall, the results of this research show that dissonance is not a phenomenon restricted to a particular culture or region within a culture (see Kitayama, Ishii, Imada and Takemura, 2006). Rather, it is a general process that people from East and West experience. However, the more the interpersonal consequences of people's choices are accessible and focused, the more important the situation is to people from interdependent cultures. Having others live with the negative features of a chosen alternative or relinquish the positive features of a rejected alternative are more aversive than having made such choices for oneself. For people in independent cultures, the consequences of decisions for oneself are sufficiently important for them to invoke the dissonance process without recourse to how others might feel.

Vicarious dissonance in East and West

In Chapter 6, we examined cognitive dissonance that is experienced on behalf of someone else. Called vicarious cognitive dissonance (Cooper and Hogg, 2007; Monin et al., 2004; Norton et al., 2003), this is a state of arousal that occurs in a member of a social group when a prototypical fellow group member acts in a way that produces an aversive consequence. This vicarious experience is quintessentially social; it is based on the social bond of group membership and transfers the state of arousal from the person engaged in the act to the group member who is observing it. It would seem to be another instance in which people from interdependent cultures should manifest cognitive dissonance.

We can contrast vicarious dissonance to personal dissonance in the induced compliance situation. In the latter, people are asked to make a statement that they do not agree with and that statement is typically shown to someone with decision-making authority. In independent cultures, the measurement of this act against normative standards suggests that an aversive consequence may well occur and dissonance is therefore aroused. It is not clear that such an act would always produce dissonance in an interdependent culture. However, in vicarious dissonance, the situation is pointedly social and the interdependent bond among group members is heightened. It is here that members of an interdependent culture should experience heightened dissonance.

New data collected in Korea support this conclusion. Chong and Cooper (2007) asked students at Korea University in Seoul, South Korea, to

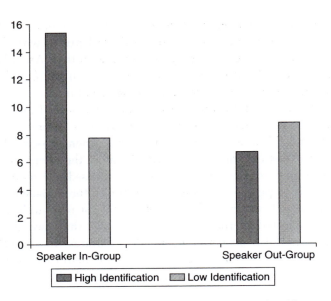

Figure 7.4   Attitudes toward a tuition increase at South Korean universities

participate in a study on the effect of increased tuition rates at their university. The study was run by a Korean-speaking researcher in the Korean language, but was a faithful replication of the study reported by Norton et al. (2003). Participants were recruited as part of a study on linguistic subcultures. They believed that they were overhearing another student from either their university, or Yonsei University, agree to make a speech in favor of increasing tuition for university students in South Korea. Needless to say, Yonsei University was selected as the alleged home university of the other student because the two universities are perceived as rival universities in South Korea. Korea University participants who believed the other student was from Yonsei believed that they were witnessing an *out-group* member deliver the speech; students who believed the speaker was from Korea University believed they were overhearing an *in-group* member. As in the Norton et al. (2003) study, whose procedure was provided in more detail in the previous chapter, the speechmaker either was asked, or told, to make a pro-tuition speech which, in turn, was to be used by the Dean of the university in forming his own policy about tuition increases. The participants then indicated their own attitude toward the proposal to increase tuition. Recall that Norton et al. found that the stronger the participants' identification with the in-group, the stronger was the effect of vicarious dissonance. Therefore, Korea University students' strength of identification with Korea University was also measured.

The results, depicted in Figure 7.4, strongly support the existence of vicarious dissonance in the interdependent society of South Korea. Korea

University students changed their attitudes to become more favorable to a tuition increase when a pro-tuition statement was made by an in-group member who freely decided to make the speech. Moreover, as predicted, the stronger the students' identification with their in-group, the more they changed their attitudes.

It is interesting that another study run by Chong and Cooper (2007) at Korea University using a similar personal dissonance paradigm showed no attitude change at all. Students from Korea University were asked, or were told, to make a speech favoring tuition increases at all Korean Universities. In the high choice conditions, all of the students agreed to make the speech. Yet, attitudes measured following the pro-tuition statement showed no change on the tuition question. Apparently, choosing to make a speech in favor of an unwanted policy did not produce dissonance in this study; however, as shown in Figure 7.4, when the highly interpersonal vicarious dissonance procedure was invoked, the Korean students showed the effects of cognitive dissonance.

Conclusions about the role of culture in cognitive dissonance

The research on the effect of culture on cognitive dissonance has illuminated a particularly interesting issue that has both broadened and limited the way we think about cognitive dissonance. What began as a warning that not all social processes exist in all cultures (Heine and Lehman, 1997) has evolved into an invitation to examine how various cultures define what is appropriate interpersonal behavior and what is not. If, as I suggested in Chapter 5, dissonance is activated by measuring one's behavior and finding that it falls short of normative or personal standards, then it is important to know just what those standards are. This cannot be done in a vacuum. The norms, rules, and expectations of a culture affect people's personal standards (what they expect of themselves) and normative standards (what they believe others expect of them), although by definition culture probably affects the latter more than the former.

The fact that dissonance is affected differently in different cultures further demonstrates that purely logical inconsistency between cognitive elements is not sufficient to arouse dissonance. Rather, it is the collision of freely chosen behavior with normative and personal standards that give rise to the unpleasant state of dissonance. Behavior that violates normative standards in one culture may be perfectly consistent with normative standards in another. Whether behavior and attitudes are logically consistent or not, dissonance will be aroused only when the behavior violates standards and those, in turn, exist not in a vacuum but in a social context.

The effect of race on cognitive dissonance: some new data

Differences abound within cultures as well as across cultures. One of those differences is race. In the United States in particular, racist attitudes, beliefs, and behaviors have left a legacy of hostility and discrimination against the minority Black population from the time Blacks were first imported as slaves several centuries ago. At the turn of the twentieth century, W.E.B. Du Bois (1903) wrote eloquently of the dilemma of being Black in America. Slavery was long gone, but the situation of Blacks in America was nonetheless psychologically precarious. Du Bois introduced the term 'double-consciousness' to articulate the underlying contradiction, or psychological incompatibility, between simultaneously being an American and a Negro. Unlike Whites, Black Americans are not only confronted with these contradictions in everyday life, but must learn to tolerate them as well. In *The Souls of Black Folks*, Du Bois wrote:

> It is a peculiar sensation, this double-consciousness, this sense of always looking at one's self through the eyes of others, of measuring one's soul by the tape of a world that looks on in amused contempt and pity. One never feels his twoness – an American, a Negro; two souls, two thoughts, two unreconciled strivings; two warring ideals in one dark body, whose dogged strength alone keeps it from being torn asunder. (Du Bois, 1903: 102)

Although Du Bois wrote more than a century ago, double-consciousness is still relevant to the Black experience in the United States. The historical inconsistency between the famous phrase in the Declaration of Independence that 'All men are created equal' and the reality of the Black experience in antebellum America has been replaced by the inconsistency between the philosophy of equal opportunity and the reality of poverty, underemployment, and discrimination. In short, to live in twenty-first century America as a member of a minority group is to experience the double consciousness that frequently treats one as equal in philosophy and less than equal in practice. Would it be surprising, under these circumstances, to find that racial minorities build a greater tolerance to inconsistency than do Whites?

Diana Hill's (2005) thesis was designed to test this question. Since there were no previous studies that systematically examined racial differences in the experience and reduction of cognitive dissonance, Hill took the straightforward approach of assigning Black and White students to high- and low-choice conditions in a typical induced compliance study. The students were told that the Dean's office was considering recommending a large increase in the cost of college tuition for the following year and wanted to assess what the arguments were on both sides of the issue. In a manner similar to Cohen's (1962) and Linder et al.'s (1967) research that we presented in the

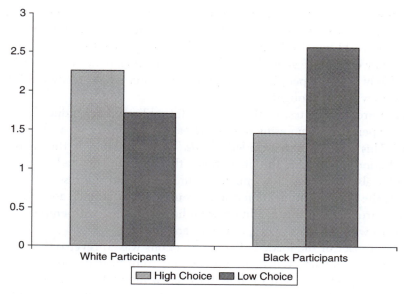

Figure 7.5   Attitude change by Black and White participants
Source: Hill (2005)

first two chapters, Hill told students that the best way to determine what the arguments are on both sides of the issue was to have college students write strong and forceful arguments favoring one side. Half of the students were asked if they would be willing to write in favor of the tuition increase; the other half were told to do so.

Attitudes toward the tuition increase were measured immediately after the writing of the counterattitudinal essays. The results confirmed Hill's hypothesis that Whites and Blacks would respond differently to the inconsistency. Figure 7.5 shows that, in the high choice conditions, White students became more favorable to an increase in tuition. Relative to the low-choice conditions, White students who wrote in favor of a tuition increase became significantly more in favor of that position. Not so for Blacks. What was surprising about the data in Figure 7.5 is that Black students expressed greater support for the tuition increase in the low-choice rather than the high-choice conditions.

Hill reasoned that Black students experienced little dissonance because their experience in a world of double-consciousness convinces them that their actions are not likely to have any effect on society's institution. Here they were in an institution which, by and large, is comprised of a majority of White students, run by White administrators, and overseen by a Board of Trustees that, like its students and administrators, are mostly White. That is,

CULTURE, RACE, AND COGNITIVE DISSONANCE

it was an institution like most institutions in a predominantly White society. Hill argued that for the Black participants who have grown used to negotiating a world run by Whites, it was less likely that they thought their opinion would make an iota of difference to the final policy outcome. It was less likely that the people running the institution would really care about what they felt or thought.

As a preliminary test of this notion, Hill replicated her induced compliance experiment again using tuition increase at the university as the attitude issue. This time, she also included a *loaded affect* condition. In this condition, in addition to stressing the high choice that the students had, the experimenter also conveyed how much the university and the researcher cared about the way the students felt and thought about an increase in tuition. The instructions in this condition were heavily loaded with emphasis on a concern with students' voice, thoughts, and feelings.

The impact of the loaded affect instructions was to reverse the findings with Black students. When the instructions were loaded with words that conveyed special concern for how they felt while performing the task and how they felt about tuition increases, Black students changed their attitudes following the induced compliance task. Like the White students whose attitudes are depicted in Figure 7.5, they changed their attitudes to become more favorable to tuition increases. Without the loaded affect instructions, Black students showed very much the same pattern as they had shown in the first experiment and did not change their attitudes on the tuition issue.

At this writing, it is premature to say that we know precisely what the differences between Black and White responses are due to in the laboratory. But the writings of W.E.B. Du Bois tell us that the cultural experiences of Black and White Americans are not the same. Although there is considerable overlap in the cultural worldviews of Black and White students, there are also differences based on two decades of personal history and centuries of different cultural histories. Those differences manifest themselves in people's tolerance of inconsistency and their belief that their opinions can make a difference in the policies of society's institutions. As such, the perceived consequences of attitude-inconsistent behavior on one's self-standards will differ markedly – markedly enough to account for racial differences in the experience of cognitive dissonance.

Social class and cognitive dissonance: education makes a difference

European American society puts a premium on people's ability to take control of their own fate, to express and actualize their sense of self, and in the words of the advertisements for the United States Army, 'to be all that you can be.' It is, as Markus and Kitayama (1991) reasoned, an agentic society. We have also seen that within the larger culture, there exist smaller yet identifiable subcultures whose shared representation of self and society may be somewhat different. For Black Americans, the long history of relative powerlessness may have given rise to a self-representation in which the consequences of attitudinal inconsistency are different from those of White Americans. Alana Snibbe and Hazel Markus recently suggested that differences in social class may also establish conditions that result in different reactions to situations that research has shown to create cognitive dissonance.

Snibbe and Markus (2005) reasoned that, although European American culture is generally agentic, such that people take responsibility for who they are and what they do, there are subcultural differences in what it means to be agentic. A person's social class may determine what he or she expects to be agentic about. For example, previous research supports the general notion that people in European American societies value being independent, but different social classes interpret the word 'independent' differently. For people higher in socioeconomic status (SES), the world is a place in which people make choices about their lives: where to live, what to do as a profession, what to purchase with disposable income, what to do with one's leisure time. For people from lower socioeconomic situations, there are fewer choices to be made: there is less disposable income, fewer choices about mobility, and less leisure time.

Interestingly, research also shows that people low in SES are not any less happy than people higher in SES and are just as satisfied with their lives (Davis, 1983; 2004; Rossi, 2001). One reason for the similar sense of satisfaction may be that people low in SES experience a different sense of what is important than people who are high in SES. Snibbe and Markus (2005) argue that for people low in SES, the most important expression of independence and agency is maintaining personal integrity and steeling themselves against a changing and hostile environment, whereas for people high in SES, it is expressing their uniqueness and influencing their environment. In this view, having and expressing choices are far more important for people of higher socioeconomic classes than for people of lower socioeconomic classes. Expression of choice is not as major a feature of the agentic self for the lower SES subculture as it is for those people from higher SES.

Snibbe and Markus then argue that people from a high SES subculture are particularly prone to experiencing cognitive dissonance after having made a choice, relative to those from low SES groups. High SES people expect to make the right choices; when they act on the environment, the quality of their choices is a reflection on their sense of self. Low SES people are simply less concerned about the consequences of their choices as a reflection on themselves. If people are asked to choose between two highly attractive alternatives, the lower SES person may be content with his or her selection and move on. According to Snibbe and Markus, it is the higher SES person who is so in need of being sure that he or she made the perfect decision, that the attractiveness of the chosen alternative must be psychologically increased and the attractiveness of the rejected choice must be psychologically demeaned.

Snibbe and Markus (2005) conducted a cognitive dissonance experiment by recruiting participants from higher and lower SES groups and asking them to choose a gift between two attractive CDs from a list of ten CDs. In order to operationalize SES, Snibbe and Markus used the participants' level of educational attainment. It should be noted that this is far from a complete assessment of socioeconomic status, but it is a component of SES that has frequently been used as an indicator of SES (Matthews, Kelsey, Meilahn, Kuller, and Wing, 1989; Ross and Wu, 1995). Participants were considered to be in a high SES group if they had attained at least a bachelor's degree in a four-year college. The level of educational attainment of the low SES group was no greater than high school.

The dissonance-provoking task need not be presented in detail for it faithfully followed the procedures used by others (e.g., Brehm, 1956; Steele, Spencer, and Lynch, 1993) in the free-choice paradigm of dissonance. Participants rated the music CDs, were allowed to choose between their fifth and sixth ranked CD as a present to take home, and then re-ranked the ten items. The results, presented in Figure 7.6, show the amount of change in the ranking by those whose highest educational attainment was high school (HS group) and those whose highest attainment was at least a bachelor's degree (BA group.) The results reveal that for people in the BA group, the differences predicted by dissonance theory and found many times in the psychological literature were obtained. The chosen CD became more attractive; the rejected alternative became less attractive. But note what happened for people with only a high school education. Consistent with Snibbe and Markus's (2005) prediction, they showed no apparent need to justify their choice by extolling the values of the alternative they selected. An unpredicted finding occurred for the unchosen alternative, however. HS participants derogated the unchosen alternative just as much as the BA participants did, suggesting an attempt to justify their choice by a somewhat different mechanism than that chosen by the BA participants.

Snibbe and Markus's (2005) provocative results add to the fascinating interaction between culture and dissonance. Clearly, their results address differences in how people with different degrees of education respond to cognitive dissonance. It is not clear whether the differences between the two groups in their study were due to levels of income or were connected specifically and intrinsically to differences in educational attainment. Indeed, income level and educational attainment were not correlated in their data. Nonetheless, Snibbe and Markus's (2005) results point to an

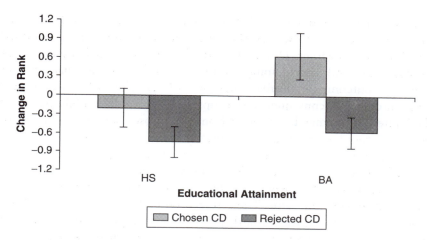

Figure 7.6   Spreading of choice alternatives as function of educational attainment (social class)
Source: Snibbe and Markus (2005)

additional challenge for understanding how subcultural distinctions in society affect the expression of cognitive dissonance.

Jack Brehm's question: a reprise

And so, long ago, I was asked a question to which I had no answer. At that time, no one had ventured an analysis of cognitive dissonance based on culture or subculture. No one had suggested that different groups in the world's or a country's population would differ in their reactions to inconsistent behavior.

The answer to Jack Brehm's question is still a puzzle awaiting its final solution. Phenotypically, we know that the manifestations of cognitive dissonance take different forms in different cultures. This is just another way of saying that the data look different when we compare East Asians to European Canadians, Black Americans to White Americans, or highly educated compared to less educated participants. To understand whether the *process* of cognitive dissonance is different, however, requires a careful answer to the question 'What is cognitive dissonance?' And this is the question I have tried to address in this book. If we take the view that cognitive dissonance is solely a process of resolving inconsistency, the data from the studies we have looked at in this chapter may convince us that dissonance is restricted to a particular class, race, and culture. However, if, as I have argued, we take the view that cognitive dissonance is aroused when people

CULTURE, RACE, AND COGNITIVE DISSONANCE

compare the consequences of their behavior to a standard and find the results unsatisfactory, then the pieces of the cultural and subcultural puzzles come together. Different cultural groupings weigh their desires, expectations, and shortcomings differently. What is an unacceptable, unwanted outcome to a Korean might be different from what is unwanted by a European. A consequence that upsets an upwardly mobile person in the United States may be different from what upsets a person whose class or caste determines his or her outcomes in India.

The generic process of cognitive dissonance probably transcends limitations of culture and subcultures. The underlying, generic process that motivates a person to action when the consequences of his or her behavior are unwanted remains the same. The research on culture and cognitive dissonance has come a long way toward appreciating that the specific events that arouse dissonance for a particular person in a particular place at a particular time may be different from what arouses dissonance in another. Culture, race, and class provide important windows into these differences.

Do we all experience dissonance? After several decades, I think the answer is yes.

8

COGNITIVE DISSONANCE
IN TODAY'S WORLD

As we have seen throughout this volume, cognitive dissonance theory has been an active field of study for five decades. The phenomenon, once thought controversial, has become widely accepted. Old controversies have ended and new ones have emerged as we continue to understand more about its limits and its underlying process. Throughout this time period, it is not surprising that the theory has been used as an analytic tool outside the laboratory to try to understand some of the causes of major world events from politics (Brace, 2005) to terror (Master, 2005). It has pervaded the popular press as well, being used as an analytic tool not only by psychologists but also by such media outlets as the editorial page of the *New York Times*.

One of the fascinating aspects of cognitive dissonance is that it often helps us make sense out of non-obvious events. Indeed, dissonance burst onto the scene at the end of the 1950s precisely because of its ability to predict seemingly non-obvious dependent measures in the laboratory. It is not surprising then that dissonance is invoked to explain some of the extraordinary events that occur outside of the laboratory. The problem for the scientist is that the explanations are post hoc, contain no data, and have no control groups. With this admission, I shall nonetheless open the current chapter by engaging in one of those post hoc explanations.

In the remainder of the chapter, I shall use the lens of cognitive dissonance to understand a process that typically lies outside of the realm of experimental social psychology – i.e., psychotherapy. In that section, I shall advance the thesis that, to the extent that psychotherapy is effective, it is precisely because of the arousal and reduction of cognitive dissonance. Adhering more to the scientific tradition of dissonance theory, I shall offer some data to support that claim. Finally, the third section of the chapter will consider how we may deliberately use what we know about cognitive dissonance to change attitudes and behaviors relevant to our health.

Cognitive dissonance and an American presidency

On a cold afternoon in mid-December 1998, the Judiciary Committee of the United States House of Representatives voted four Articles of Impeachment against President William Jefferson Clinton. He was accused of perjurious testimony, obstruction of justice, and the misuse of his office in attempts to cover up his relationships with Monica Lewinsky and Paula Jones. The full House of Representatives approved two of the Articles of Impeachment, turning down the other two. Less than two months later, the Senate of the United States refused to convict the President of either count.

Could the reduction of cognitive dissonance amongst American voters have helped to save the Clinton presidency? I think so (Cooper, 1999). Let's look at why.

The months preceding the vote by the House of Representatives had not gone well for Bill Clinton. An investigation into a land development deal had been broadened considerably to include his involvement with the Senate intern, Monica Lewinsky, and an Arkansas clerk named Paula Jones. Embarrassing incidents made headlines on a daily basis throughout 1998. Perhaps sensing a political knockout of the President, the Republican-controlled House of Representatives voted overwhelmingly (363 to 63) to authorize its Judiciary Committee to investigate the possibility of impeachment. The news continued to worsen for the President who had sworn to a national television audience that he 'never had sexual relations with that woman, Monica Lewinsky.' In July 1998, he apologized to the nation for lying about his relationship.

Public opinion polling, which took the pulse of the nation on an almost daily basis, showed an amazing result. Yes, people were angry and/or disappointed with the President's behavior. Some were angry about his marital infidelity; some were angry about abuse of power through sexual contact with a young intern; some were angry that the contact took place in the White House; some were forgiving of the sexual contact but angry or disappointed by his not telling the truth about it. Critics and detractors of the President waited for the cumulative weight of the evidence to turn into widespread disapproval of his presidency, but the predicted decline in his job approval rate never occurred. Despite people's disapproval of his actions with Ms Lewinsky, his overall popularity went steadily skyward. It seemed that with every allegation and revelation, the President's popularity increased rather than decreased. By late December 1998, Clinton's job approval rate stood at one of the highest ever achieved by a second-term president at that stage of his presidency.

Far be it for an experimental social psychologist to understand how members of Congress cast their votes. What is clear after a season of negative presidential news and climbing presidential popularity is that the full House of Representatives voted for only two of the four articles of impeachment, the

Senate of the United States proceeded to trial very quickly, and the Articles of Impeachment, requiring a two-thirds Senate vote to remove the President, failed to achieve a simple majority vote on either article. Case closed.

The irony of public opinion in 1998–1999 was that people overwhelmingly thought that the President had engaged in unsavory behavior and agreed that each new revelation was negative. No one praised the President for his behavior and few found the totality of his explanations acceptable. Nonetheless, the public separated its opinion of the President's personal conduct from his role as President of the United States. They disapproved of the former but approved of the latter. Although there are no official correlations available for the public opinion data, it seemed that the more negative the personal allegations, the more positive his presidential approval became.

The psychology of effort justification: a reprise

Based on our laboratory studies of cognitive dissonance, we might have the feeling that we've seen a parallel phenomenon before. Aronson and Mills (1959) introduced us to the concept of *effort justification* (see Chapter 1). The more onerous it becomes to achieve a desired goal state, the more attractive the goal becomes. In Aronson and Mills's study, students made the choice to enter a sexual discussion club and, as they had been told, there were some onerous steps they had to take prior to gaining entry. Specifically, the students knew they had to pass a screening test in order to join their colleagues in the club. The more onerous, difficult, or noxious the screening test, the more the students came to believe that the club was fun, the discussion interesting, and their colleagues articulate and fun. Might the elevation in Bill Clinton's popularity following the revelations about Monica Lewinsky have been based on the same process?

First, a caveat is necessary. Experimental social psychologists are uncomfortable with explanations that do not rely on control groups and random assignment to condition. We are uncomfortable retrofitting our explanations to accommodate historical events. In this chapter, we may take some liberties and apply a dissonance analysis where the parallel seems striking. Such is the case with attitudes toward Bill Clinton following the Monica Lewinsky episode.

When more of a bad thing is a good thing

In Chapter 4 I presented a study that I conducted years ago (Cooper, 1971), which extended some of the principles expressed by Aronson and Mills (1959). The central notion of my study was that people experience cognitive dissonance when they choose a course of action that has potentially unwanted elements and those unwanted elements then come to pass. It is ipso facto an aversive consequence of your choice behavior to have caused an unwanted event to occur. Dissonance occurs to the extent that you chose to engage in the action and to the extent that the consequences of your action were foreseeable. Here is an illustration: suppose you decide to take a hike in the woods with a friend. You could ask any number of friends, but you choose one particular person whom you think would be fun to have along. You know she has a tendency to become fatigued because of allergies. Her allergic reactions do not occur frequently and you hope they will not occur on this hike. But they do. Your friend, rather than having the good time you hoped she would have, is rather miserable and you find yourself spending much of your effort encouraging her through the rest of the afternoon's walk.

You would be in a state of cognitive dissonance. Your decision to ask your friend to join you turned out to have negative consequences for her and you. You made her uncomfortable and it ruined the pleasure of your trip. But the decision to take this particular friend was yours. What is more, you knew about her allergy when you asked her. In terms of dissonance theory, you made a decision whose consequences were foreseeable. It is not that you knew they *would* occur, just that they *might* occur, and you now experience dissonance. To alleviate the dissonance and justify the decision, you conclude that you really enjoyed the trip after all and, despite your friend's allergic reaction, you really enjoyed her company.

In my study, I had participants come to the laboratory in groups of six to play a competitive game. Each participant understood that they would be playing with a partner chosen at random from the other five participants. The game was an intellectual task such that speed and accuracy were important. The outcome of a pair of students would depend on the speed and accuracy of each member of the team. Successful performance by both players would earn money for each of them. Poor performance by either member of the pair would cause both members to lose money. Before breaking into teams, each participant was told something about the person from the group of six who had been chosen to be their partner. Each player was given information to suggest that the partner had a personality trait that, if manifested during the game, could be trouble – i.e., could cause the partners to lose money during the game. Some participants had a chance to choose to stay with the partner or choose another partner; other participants had no choice.

As the game was played, it turned out that all partners did indeed manifest a trait that caused the participant to lose money. For some of the participants, it was precisely the trait they had been told about; for the other participants, it was a trait that was totally different from what they had been led to expect. Our prediction was that, when asked at the end of the study, participants who chose to stay with their partner despite their potentially money-losing trait, would come to value them as a partner and find them more attractive and likeable. This is what occurred, as long as the trait was foreseeable. If it was an unforeseeable trait (i.e., 'I had no way of knowing she would be like *this!*'), then dissonance did not occur.

Recalling the data presented in Figure 4.2, we also found that the more aversive the consequence, the greater the liking. The more money the participant lost because of her partner's foreseeable trait, the greater was the liking. The reverse was true for the unforeseeable trait: the more money the partner caused the participant to lose due to a trait they could not have foreseen, the less the participant liked the partner.

Granting a few reasonable assumptions, the psychological situation confronting citizens in the United States in 1998 was similar to that confronting participants in my study. Bill Clinton was elected for a host of reasons. Some found him intelligent, others found him charming, others found him more 'in touch' with ordinary people than the incumbent, George H.W. Bush, or Clinton's challenger in the 1996 election, Bob Dole. Very few people voted for Bill Clinton because of his unassailable morality or marital fidelity. By 1996, Clinton had already been sued by Paula Jones and accused by other women of sexual improprieties while Governor of Arkansas. It would not be much of a stretch to say that marital infidelity and sexual wandering were foreseeable aspects of Clinton's next four years in office. But in 1996, Clinton was reelected to the presidency in a landslide.

It would have been difficult to claim that some form of moral lapse was completely unforeseeable when Clinton was voted back into office in 1996. It is quite reasonable to conclude that voters who chose to return Clinton to the White House were in a state of dissonance when they learned of the Monica Lewinsky affair. And much like the participants in my study who elevated their liking of their partner, we citizens in 1998 reduced dissonance by increasing our liking for the man we had chosen. And the more allegations we heard, the more dissonance we needed to reduce, and the more we liked him.

Reactions to a major political event like the Clinton impeachment are multiply determined. There were important political considerations including worry over the trauma of convicting a sitting president and the political fallout of such an outcome. However, it seems that public opinion in Clinton's favor during the winter of 1998–1999 turned the outcome of the Congressional process in his favor. It may well have been that dissonance reduction contributed to the saving of a presidency.

Cognitive dissonance and mental health: what makes psychotherapy work?

Psychotherapy is a set of procedures designed to change people's attitudes, emotions, and behaviors. The goal of psychotherapy can differ from approach to approach, with some emphasizing the actualization of the real self (Rogers, 1961), others emphasizing the unlocking of hidden and repressed memories (Freud, 1933) and others focusing on changing behaviors (Wolpe, 1967) and cognitions (Beck, 1976; Ellis, 1975). Regardless of their founding principles or underlying processes, most therapies seek to change people's maladaptive reactions to their social world to more adaptive responses.

Although the ultimate goal of psychotherapy is similar from therapy to therapy, the procedures can vary radically. Even for patients with similar complaints, the process of what they must undergo will differ markedly, depending on the theoretical orientation of the therapist. In classical psychoanalysis, for example, a patient may spend many months learning the technique of free association, allowing all thoughts, memories, and impulses to be brought into the therapy room without censorship of any kind. Years of free associating may then ensue in which the patient, with the aid of the analyst, is brought to understand the secrets that have been repressed in the unconscious since childhood. It is a difficult and often emotionally wrenching process. In the end, a patient who is afraid to go out of doors, for example, may come to understand the reason for his or her agoraphobia and learn to cope with leaving the house.

Had the same patient entered the office of a modern cognitive therapist, he or she would have been guided through a process of relabeling and relearning the meaning of his or her behavior as well as relearning the meaning of others' behavior in the social environment. In the office of a behavior therapist, the patient might learn the techniques of reciprocal inhibition (Wolpe, 1967). This patient would learn muscle relaxation techniques that would enable his or her behavior toward the out of doors to change. Or, a patient could choose an implosive technique (Stampfl and Levis, 1967) where he or she could be brought face to face with a feared object, such as going out of doors, experience the rush of excessive anxiety, and as a result, learn to extinguish her or his fear.

Despite the radically different theoretical underpinnings of various psychotherapies and despite seemingly different procedures within the consulting room, each therapy claims a reasonable and roughly similar success rate for achieving change (Bergin, 1971; Smith and Glass, 1977). Are therapies really so different? At a surface level, yes; at a deeper level, perhaps not. One common component of psychotherapies is that they occur in an interpersonal arena, with a therapist attempting to influence the attitudes, emotions, and/or behaviors of the patient. This implies that social psychological principles may be at work in an effective psychotherapy. Second, psychotherapies entail a person working hard, expending effort, time, and money in order to achieve a goal. And third, the therapies and therapists are selected by an act of free choice by the patient. This set of underlying factors –

choice and effort in a social context – has the familiar combination of principles that activate cognitive dissonance (Cooper and Axsom, 1982).

Choosing a therapy

When we make choices in our life, cognitive dissonance propels us to spread the attractiveness of the alternatives (Brehm, 1956). The chosen item seems more attractive and the rejected alternative seems less attractive than they did before the choice. In Chapter 1, we discussed Brehm's study in which participants chose a gift from among a set of attractive alternatives. If a participant chose a toaster, the toaster became more attractive than it had seemed prior to the choice.

An intriguing extension of this study would have been to see if people not only became more excited about the toaster but also about the toast. Did people enjoy going home to put bread in their new toaster, spreading jam on the toast's golden brown surface and savoring the taste? Did a person who decided to purchase a Corvette instead of a BMW not only enjoy the Corvette more but also driving with speed? If these reasonable extensions of the consequences of free choice are true, they suggest one of the active ingredients in psychotherapy: freely choosing the therapy to attend makes the therapy more attractive and motivates the clients to be successful.

A study by Mendonca and Brehm (1983) addressed this issue. Mendonca worked with children who were overweight and whose parents wished to enroll them in a weight control program. This was not a laboratory study with college students making choices among consumer items. These were children between 8 and 15 years of age who were severely overweight, averaging about 48 lbs more than normal for their height and age. The therapy, too, was very real. Known as 'Take Control,' it was a comprehensive eight-week group therapy program run in groups of three to four children.

Mendonca's experimental manipulation was to allow some children to choose their therapy while other children believed the therapy was assigned. In the choice group, the children were led to believe that there were three different therapies available to them featuring different leaders and different activities. They could choose the one that seemed best to them. In reality, all choices were described in a way that, no matter which they chose, they were enrolled in Take Control. In the no-choice condition, the children were told that they would be given the Take Control therapy. Children who believed they had chosen the therapy were mixed into the same group sessions as the children who believed they had had no choice.

Figure 8.1 shows the results of Take Control therapy. Following the eight weeks of the program, children who believed they had chosen their therapy lost more weight than the no-choice children. As the bars on the right side

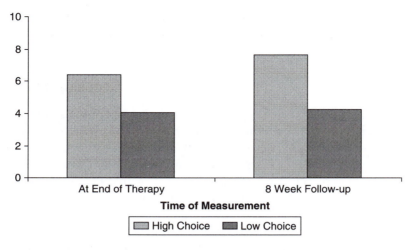

Figure: 8.1   Weight loss as a function of choice to participate in therapy
Source: Mendoca and Brehm (1983)

of Figure 8.1 show, the effect was maintained four weeks after the therapy was concluded.

Mendonca' and Brehm's study is suggestive that effort justification may be a factor in psychotherapy. Weight loss occurred in choice conditions more than in no-choice conditions, suggesting that dissonance was at work which, in turn, made the goal of the therapy (losing weight) more attractive. Two issues with this fascinating study make its conclusions tentative, however. The first is that there was no control group of children who received no treatment at all. We do not know if, during an eight-week period, severely overweight children may show a regression to the mean – i.e., tend to lose some of their excess weight no matter what they do. Hypothetically, if control children lost 10 lbs during the same period, then the conclusion of the study would be quite different. A second issue involved an unfortunate and unintended accident of prior motivation. Despite attempts to randomize the selection of children into the choice and no-choice groups, it turned out that children's reported motivation to lose weight, even before the study began, was higher among the children in the choice group than in the no-choice group. Nonetheless, this study is at least suggestive that dissonance processes may facilitate the effectiveness of psychotherapy.

To touch a snake: effort justification and the reduction of phobia

All therapies require work. Whether it is coming face to face with your anxiety in an implosive therapy, acquainting yourself with your repressed memories and desires in psychoanalysis, or talking about your most threatening interpersonal interactions in cognitive therapy, all involve effort. All involve the expenditure of time, and most involve the expenditure of money. Effort, as we conceptualized the concept previously in this book, is anything a person finds noxious and would rather not do. Therefore, whether a therapy costs you physical effort, emotional effort, time away from your work, friends and family, or costs you a high proportion of your income, the therapy involves effort in the psychological meaning of the term.

The proposal from cognitive dissonance theory is based on the element common to all therapies – effort. The attractiveness of the therapy, the motivation to achieve its goals, and the attractiveness of the goals themselves will increase as a function of the expenditure of effort. Voluntarily spending time, money, emotional, or physical effort arouses the uncomfortable tension state of dissonance, which can be reduced by enhancing the value of what the effort is for – the goal state for which a client has come to psychotherapy.

Imagine a person who is afraid of an object and wants help to overcome that fear. He attends a therapy that requires effort. Depending on the therapy, he reveals his innermost thoughts, confronts his anxiety, spends his time, and perhaps his money. Dissonance theory predicts the client will be motivated to justify these noxious expenditures by becoming more motivated to reach his goal and ultimately find the goal more attractive (i.e., the object of which he was formerly afraid). This will be true regardless of what the effort consists of, provided that it was engaged in freely.

I ran two studies designed to assess this notion (Cooper, 1980). In the first study, I asked for volunteer participants who were afraid of snakes and who would be willing to engage in an experimental therapy designed to alleviate the fear. When they arrived at the laboratory, the volunteers were greeted by a female experimenter who introduced them to Oz, a 6-foot boa constrictor curled up sweetly in a glass tank at one end of the room. The experimenter asked the participant to walk to Oz's side of the room and pet it. She demonstrated by walking to Oz's tank, taking the cover off and gently petting the snake. (Boas are non-poisonous snakes and are typically gentle and docile. Exceptions to that account can be left to another occasion. Suffice it to say that no one was ever injured in any way by the snake.) Any participant who could follow suit and pet the snake was eliminated as not being snake phobic. This exercise also provided us with an initial pre-measure: surreptitious marks along the baseboard allowed us to measure the distance the participants could come to the snake prior to any therapeutic intervention.

The experimenter then routinely informed half of the participants that she would take them to an adjoining room where the experimental therapy would proceed. 'What we will do now,' she explained, 'is proceed to the next room where our therapist will run you through the experimental therapy. I should let you know that it might be difficult or effortful for you.' For the other half of the participants, assigned to the choice condition, she continued, 'If you would rather stop now and not proceed to the therapy, that is perfectly all right. Would you like to stop now?' None of the participants chose to stop.

Therapeutic interventions

Implosion

One of our therapeutic interventions was modeled after Stampfl and Levis's (1967) system of implosive therapy. The central idea of implosive therapy is to have a client face his or her feared object as directly as possible, allow the client to become flooded with anxiety and, by facing this noxious emotion, extinguish the fear. In a true implosive therapy session, the therapist uses his or her ingenuity to concoct situations that will flood the patient with anxiety. London summarized this approach colorfully by explaining that the 'therapist creates the most thoroughgoing catalogue of horrors imaginable, perhaps as rich a collection of lore as was ever composed and narrated for the singular purpose of evoking nauseous terror from even the bravest of men' (London 1967: 102–103).

Okay, in the laboratory with our college students, we stopped short of creating nauseous terror in the hearts of our students. What we did to emulate an implosive therapy session was to have the participants examine a list of events that make typical snake phobics very nervous. One event, for example, was 'I am on a camping trip. I am in my sleeping bag. I hear a rustling in the leaves nearby. Then I feel something slithering up my leg.' If a student chose this scene as one that made him particularly anxious, the experimenter and the participant then acted out the scene in the laboratory. The lights were dimmed, a sleeping bag was put on the floor, and the scene was enacted. The acting out of anxiety-producing scenes lasted for 40 minutes.

At the conclusion of the 40 minutes of therapy, the participant was escorted back to the office of the first experimenter. As before, the experimenter asked the student to walk to the snake, remove the glass top, and pet Oz. How close they could come, compared to how close they came before the therapy, served as our dependent measure. We predicted that the high-choice participants would come closer to the snake than would low-choice participants.

Our own therapy 'brew': physical exercise therapy

There was another set of conditions in the study. If effort justification underlies the change in psychotherapy, then it should not matter what the effort is. It should not even matter if the effort makes much sense or is a part of any published therapy. In this vein, we concocted our own therapeutic procedure: physical exercise. In this therapy, we had our participants spend 40 minutes doing purely physical tasks. They ran in place for 10 minutes, wound a yo-yo (a rope connected to a stick with a 5-lbs weight attached to the rope) and jumped rope. These tasks were physically rather than emotionally exhausting and, like the implosive therapy, lasted for a total of 40 minutes. (In order to provide some words of explanation for why they were being asked to engage in physical activity, we explained that physical exercise was related to autonomic reactivity and that autonomic sensitivity is related to emotion and fear.) Like the implosive therapy participants, they were then escorted to the office of the first experimenter and asked to approach Oz.

How close could participants come to Oz? Recall that our prediction is for a main effect for choice. Regardless of the kind of effort – whether it was emotional and derived from an existing method of psychotherapy actually used with clients, or a purely physical set of activities with no apparent relationship to therapy – participants who chose to engage in the effort would experience dissonance. Participants who had no choice would not experience dissonance. The reduction of dissonance was predicted to result in greater ability of the participants to push themselves closer to Oz. Figure 8.2 shows that this is precisely what happened. On average, the high-choice participants were able to get more than 10 feet closer in the physical exercise condition and nearly 9 feet closer in the implosive therapy condition than prior to the therapy. Low-choice participants could only get approximately 1 foot closer to the snake. A no-therapy control group was also run. These participants were told that the equipment necessary for conducting the therapy had not arrived. They waited in a comfortable room for 40 minutes and then were asked to approach the snake again. The improvement of the control participants was like the low-choice condition, approaching approximately 1 foot closer (11.8 inches) to Oz than they had previously.

Becoming assertive

A second experiment extended the same design to a different problem – the problem of assertiveness. We recruited for participants who felt they had a problem with being sufficiently assertive. Examples might be feeling embarrassed to tell a store clerk that you did not get back enough change or telling the salesperson in the shoe store that you do not like any of the styles she is showing you.

As in the snake phobia study, we conducted a factorial experiment in which we manipulated decision freedom to participate in the experimental therapy and the type of effort involved in the therapy. As our example of a

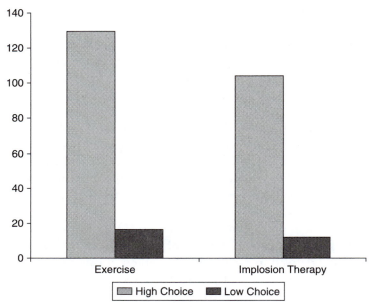

Figure 8.2   Improvement in approach to a snake (in inches) as a function
of therapy type and choice
Source: Cooper (1980)

legitimate therapy used frequently for treatment for assertive anxiety, we
used a role-playing procedure called 'assertiveness training' (Salter, 1949).
The alternative therapy was our physical effort therapy that we used in the
snake phobia experiment. At the end of the therapy session, we thanked
participants and, as promised, paid them for their participation. Except …
we paid them only half of what we had promised them. The question was,
how *assertive* would participants be after realizing they had not been paid
the amount they were promised?

Figure 8.3 shows that the results parallel our snake phobia experiment.
Participants' verbal and non-verbal responses were coded on a five-point
rating scale by observers who did not know what therapy or choice condition the participants had been in. Higher numbers indicated more assertive
responses. As in the snake phobia study, the results showed a main effect for
choice. Participants, who came to the session because of reluctance to be
assertive, acted in a more assertive fashion if they freely decided to engage
in an effortful situation; whether the therapy was assertiveness training or
simple physical exercise made no difference. The act of freely committing
effort for the goal of becoming more assertive successfully resulted in
greater assertiveness.

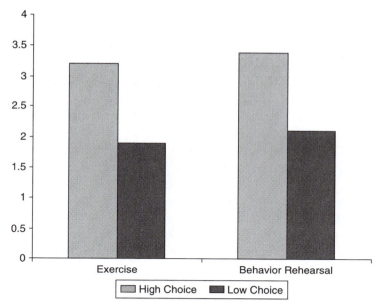

Figure 8.3 Degree of assertiveness after training
Source: Cooper (1980)

Losing weight to reduce dissonance

The two studies reported by Cooper (1980) show that the expenditure of effort under choice conditions can lead to therapeutic change. Although the results are consistent with the classic findings of Aronson and Mills (1959), they did not address the dissonance prediction that higher degrees of effort result in greater degrees of change. Aronson and Mills had examined the attractiveness of the discussion group following low and high effort. There was no low-effort condition in the Cooper (1980) studies. Axsom and Cooper (1985) sought to extend the earlier work by showing that the degree of effort a person expended was related to the degree of change toward the desired goal. We also sought to extend the reach of the cognitive dissonance therapy to a different problem that affects people's lives – namely, obesity.

Our participants were not students, but rather volunteers from the local community who responded to newspaper advertisements. The participants were between 15 and 30 lbs overweight. Of course, we could not use a physical exercise therapy for this group because the physical effort, per se, would affect weight loss. Therefore, we invented what some might call a bizarre form of therapy called 'cognitive effort therapy.'

In the *high-effort* condition, we asked the participants to do a number of tasks that had been pre-rated to be difficult and taxing. However, none of the tasks required any physical exercise. One of the cognitive tasks was to look at pairs of parallel lines presented very quickly and to determine which of the two lines was slightly off its vertical axis. Another task was repeating tongue-twisters such as 'She sells sea shells by the seashore' with delayed auditory feedback. That is, they could hear their own voice being played back to them, via a set of headphones, at a delay of 316 ms. If you try some of these tasks at home, you will see how intensely difficult they are.

We invented a bogus cover story to relate these bizarre but effortful activities to the goal of weight loss. We stressed to the participants that the tasks were designed to arouse their autonomic, psychophysiological systems, which in turn was expected to help them control their weight. It seemed important to connect the effortful procedures to the goal, just as Aronson and Mills (1959) had connected the effort involved in their screening task with the goal of joining the group.

In a *low-effort* variation of this procedure, the participants were given the same cover story about psychophysiological arousal and weight loss. They were given substantially similar cognitive tasks to perform, but they were made much easier. The nearly parallel lines were on the screen for a much longer duration and the delayed auditory feedback for tasks such as the tongue twisters was set at a much shorter duration such that it did not interfere materially with people's ability to recite the statements. We also ran a *control* condition in which participants who had volunteered for the study were put on a waiting list and given no tasks to perform.

The weigh-in

After three weeks, high-effort, low-effort and control participants were brought back for the big weigh-in. The scale showed our results in pounds. Control subjects gained 0.18 lbs during the three weeks, low-effort subjects lost 0.82 lbs and high-effort subjects lost 1.76 lbs. These differences were admittedly small but statistically reliable. Danny Axsom and I were both happy and disappointed. We were happy that the results followed a dissonance prediction: the greater the amount of effort that was involved in our therapy, the more weight was lost by participants. There was also something satisfying about seeing the result occur on a genuine, physical scale. On the other hand, losing less than 2 lbs in the high-effort condition is hardly an advertisement for the efficacy of our treatment.

On the other hand, only three weeks had transpired between the initial and final measurement. We decided to locate our participants six-months after the study had ended. We had not had any contact with the participants during the six-month interval and the participants had no expectation that we were

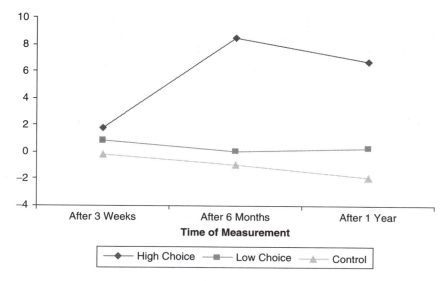

Figure 8.4   Weight loss (in lbs) by effort condition
Source: Axsom and Copper (1985)

going to call them for a follow-up. Whatever had happened during the cognitive effort session clearly continued during the intervening time period. Figure 8.4 shows that after six months, high-effort participants had lost nearly 7 more pounds, bringing their total weight loss to 8.55 lbs. By contrast, low-effort participants had lost a statistically negligible amount (0.07 lbs), and control participants had gained a negligible amount (0.94 lbs).

When we interviewed our participants, we heard a chorus of similar statements from the high-effort participants. They told us that when they left our laboratory, they were convinced that our parallel-lines, tongue twister, and other similar tasks simply did not work. However, they had decided that they now must really *do* something about their weight. The precise steps that the participants took differed widely. Some joined a gym, one decided to keep careful records of food intake, another decided to cut out all sugars from her diet. What was common to most of the comments, however, was their increased determination to succeed finally at their goal of reducing their weight. And that is how we believe the dissonance resulted in weight loss. By voluntarily expending effort to achieve a goal, cognitive dissonance was automatically aroused. To reduce it, the participants changed their evaluation of the goal. Weight loss was desirable before the study; after it, weight loss was an extremely important goal. It was important enough to take drastic action to achieve it, whether it was in the form of more exercise or healthier eating habits. Surely, the participants were correct that our

COGNITIVE DISSONANCE IN TODAY'S WORLD

procedures did not help them (directly) to lose weight. What they did not see was that it was the effortful procedures for which they had volunteered, and which were repeated session after laborious session, that had caused them to raise their determination to achieve their goal of losing weight.

Combining choice and effort: putting the variables together

A study by Axsom (1989) finally put the variables of choice and effort together in a single study. In the three psychotherapy studies we have discussed, we have seen evidence for psychotherapeutic change when people engaged in a highly effortful procedure under conditions of high, rather than low choice (Cooper, 1980). In the weight loss study (Axsom and Cooper, 1985), we have seen people become more committed to change when effort was high rather than low, but the magnitude of choice was always set high. Each of the studies implied the interaction. The full prediction is that dissonance occurs when, and only when, the magnitude of choice to engage in the therapy is high and the therapeutic activity contains high rather than low effort.

Axsom conducted a study in which the participants were snake phobic and seeking a way to reduce that fear. Like the procedure used in the Cooper (1980) study, participants had either high or low choice to take part in what they were told was a potentially effortful and difficult procedure. Instead of having two different types of therapy that were both highly effortful, Axsom used a laboratory variation of Wolpe's (1967) behavioral therapy and varied the magnitude of effort that the therapy contained. Axsom's study was the real 2 x 2 factorial design: Participants were in one of four conditions consisting of either high and low choice and either a high or low degree of effort contained in the behavioral therapy.

The outcome measure in the study was the change in participants' ability to approach a 5-ft New Jersey garden snake. The results are shown in Figure 8.5. The results clearly show that only one therapy condition was successful, namely when people freely chose to engage in a highly effortful procedure in order to approach the snake. Dissonance was created by taking personal responsibility for engaging in the highly effortful task, and was reduced by participants' pushing themselves to get closer to the snake.

A final question to ask is whether we are certain the results of the therapy studies were due to the arousal of cognitive dissonance. Dissonance certainly predicted the outcome, but there is another step that can help confirm that the changes people made in their behavior were at the service of reducing dissonance. In the conceptual model of dissonance, change is motivated by arousal. As we saw in Chapter 3, the misattribution research paradigm helped social psychology determine that dissonance truly was

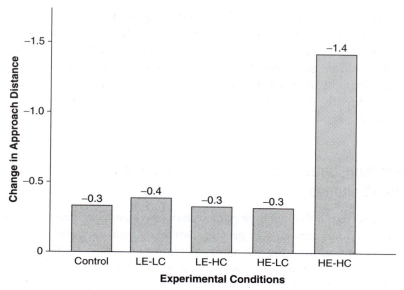

Figure 8.5   Change in approach to a snake as a funtion of choice and effort

Source: Axsom (1989)

based on a state of aversive arousal. When arousal was falsely attributed to an external stimulus such as a pill, room lighting, or poor ventilation, the attitudinal consequences of dissonance disappeared.

Axsom (1989) conducted a second study in which he allowed some participants in an effortful therapy program to falsely attribute their arousal to the hot, poorly ventilated, windowless room that they were in. Participants in this study were Rutgers University students who wanted to participate in research on an experimental procedure designed to alleviate their fear of public speaking. They were given either high or low choice to engage in the therapy process that was either high or low in its degree of effort. The third variable in the study was whether people were encouraged to think that the therapeutic room was unduly uncomfortable. This provided the opportunity for misattribution and it was made salient for half of the students. At the end of the study, the participants were asked to give a public speech. The word count and fluency of the speech were assessed. Dissonance, and therefore improvement in speech fluency, was expected for those participants in the high-choice condition whose therapy was highly effortful, thus replicating the previous research. However, that effect was expected to disappear when participants could misattribute their arousal to the uncomfortable room.

COGNITIVE DISSONANCE IN TODAY'S WORLD

The results confirmed Axsom's predictions. Participants gave longer and more fluent speeches in the high-choice, high-effort condition, but only when there was no misattribution stimulus present. When the students' arousal could be attributed to the room rather than to volunteering for a difficult therapy, there was no improvement in the students' speech dysfluency. Apparently, the effort justification results in psychotherapy are due to the arousal property of dissonance.

Advocating better health: a role for dissonance induced change

Physicians constantly urge their patients to exercise, stop smoking, eat healthier food, and take measures to protect themselves from excessive exposure to sun radiation and from the risk of sexually transmitted diseases. Governments around the world, with cooperation from advertising councils and corporate sponsors, spend vast amounts of resources to communicate public health messages. There are numerous psychological models of persuasion that have been used, with varying degrees of success, to effect change in health-related attitudes and behaviors (Salovey & Rothman, 2003).

The problem of achieving greater compliance with health-related messages is not an easy one, partly because people already agree with the overall proposition in the message. Most people believe that they should stop smoking or eat healthier foods. Most people agree they should wear sun block when exposed to the sun and most sexually active people agree that they should use condoms to reduce the risk of HIV and other sexually transmitted diseases. Being persuasive about the need to use condoms, for example, may not actually produce greater condom use. Being persuasive about using sun block may not lead to more frequent use of the product. People already agree; it's getting them to take the next step that presents the problem.

Recent evidence suggests that cognitive dissonance may be an effective means of inducing changes in both behavior and attitudes toward greater compliance with positive health messages. The work suggests that dissonance may be one more effective arrow in the quiver of techniques that health professionals can use to trigger healthier behaviors.

Hypocrisy as an instance of cognitive dissonance

Imagine that you are asked to make a statement urging others to use sun block every time they go to the beach or have an extended time in the sun. You have heard about the research linking exposure to ultraviolet radiation to carcinoma and melanoma. You know that the former is dangerous and the latter is frequently lethal. You have no problem making this statement, making it in public, allowing it to be used to convince others to use sun block. Do you actually use sun block every time you have extended exposure to the sun? Well, despite your noble attempts, you may have forgotten on one occasion (or more). The knowledge that you advocated the use of sun block, knowing that you do not always comply with your own advice, is hypocritical.

Elliot Aronson, Jeff Stone, and their colleagues (Aronson, 1999; Dickerson et al., 1992; Fried and Aronson, 1995; Stone et al., 1994) suggested that, under the appropriate conditions, the hypocrisy in the example above would be experienced as cognitive dissonance. There are two conditions necessary to turn the hypocrisy into dissonance:

1 You must be personally responsible for making the pro-attitudinal statement.
2 Your prior discrepant behavior needs to be brought to your attention – i.e., made accessible.

Under those conditions, dissonance will ensue. The aversive consequence comes from the reminder of the prior behavior. Recalling that you did not use sun block comes up short when measured against either personal or normative standards. Especially considering your current advocacy in favor of the 'always-use-sun block' position, the reminder of your prior behavior is a salient, unwanted event.

The most direct way to reduce the dissonance is to change your future behavior to make it consistent with your attitude. You will become more likely to purchase and use sun block as a consequence of reducing dissonance. In addition, you might express even more extreme attitudes on the issue, now being more certain than ever that sun block should be used whenever you go out of doors in the day time.

That is the theory, and the results of several experiments generally support the predictions. We'll return to the specific health issue of sun block later in this chapter. First, let's look at a study that focused on the prevention of HIV by encouraging the purchase of condoms by sexually active college students. Stone, Aronson, Crain, Winslow and Fried (1994) recruited unmarried college students who indicated they had been heterosexually active within the previous three months. The participants in the *hypocrisy* condition were asked to agree to make a videotape that would be shown to high school students advocating safe sex practices. The participants crafted their own speech and then delivered it in front of a video camera. In a second condition, the participants were asked to think about what they might say in a persuasive message about safe sex practices, but were not asked to make a public speech.

After completing the speech (or thinking about such a speech), some of the participants were made *mindful* of times that they did not engage in safe sex practices. The experimenter explained that it was important to know more about the circumstances that made condom use difficult. They read a list of common reasons that people give for failing to use condoms and were asked to identify circumstances that surrounded their own past failure to use condoms. The other half of the participants were not made mindful of past failures to use condoms.

After finishing their participation, the students were thanked. The experimenter remarked that the agency sponsoring the research wanted to make condoms available for purchase at a large discount. The participants were given an opportunity to purchase as many condoms as they wished, in total privacy, before leaving the study. Stone et al. (1994) predicted that the participants who were in the throes of cognitive dissonance would be motivated to alleviate their dissonance by behaving more in line with their attitudes. That is, participants in all conditions approved of using condoms for safe sex practice, but it was the participants who publicly advocated it *and* were made mindful of past occasions in which they did not use them, who would be motivated to purchase more condoms.

The results of condom purchase are shown in Figure 8.6. As predicted, more than 80 percent of the participants in the hypocrisy condition purchased condoms before leaving the building, whereas fewer than 50 percent purchased the condoms in the other conditions. Readers will note, of course, that the purchase of condoms is not precisely the same as using condoms. As Stone et al. remarked,

> AIDS researchers ... cannot measure condom use in the most direct manner; that is, we cannot crawl into bed with our subjects during their lovemaking ... Purchasing condoms is not identical to using condoms, but it is a crucial step between holding positive attitudes toward condom use and the practice of safer sex. (Stone et al., 117–118)

And, indeed, the hypocrisy created by the public, pro-attitudinal speech and the reminder of past failures to act in accordance with their attitudes, motivated purchasing behavior that increased participants' access to the condoms.

Arousing dissonance through hypocrisy procedures has proven to be a robust way to accomplish pro-social behavior change. In a follow-up study, Stone, Wiegand, Cooper and Aronson (1997) showed that the behavior change is focused and specific, relating to the specific domain implicated by the hypocrisy. These investigators replicated the earlier Stone et al. (1994) study, but gave people an opportunity to make themselves feel better in other ways, such as by donating money to a homeless shelter. They found that participants' behavior was directed specifically to the issue implicated

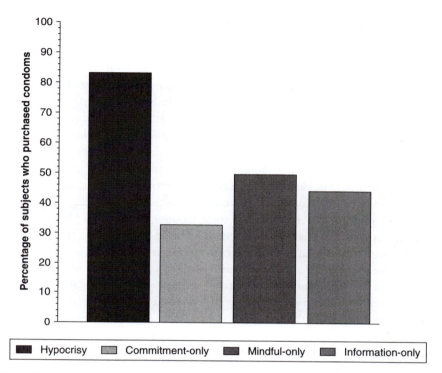

Figure 8.6   Percentage of participants who purchased condoms
Source: Stone, Wiegand, Cooper, and Aronson (1997)

in the hypocrisy. In the high-hypocrisy conditions, participants again purchased more condoms as the way to alleviate their dissonance.

Hypocrisy induction has been applicable to a broad array of domains. In
the very first hypocrisy study, Dickerson et al. (1992; see Chapter 4)
aroused hypocrisy and succeeded in getting university women to take
shorter showers during a drought emergency. In a study by Fried and
Aronson (1995), students who were made to feel hypocritical about litter-
ing the environment volunteered to make phone calls for an anti-littering
campaign. Hing, Li, and Zanna (2002) found that, in order to alleviate their
hypocrisy, aversive racists reduced prejudiced responses to Asian students at
a Canadian university, and Fointiat (2004) was able to use the hypocrisy
paradigm in Provence to gain greater compliance with anti-speeding cam-
paigns on the roads in France. Overall, inducing dissonance through
hypocrisy is both interesting theoretically and seems to be an encouraging
way to achieve behavior change in valued, pro-social directions.

From hypocrisy to vicarious hypocrisy

In Chapter 6 we discussed the idea of vicarious cognitive dissonance – i.e., experiencing dissonance on behalf of other people in your in-group. We saw evidence that when a person witnesses a fellow group member act in a dissonance-arousing manner, the witness experiences an unpleasant affect vicariously and accordingly changes his or her attitude to reduce the dissonance. The same experience of vicarious dissonance occurs when witnessing a fellow group member acting hypocritically. The experience of vicarious hypocrisy leads to taking behavioral steps to reduce the dissonance. Potentially, then, vicarious hypocrisy, can be another method of encouraging people to take action to improve their health.

In an experiment by Fernandez, Stone, Cooper, Cascio, and Hogg (2007), students at the University of Arizona were asked to listen to a speech made by another student that encouraged people to use sun block as a preventative measure for skin cancer. The participants were told that the University of Arizona was collaborating with rival university, Arizona State, on a project to develop effective public service announcements designed to convince high school graduates to use sun block as protection against skin cancer. Flattering the participants, the experimenter praised the ability of college students to serve as more persuasive role models than doctors and public health officials.

The experimenter explained that public service announcements had already been made by college students during the previous phase of the study, and the purpose of the current session was to offer an assessment of the messages. Participants listened to a tape recording of a female student who made a strong speech advocating the use of sun block every day to protect against the threat of melanomas. Of course, all participants heard precisely the same speech but the cover story allowed us to vary whether the hypocritical speechmaker was allegedly from the person's in-group (Arizona) or from the rival out-group (Arizona State). The speech concluded with the statement, 'No matter how busy you think you are with school or work, you can and should always wear sunscreen to reduce your risk of cancer.'

In the *target-advocacy* condition, the recording ended after the statement was complete. However, in the *target-hypocrisy* condition, the strong statement at the end of the speech laid the groundwork for demonstrating the target's inability to practice what she had preached. For participants in the target-hypocrisy condition, the tape continued with the researcher explaining that it would be helpful to know more about why college students fail to use sunscreen every time they spend time in the sun. He indicated that researchers in the sunscreen program had made a list of common reasons people use for not applying sunscreen. The target asked to see the list and

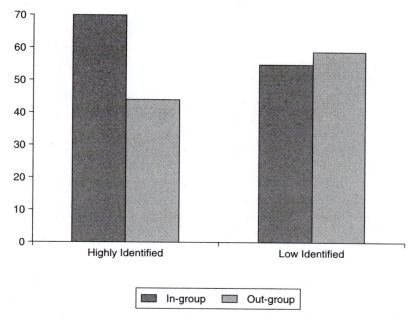

Figure 8.7   Percentage of women redeeming their coupons for sun screen
Source: Adapted from Fernandez et al. (2007)

then responded, 'Yeah, it's true for me. I can see some of the major reasons why I don't use sunscreen regularly right here on the top. I sometimes forget it in my car, or in the house … or I'm in too much of hurry to stop and put it on before I go out.' In this way, the target, who has already advocated the consistent use of sunscreen whenever one goes out of doors, publicly admits to behavior that contradicts the statement. From our previous research, we predicted that the participant would experience vicarious dissonance from overhearing another student confess to the hypocrisy – but only if the fellow student was from the participant's in-group. The hypocrisy of students from the rival institution, Arizona State University, should not lead to vicarious hypocrisy.

At the conclusion of the research session, participants were asked about their attitudes toward always using sunscreen and the strength of their intention to use sunscreen in the future. Finally, all participants were given a coupon that they could redeem for free bottles of sunscreen. All they needed to do was to send a confirmation of their desire to have the free sample to the e-mail address listed on the coupon. The e-mail address belonged to the researchers and we were able to tally the number of people who actually tried to acquire the sunscreen. (And we did send them their free bottle of sunscreen!)

The results of the study were exciting (at least for the women in the sample; men seemed to want no part of having sunscreen). Female participants' attitudes at the end of the study became more ardent that sunscreen should always be used – provided that the target speaker was from the in-group and the participant felt highly attracted to that in-group. Behavior was also affected. As shown in Figure 8.7, in the condition in which the University of Arizona participant felt highly identified with her university, witnessing the in-group speaker admit to her hypocrisy resulted in 70 percent of the participants emailing their request for their complimentary sunscreen. By contrast, only 54 percent of the other participants bothered to reclaim their coupons.

An as-yet untested aspect of the vicarious hypocrisy situation is the possibility that a single instance of advocacy in which an in-group member reveals past transgressions may translate broadly to all members who are strongly identified with their group. One advantage of a public service announcement on television or other media is that a single showing can be used to reach many citizens. The vicarious hypocrisy program would enable prototypical group members to advocate what they strongly believe, but by admitting to prior inconsistent behaviors, may induce vicarious dissonance in their entire group, leading to more positive behaviors toward cancer prevention, the spread of HIV, and other important health issues.

AFTERWORD

Toward a Modern Theory of Dissonance: What Have We Learned?

Fifty years ago, Leon Festinger taught us that we have a drive to rid ourselves of cognitive inconsistency. In so doing, he introduced the concept of cognition into social psychology and allowed us to see the occasions in which the discomfort that arose from cognitive inconsistency led us to change our view of the world. Sometimes, it made us alter the importance of our cognitions, sometimes it made us seek new information but, most frequently, it caused us to change our attitudes. Festinger and his colleagues pushed this elegantly straightforward principle wherever it would go, generating data to show us some of the subtle consequences of our pursuit of consistency. And, in no small measure, that elegantly straightforward theory rose to the level of a super-theory because it frequently led us to realize the limits of other principles, such as reinforcement, that had too often been left unquestioned and untested.

In his address to the 95th Annual Convention of the American Psychological Association in New York City in 1987, Festinger explained that he had left the field of social psychology in part because he felt so wedded to his statement of dissonance theory that, if he stayed in the field, he would have ended up defending every word of his original statement. And he did not think that was a good thing. 'Let me put it clearly,' he stated. 'The only kind of theory that can be proposed and ever will be proposed that absolutely will remain inviolate for decades … is a theory that is not testable. If a theory is at all testable, it will not remain unchanged. It has to change.'

And *change* is what this book has been about. Dissonance is no longer Festinger's inconsistency model, although it owes that model an enormous debt. The realm of dissonance is no longer restricted to comparing cognitions with one another to examine their logical consistency or inconsistency; it now includes considerations of responsibility for action, the consequences of our behavior, and our self-views. Modern theories of social cognition, motivated reasoning, and the self all play a role in understanding what cognitive dissonance is all about.

The state of play of cognitive dissonance

There is no single direction of change that has captured the consensus of all social psychologists. Many distinguished researchers have taken the position that no change was needed and that dissonance is still a function of inconsistent cognitions (e.g., Beauvois and Joule, 1999; Harmon-Jones, Brehm, Greenberg, Simon, and Nelson, 1996), some think it is a subcategory of self-affirmation (Steele, 1988; J. Aronson, Cohen, and Nail, 1999) and others believe it is a theory about self-expectations (Aronson, 1992; 1999).

In my view, the evidence leads to the conclusion that dissonance is a state of arousal that occurs when a person acts responsibly to bring about an unwanted consequence. The measuring rod for deciding if a consequence is undesired can be the internalized standards of one's society, culture, or family, or it can be very personal standards that have been generated by what one thinks of oneself. Either measuring rod is possible, but the playing field is not even. It tilts toward normative standards unless something in the environment specifically makes personal standards particularly accessible.

The legacy of cognitive dissonance

Cognitive dissonance has already left many legacies in its wake, and there will almost certainly be more. Its legacies have been both practical and theoretical. At the theoretical level, cognitive dissonance helped us to see the limits of certain other principles that had been thought to be ubiquitously universal, such as reinforcement and learning theories. But more important, cognitive dissonance has informed, and been informed by, a host of other theories. Kunda's (1990) motivated cognition theory, Steele's (1988) self-affirmation theory, Tesser's (1990) self-evaluation maintenance theory, and Higgins's (1989) self-discrepancy theory are but some of the examples. Each of those theories was grounded in dissonance theory and each of those theories has left its imprint in the evolution of dissonance.

In addition, cognitive dissonance research added methodological innovations to social psychology, including an emphasis on high-impact research in which meaningful and elaborate social situations were made very real to participants in experimental settings. But, even with its emphasis on the experimental method, research spawned new ways of examining derivations made by the theory, including use of connectionist modeling (Schultz and Lepper, 1996).

On a more practical scale, dissonance has been used as a lens through which to view child-rearing practices, economic behavior (Quattrone and Tversky, 2004), political behavior, and psychopathology, as well as the other issues that were highlighted in Chapter 8. Through the lens of dissonance, we have also been able to gain more insights into the role of culture on our social behavior, and the effects have been reciprocal. The study of culture has helped us understand what is meant by dissonance.

The future of dissonance

There are avenues left unexplored. Is dissonance learned and, if so, how is it learned? How widespread is vicarious cognitive dissonance and how close will it come to fulfilling the promise we discussed in Chapter 6 for using the approach to change attitudes and behaviors in pro-social directions? Will it lead to techniques that can be used on a wide-scale basis for encouraging people to take better care of their physical and mental health? Will individual and cultural differences reveal fundamental differences in how dissonance is experienced or will the differences in the expression of dissonance lead to a greater understanding of individuals and culture?

Finally, what theoretical challenges will cause us to see that at least some parts of even the most modern versions of dissonance theory, such as the Self-Standards Model, are simply wrong or need repair?

Festinger explained, 'All theories are wrong … One asks, "How much of the empirical realm can it handle and how must it be modified and changed as it matures.?"' Festinger would have been pleased to see his theory mature, to see it cast off some of the assumptions that were contradicted in the empirical realm and replaced by more comprehensive views. As it matured, it began to look less and less like the edifice Festinger had constructed and more like a multifaceted structure that took behavior as its base and considered consequences, responsibility, and the self. I think Festinger would have smiled appreciatively at the maturation.

And one thing more. Because all theories are wrong, the current one will undoubtedly be only a way-station to a future evolution.

REFERENCES

Abelson, R.P., Aronson, E., McGuire, W., Newcomb,T., Rosenberg, M., and Tannenbaum, P. (eds) (1968). *Theories of Cognitive Consistency: A Sourcebook*. Chicago, IL: Rand McNally.

Aronson, E. (1968) 'Dissonance theory: progress and problems,' in R.P. Abelson, E. Aronson, W.J. McGuire, T.M. Newcomb, M.J. Rosenberg, and P.H. Tannenbaum (eds), *Theories of Cognitive Consistency: A Sourcebook*. Chicago, IL: Rand McNally, pp. 5–27.

Aronson, E. (1992) 'The return of the repressed: dissonance theory makes a comeback,' *Psychological Inquiry*, 3 (4): 303–311.

Aronson, E. (1999) 'Dissonance, hypocrisy, and the self-concept,' in E. Harmon-Jones and J. Mills (eds), *Cognitive Dissonance: Progress on a Pivotal Theory in Social Psychology*. Washington, DC: American Psychological Association, pp. 103–126.

Aronson, E. and Carlsmith, J.M. (1962) 'Performance expectancy as a determinant of actual performance,' *Journal of Abnormal and Social Psychology*, 65 (3): 178–182.

Aronson, E. and Carlsmith, J.M. (1963) 'The effect of the severity of threat on the devaluation of forbidden behavior,' *Journal of Abnormal and Social Psychology*, 66: 584–588.

Aronson, E. and Mills, J. (1959) 'The effect of severity of initiation on liking for a group,' *Journal of Abnonnal and Social Psychology*, 59(2): 177–181.

Aronson, J, Blanton, H., and Cooper, J. (1995) 'From dissonance to disidentification: selectivity in the self-affirmation process,' *Journal of Personality and Social Psychology*, 68 (6): 986–996.

Aronson, J., Cohen, G., and Nail, P.R. (1999) 'Self-affirmation theory: an update and appraisal,' in E. Harmon-Jones and J. Mills (eds), *Cognitive Dissonance: Progress on a Pivotal Theory in Social Psychology*. Washington, DC: American Psychological Association, pp. 127–147.

Axsom, D. (1989) 'Cognitive dissonance and behavior change in psychotherapy,' *Journal of Experimental Social Psychology*, 25 (3): 234–252.

Axsom, D. and Cooper, J. (1985) 'Cognitive dissonance and psychotherapy: the role of effort justification in inducing weight loss,' *Journal of Experimental Social Psychology*, 21 (2): 149–160.

Baumeister, R.F. (1999) *The Self in Social Psychology*. New York, NY: Psychology Press.

Beauvois, J. and Joule, R.V. (1999) 'A radical point of view on dissonance theory,' in E. Harmon-Jones and J. Mills (eds), *Cognitive Dissonance: Progress on a Pivotal Theory in Social Psychology*. Washington, DC: American Psychology Association, pp. 43–70.

Bergin, A.E. and Lambert, M.J. (1978) 'The evaluation of therapeutic outcomes,' in S.L. Garfield and A.E. Bergin (eds), *Handbook of Psychotherapy and Behavior Change*, vol. 2. New York: Wiley.

Bem, D.J. (1965) 'An experimental analysis of self-persuasion,' *Journal of Experimental Social Psychology*, 1 (3): 199–218.

Bem, D.J. (1967) 'Self perception: an alternative interpretation of cognitive dissonance phenomena,' *Psychological Review*, 76 (3): 183–200.

Bem, D.J. (1972) 'Self-perception theory,' in L. Berkowitz (ed.), *Advances in Experimental Social Psychology'*, vol. 6. New York: Academic Press, pp. 1–62.

Berkowitz, L. and Devine, P.G. (1989) 'Research traditions, analysis, and synthesis in social psychological theories: the case of dissonance theory,' *Personality and Social Psychology Bulletin*, 15 (4): 493–507.

Blanton, H., Cooper, J., Skurnik, I., and Aronson, J. (1997) 'When bad things happen to good feedback: exacerbating the need for self-justification with self-affirmations,' *Personality and Social Psychology Bulletin*, 23 (7): 684–692.

Blanton, H., Pelham, B.W., DeHart, T. and Carvalllo, M. 'Overconfidence as dissonance reduction,' *Journal of Experimental Social Psychology*, 37: 373–385.

Bodley, J.H. (1994) *Cultural Anthropology: Tribes, States and the Global System.* NY: McGraw-Hill.

Brace, P. (2005) 'Out of touch: the presidency and public opinion,' *Political Psychology*, 26 (3): 486–487.

Brehm, J.W. (1956) 'Postdecision changes in the desirability of alternatives,' *Journal of Abnormal and Social Psychology*, 52 (3): 384–389.

Brehm, J.W. and Cohen, A.R, (1962) *Explorations in Cognitive Dissonance*. Oxford: Wiley.

Brehm, J.W. and Jones, R.A. (1970) 'The effect on dissonance of surprise consequences,' *Journal of Experimental Social Psychology*, 6 (4): 420–431.

Carlsmith, J.M., Collins, B.E., and Helmreich, R.L. (1966) 'Studies in forces compliance: I. The effect of pressure for compliance on attitudes change produced by face to face role playing and anonymous essay writing,' *Journal of Personality and Social Psychology'*, 4 (1): 1–13.

Chapanis, N.P. and Chapanis, A. (1964) 'Cognitive dissonance,' *Psychological Bulletin*, 61 (1): 1–22.

Chong, J. and Cooper, J. (2007) 'Cognitive dissonance and vicarious dissonance in East Asia: Can I feel your discomfort but not my own?' Poster presented at the meeting of the Society for Personality and Social Psychology, Memphis, TN.

Cohen, A.R. (1962) 'A dissonance analysis of the boomerang effect,' *Journal of Personality*, 30 (1): 75–88.

Cooper, J. (1971) 'Personal responsibility and dissonance: the role of foreseen consequences,' *Journal Personality and Social Psychology*, 18: 354–363.

Cooper, J. (1980) 'Reducing fears and increasing assertiveness: the role of dissonance reduction,' *Journal of Experimental Social Psychology*, 16: 199–213.

Cooper, J. (1998) 'Unlearning cognitive dissonance: toward an understanding of the development of cognitive dissonance,' *Journal of Experimental Social Psychology*, 34: 562–575.

Cooper, J. (1999) 'Unwanted consequences and the self: in search of the motivation for dissonance reduction,' in E. Harmon-Jones and J. Mills (eds), *Cognitive Dissonance: Progress on a Pivotal Theory in Social Psychology*. Washington, DC: American Psychological Association, pp. 149–175.

Cooper, J. and Fazio, R.H. (1984) 'A new look at dissonance theory,' in L. Berkowitz (ed.), *Advances in Experimental Social Psychology*, vol. 17. Orlando, FL: Academic Press, pp. 229–264.

Cooper, J. and Fazio, R. (1989) 'Research traditions, analysis, and synthesis: building a faulty case around misinterpreted theory,' *Personality and Social Psychology Bulletin*, 15: 519–529.

Cooper, J. and Goethals, G.R. (1974) 'Unforeseen events and the elimination of cognitive dissonance,' *Journal of Personality and Social Psychology*, 29 (4): 441–445.

Cooper, J. and Hogg, M.A. (2007) 'Feeling the anguish of others: A theory of vicarious dissonance,' in M.P. Zanna (ed.), *Advances in Experimental Social Psychology*, 39, San Diego, CA: Academic Press.

Cooper, J. and Scalise, C.J. (1974) 'Dissonance produced by deviations from life-styles: the interaction of Jungian typology and conformity,' *Journal of Personality and Social Psychology*, 29: 566–571.

Cooper, J. and Worchel, S. (1970) 'The role of undesired consequences in the arousal and cognitive dissonance,' *Journal of Personality and Social Psychology*, 16: 312–320.

Cooper, J., Fazio, R.H., and Rhodewalt, F. (1978) 'Dissonance and humor: evidence for the un differentiated nature of dissonance arousal,' *Journal of Personality and Social Psychology*, 36: 280–285.

Cooper, J., Zanna, M.P. and Goethals, G.R. (1974) 'Mistreatment of an esteemed other as a consequence affecting dissonance reduction,' *Journal of Experimental Social Psychology*, 10: 224–233.

Cooper, J., Zanna, M.P. and Taves, P. (1978b) 'Arousal as a necessary condition for attitude change following induced compliance,' *Journal of Personality and Social Psychology*, 36: 1101–1106.

Croyle, R. and Cooper, J. (1983) 'Dissonance arousal: physiological evidence,' *Journal of Personality and Social Psychology*, 45: 782–791.

Davis, K.E. and Jones, E.E. (1960) 'Change in interpersonal perception as a means of reducing cognitive dissonance,' *Journal of Abnormal and Social Psychology*, 61 (3): 402–410.

Davis, M.H. (1983) 'Measuring individual differences in empathy: evidence for a multidimensional approach,' *Journal of Personality and Social Psychology*, 44: 113–126.

Davis, M.H. (1994) *Empathy: A Social Psychological Approach*. Boulder, CO: Westview Press.

Dickerson, C.A., Thibodeau, R., Aronson, E., and Miller, D. (1992) 'Using cognitive dissonance to encourage water conservation,' *Journal of Applied Social Psychology*, 22 (11): 841–854.

Du Bois, W.E.B. (1903) *The Souls of Black Folk*. Chicago: A.C. McClurg & Co.

Elkin, R.A. and Leippe, M.R. (1986) 'Physiological arousal, dissonance, and atti-tude change: evidence for a dissonance-arousal link and a "Don't remind me" effect,' *Journal of Personality and Social Psychology*, 51 (1): 5–65.

Elliot, A.J. and Devine, P.G. (1994) 'On the motivational nature of cognitive disso-nance: dissonance as psychological discomfort,' *Journal of Personality and Social Psychology*, 67: 382–394.

Ellis, A. (1975) 'Does rational-emotive therapy seem deep enough?,' *Rational Living*, 10 (2): 11–14.

Elms, A.C. and Janis, I.L. (1965) 'Counter-norm attitudes induced by consonant vs. dissonant conditions of role-playing,' *Journal of Experimental Research in Personality*, 1 (1): 50–60.

Fazio, R.H., Zanna, M.P., and Cooper, J. (1977) 'Dissonance and self-perception: an integrative view of each theory's proper domain of application', *Journal of Experimental Social Psychology*, 13: 464–479.

Fernandez, N. Stone, J., Cascio, E., Cooper, J. and Hogg, M.A. (2007) 'Vicarious hypocrisy: The use of attitude bolstering to reduce dissonance after exposure to a hypocritical ingroup member.' Paper presented at the meeting of the Society for Personality and Social Psychology, Memphis, TN.

Festinger, L. (1954) 'A theory of social comparison processes,' *Human Relations*, 7: 117–140.

Festinger, L. (1957) *A Theory of Cognitive Dissonance*. Evanston, IL: Row, Peterson.

Festinger, L. and Carlsmith, J.M. (1959) 'Cognitive consequences of forced compliance,' *Journal of Abnormal and Social Psychology*, 58: 203–210.

Festinger, L., Riecken, H.W., and Schachter, S. (1956) *When Prophecy Fails*. Minneapolis: University of Minnesota Press.

Fointiat, V. (2004). '"I know what I have to do, but ..." When hypocrisy leads to behavioral change,' *Social Behavior and Personality*, 32 (8): 741–746.

Freedman, J.L. (1965) 'Long-term behavioral effects of cognitive dissonance,' *Journal of Experimental Social Psychology*, 1 (2): 145–155.

Freud, S. (1933) *New Introductory Lecture on Psychoanalysis*. Oxford: Norton & Co.

Frey, D. (1988) 'Postdecisional preference for decision-relevant information as a function of the compence ot its source and the degree of familiarity with this information,' *Journal of Experimental Social Psychology*, 17: 42–50.

Fried, C.B. and Aronson, E. (1995) 'Hypocrisy, misattribution, and dissonance reduction,' *Personality and Social Psychology Bulletin*, 21 (9): 925–933.

Galinsky, A., Stone, J., and Cooper, J. (2000) 'The reinstatement of dissonance and psychological discomfort following failed affirmations,' *European Journal of Social Psychology*, 30: 123–147.

Gerard, H.B. and Mathewson, G.C. (1966) 'The effects of severity of initiation on liking for a group: a replication,' *Journal of Experimental Social Psychology*, 2: 278–287.

Goethals, G.R. and Cooper, J. (1972) 'Role of intention and postbehavioral consequences in the arousal of cognitive dissonance,' *Journal of Personality and Social Psychology*, 23: 292–301.

Goethals, G.R. and Cooper, J. (1975) 'When dissonance is reduced: the timing of self-justificatory attitude change,' *Journal of Personality and Social Psychology*, 32: 361–367.

Goethals, G.R., Cooper, J., and Naficy, A. (1979) 'Role of foreseen, foreseeable, and unforseeable behavioral consequences in the arousal of cognitive dissonance,' *Journal of Personality and Social Psychology*, 37: 1179–1185.

Gonzales, A.E.J. and Cooper, J. (1975) 'What to do with leftover dissonance: Blame it on the lights.' Unpublished manuscript, Princeton University. Data reported in Zanna, M.P. and Cooper, J. (1976) 'Dissonance and the attribution process,' in J. H. Harvey, W.J. Ickes and R.F. Kidd (eds), *New Directions in Attribution Research*. Hillsdale, NJ: Erlbaum.

Gosling, P., Denizeau, M., and Oberle, D. (2006) 'Denial of responsibility: a new mode of dissonance reduction,' *Journal of Personality and Social Psychology*, 90 (5): 722–733.

Harmon-Jones, E. (1999) 'Toward an understanding of the motivation underlying dissonance effects: is the production of aversive consequences necessary?,' in E. Harmon-Jones and J. Mills (eds), *Cognitive Dissonance: Progress on a Pivotal Theory in Social Psychology*, Washington, DC: American Psychological Association, pp. 71–103.

Harmon-Jones, E. and Mills, J. (eds) (1999) *Cognitive Dissonance: Progress on a Pivotal Theory in Social Psychology*, Washington, DC: American Psychological Association.

Harmon-Jones, E., Brehm, J.W., Greenherg, J., Simon, L., and Nelson, D.E. (1996) 'Evidence that the production of aversive consequences is not necessary to create cognitive dissonance,' *Journal of Personality and Social Psychology*, 70: 5–16.

Heider, F. (1946) 'Attitudes and cognitive organization,' *The Journal of Psychology*, 21: 107–112.

Heine, S.J. and Lehman, D.R. (1997) 'Culture, dissonance, and self-affirmation,' *Personality and Social Psychology Bulletin*, 23: 389–400.

Higgins, E.T. (1989) 'Self-discrepancy theory: what patterns of self-beliefs cause people to suffer?,' in L. Berkowitz (ed.), *Advances in Experimental Social Psychology*, vol. 22. San Diego, CA: Academic Press, pp. 93–136.

Higgins, E.T., Rhodewalt, F., and Zanna, M.P. (1979) 'Dissonance motivation: its nature, persistence, and reinstatement,' *Journal of Experimental Social Psychology*, 15: 16–34

Hill, D.M. (2005) 'Race and cognitive dissonance: The role of double-consciousness in the experience of dissonance.' Unpublished Masters' thesis. Princeton University.

Hing, L.S., Li, W., and Zanna, M.P. (2002) 'Inducing hypocrisy to reduce prejudicial responses among aversive racists,' *Journal of Experimental Social Psychology*, 38: 71–78.

Hogg, M.A. (2001) 'Social categorization, depersonalization, and group behavior,' in M.A. Hogg and R.S. Tindale (eds), *Blackwell Handbook of Social Psychology: Group Processes*. Oxford: Blackwell, pp. 56–85.

Hogg, M.A. and Cooper, J. (2006) 'Prototypicality as a necessary factor in the experience of vicarious cognitive dissonance.' Unpublished manuscript. University of Queensland.

Hoshino-Browne, E., Zanna, A.S., Spencer, S.J., Zanna, M.P., Kitayama, S., and Lackenbauer, S. (2005) 'On the cultural guises of cognitive dissonance: the case of Easterners and Westerners,' *Journal of Personality and Social Psychology*, 89: 294–310.

Hovland, C.I., Lumsdaine, A.A., and Sheffield, F.D. (1949) *Experiments on Mass Communication (Studies in Social Psychology in World War II, vol. 3)*. Princeton, NJ: Princeton University Press.

Hovland, C.I., Janis, I.L., and Kelley, H.H. (1953) *Communication and Persuasion*. New Haven: Yale University Press.

Hull, C.L. (1952) *A Behavior System: An Introduction to Behavior Theory Concerning the Individual Organism*. New Haven, CT: Yale University Press.

Iwao, S. (1988) 'Social psychology's models of man: Isn't it time for East to meet West?' Invited address to the International Congress of Scientific Psychology, Sydney, Australia.

Jones, R.A., Linder, D.E., Kiesler, C.A., Zanna, M.P., and Brehm, J.W. (1968) 'Internal states or external stimuli: Observer's attitude judgments and the dissonance theory-self-perception controversy. *Journal of Experimental Social Psychology*, 4: 247–269.

Kelley, H.H. (1972) 'Attribution in social interaction,' in E.E. Jones, D.E. Kanouse, H.H. Kelly, R.E. Nisbett, S. Valins and B. Weiner (eds), *Attribution: Perceiving the causes of behavior*. Morristown, NJ: General Learning Press.

Kihlstrom, J.F. and Cantor, N. (1984) 'Mental representations of the self,' in L. Berkowitz (ed.), *Advances in Experimental Social Psychology*, vol. 17. San Diego, CA: Academic Press.

Kitayama, S., Ishii, K., Imada, T., Takemura, K. and Ramaswamy, J. 'Voluntary settlement and the spirit of independence: Evidence from Japan's "northern frontier,"' *Journal of Personality and Social Psychology*, 91: 369–384.

Kitayama, S., Snibbe, A.C., Markus, H.R., and Suzuki, T. (2004) 'Is there any "free" choice?: Self and dissonance in two cultures,' *Psychological Science*, 15: 527–533.

Kunda, Z. (1990) 'The case for motivated reasoning,' *Psychological Bulletin*, 108: 480–498.

Leary, M.R. and Tangney, J.P. (2003) *Handbook of Self and Identity*. New York: Guilford Press.

Lepper, M.R., Zanna, M.P., and Abelson, R.P. (1970) 'Cognitive irreversibility in a dissonance-reduction situation,' *Journal of Personality and Social Psychology*, 16: 191–198.

Linder, D.E., Cooper, J., and Jones, E.E. (1967) 'Decision freedom as a determinant of the role of incentive magnitude in attitude change,' *Journal of Personality and Social Psychology*, 6: 245–254.

London, P. (1967) 'The induction of hypnosis,' in J.E. Gordon (ed.), *Handbook of Clinical and Experimental Hypnosis*, New York: Macmillan.

Losch, M.E. and Cacioppo, J.T. (1990) 'Cognitive dissonance may enhance sympathetic tonus, but attitudes are changed to reduce negative affect rather than arousal,' *Journal of Experimental Social Psychology*, 26: 289–304.

Mackie, D.M. and Smith, E.R. (1998) 'Intergroup relations: insights from a theoretically integrative approach,' *Psychological Review*, 105: 499–529.

Mackie, D.M., Worth, L.T. and Asuncion, A.G. (1990) 'Processing of persuasive in-group messages,' *Journal of Personality and Social Psychology*, 58: 812–822.

Markus, H.R. and Kitayama, S. (1991) 'Culture and the self: implications for cognition, emotion, and motivation,' *Psychological Review*, 98: 224–253.

Matthews, K.A., Kelsey, S.F., Meilahn, E.N., Kuller, L.H., and Wing, R.R. (1989) 'Educational attainment and behavioral and biologic risk factors for coronary heart disease in middle-aged women,' *American Journal of Epidemiology*, 129: 1132–1144.

Mendonca, P. (1980) 'The effects of choice and client characteristics in the behavioral treatment of overweight chidren.' Unplublished manuscript, University of Kansas.

Mendonca, P.J. and Brehm, S.S. (1983) 'Effects of choice on behavioral treatment of overweight children,' *Journal of Social and Clinical Psychology*, 1: 343–358.

Miller, J.G. (1984) 'Culture and the development of everyday social explanation,' *Journal of Personality and Social Psychology*, 46: 961–978.

Mills, J. (1965) 'Avoidance of dissonant information,' *Journal of Personality and Social Psychology*, 2: 589–593.

Miils, J. and Jellison, J.M. (1968) 'Effect on opinion change of similarity between the communicator and the audience he addressed,' *Journal of Personality and Social Psychology*, 9: 153–156.

Monin, B., Norton, M.I., Cooper, J., and Hogg, M.A. (2004) 'Reacting to an assumed situation vs. conforming to an assumed reaction: the role of perceived speaker attitude in vicarious dissonance,' *Group Processes and Intergroup Relations*, 7: 207–220.

Nel, E., Helmreich, R., and Aronson, E. (1969) 'Opinion change in the advocate as a function of the persuasibility of his audience: a clarification of the meaning of dissonance,' *Journal of Personality and Social Psychology*, 12: 117–124.

Norton, M.I., Monin, B., Cooper, J., and Hogg, M.A. (2003) 'Vicarious dissonance: attitude change from the inconsistency of others,' *Journal of Personality and Social Psychology*, 85: 47–62.

Pallak, M.S. and Piitman, T.S. (1972) 'General motivational effects of dissonance arousal,' *Journal of Personality and Social Psychology*, 21: 349–358.

Pyszczynski, T. and Greenberg, J. (1987) 'Toward an integration of cognitive and motivational perspectives on social inference: a biased hypothesis-testing model,' in L. Berkowitz (ed.), *Advances in Experimental Social Psychology*, vol. 20. San Diego, CA: Academic Press, pp. 297–340.

Quattrone, G.A. and Tversky, A. (2004) 'Self-deception and the voter's illusion,' in E. Shafir (ed.), *Preference, Belief, and Similarity: Selected Writings by Amos Tversk*, Cambridge, MA: MIT Press, pp. 825–844.

Rhodewalt, F. and Comer, R. (1979) 'Induced-compliance attitude change: Once more with feeling,' *Journal of Experimental Social Psychology*, 15: 35–47.

Rogers, C.R. (1961) *On Becoming a Person*. Boston: Houghton Mifflin.

Rosenberg, M. (1965) *Society and the Adolescent Self-image*. Princeton, NJ: Princeton University Press.

Ross, C.E. and Wu, C. (1995) 'The links between education and health,' *American Sociological Review*, 60: 719–745.

Rossi, A.S. (2001) *Caring and Doing for Others: Social Responsibility in the Domains of Family, Work, and Community*. Chicago, IL: University of Chicago Press.

Sakai, H. (1981) 'Induced compliance and opinion change,' *Japanese Psychological Research*, 23: 1–8.

Sakai, H. and Andow, K. (1980) 'Attribution of personal responsibility and dissonance reduction,' *Japanese Psychological Research*, 22: 32–41.

Salovey, P. and Rothman, A.J. (eds). *Social Psychology of Health*. New York: Psychology Press.

Salter, A. (1949) *Conditioned Reflex Therapy: the Direct Approach to the Reconstruction of Personality*. Oxford: Creative Age Press.

Sanitioso, R., Kunda, Z., and Fong, G.T. (1990) 'Motivated recruitment of autobiographical memories,' *Journal of Personality and Social Psychology*, 59: 229–241.

Schachter, S. and Singer, J.E. (1962) 'Cognitive, social, and physiological determinants of emotional state,' *Psychological Review*, 69: 379–399.

Schachter, S. and Wheeler, L. (1962) 'Epinephrine, chlorpromazine, and amusement,' *Journal of Abnormal and Social Psychology*, 65: 121–128.

Scher, S.J. and Cooper, J. (1989) 'Motivational basis of dissonance: the singular role of behavioral consequences,' *Journal of Personality and Social Psychology*, 56: 899–906.

Schlenker, B.R. (1980) *Impression Management: The Self-Concept, Social Identity, and Interpersonal Relations*. Monterey, CA: Brooks/Cole.

Schultz, T.R. and Lepper, M.R. (1996) 'The consonance model of dissonance reduction,' in S.J. Read and L.C. Miller (eds), *Connectionist Models of Social Reasoning and Social Behavior*. Mahwah, NJ: Lawrence Erlbaum Associates, pp. 211–244.

Sedikides, C. and Gregg, A.P. (2003) 'Portraits of the self,' in M.A. Hogg and J. Cooper (eds), *Sage Handbook of Social Psychology*. London: Sage, pp. 110–138.

Sherman, S.J. and Gorkin, L. (1980) 'Attitude bolstering when behavior is inconsistent with central attitudes,' *Journal of Experimental Social Psychology*, 16: 388–403.

Shrauger, J.S. (1975) 'Responses to evaluation as a function of initial self-perceptions,' *Psychological Bulletin*, 82: 581–596.

Simon, L., Greenberg, J., and Brehm, J. (1995) 'Trivialization: the forgotten mode of dissonance reduction,' *Journal of Personality and Social Psychology*, 68: 247–260.

Skinner, B.F. (1953) *Science and Human Behavior*. Oxford: Macmillan.

Smith, M.L. and Glass, G.V. (1977) 'Meta-analysis of psychotherapy outcome studies,' *American Psychologist*, 32: 752–760.

Snibbe, A.C. and Markus, H.R. (2005) 'You can't always get what you want: educational attainment, agency, and choice,' *Journal of Personality and Social Psychology*, 88: 703–720.

Stampfl, T.G. and Levis, D.J. (1967) 'Essentials of implosive therapy: a learning theory-based psychodynamic behavioral therapy,' *Journal of Abnormal Psychology*, 72: 496–503.

Staw, B.E. (1974) 'Attitudinal and behavioral consequences of changing a major organizational reward: A field experiment,' *Journal of Personality and Social Psychology*, 29: 742–751.

Steele, C.M. (1975) 'Name-calling and compliance,' *Journal of Personality and Social Psychology*, 31: 361–369.

Steele, C.M. (1988) 'The psychology of self-affirmation: sustaining the integrity of the self,' in L. Berkowitz (ed.), *Advances in Experimental Social Psychology*, vol. 21. San Diego, CA: Academic Press, pp. 261–302.

Steele, C.M. and Liu, T.J. (1983) 'Dissonance processes as self-affirmation,' *Journal of Personality and Social Psychology*, 45: 5–19.

Steele, C.M., Hopp, H., and Gonzalez, J. (1988) 'Dissonance and the lab coat.' Unpublished manuscript, University of Washington.

Steele, C.M., Spencer, S.J., and Lynch, M. (1993) 'Self-image resilience and dissonance: the role of affirmational resources,' *Journal of Personality and Social Psychology*, 64: 885–896.

Stone, J. (1999) 'What exactly have I done? The role of self-attribute accessibility in dissonance,' in E. Harmon-Jones and J. Mills (eds), *Cogtiitive Dissonance: Progress on a Pivotal Theory in Social Psychology*. Washington, DC: American Psychological Association, pp. 175–200.

Stone, J. and Cooper, J. (2001) 'A self-standards model of cognitive dissonance,' *Journal of Experimental Social Psychology'*, 37: 228–243.

Stone, J. and Cooper, J. (2003) 'The effect of self-attribute relevance on how self-esteem moderates attitude change in dissonance processes,' *Journal of Experimental Social Psychology*, 39: 508–515.

Stone, J., Aronson, E., Crain, A.L., Winslow, M.P., and Fried, C.B. (1994) 'Inducing hypocrisy as a means of encouraging young adults to use condoms,' *Personality and Social Psychology Bulletin*, 20: 116–128.

Stone, J., Wiegand, A.W., Cooper, J., and Aronson, E. (1997) 'When exemplification fails: hypocrisy and the motive for self-integrity,' *Journal of Personality and Social Psychology*, 72: 54–65.

Stout, C.E. (2002) *The Psychology of Terrorism: Theoretical Understandings and Perspectives*, vol. III. Westport, CT: Praeger Publishers/Greenwood Publishing Group.

Sullivan, H.S. (1953) *The Interpersonal Theory of Psychiatry*. New York: W.W. Norton & Co.

Tajfel, H. (1982) *Social Identity and Intergroup Relations*. Cambridge: Cambridge University Press.

Tedeschi, J.T., Schlenker, B.R., and Bonoma, T.V. (1971) 'Cognitive dissonance: private ratiocination or public spectacle?,' *American Psychologist*, 26: 685–695.

Tesser, A. (1990) 'Smith and Ellsworth's appraisal model of emotion: a replication, extension, and test,' *Personality and Social Psychology Bulletin*, 16: 210–223.

Thibaut, J.W. and Keiley, H.H. (1959) *The Social Psychology of Groups*. New York: Wiley.

Thibodeau, R. and Aronson, E. (1992) 'Taking a closer look: reasserting the role of the self-concept in dissonance theory,' *Personality and Social Psychology Bulletin*, 18: 591–602.

Waterman, C.K. and Katkin, E.S. (1967) 'Energizing (dynamogenic) effect of cognitive dissonance on task performance,' *Journal of Personality and Social Psychology*, 6: 126–131.

Weaver, K.D. and Cooper, J. (2002) 'Self-standard accessibility and cognitive dissonance reduction.' Poster presented at the meeting of the Society of Personality and Social Psychology.

Wolpe, J. (1958) *Psychotherapy by Reciprocal Inhibition*. Stanford, CA: Stanford University Press.

Wolpe, J. (1967) 'Phobic reactions and behavior therapy,' *Conditional Reflex*, 2: 162.

Zanna, M.P. and Aziza, C. (1976) 'On the interaction of repression-sensitization and attention in resolving cognitive dissonance,' *Journal of Personality*, 44: 577–593.

Zanna, M.P. and Cooper, J. (1974) 'Dissonance and the pill: an attribution approach to studying the arousal properties of dissonance,' *Journal of Personality and Social Psychology*, 29: 703–709.

INDEX